Water From The Well

Lectionary Devotional
For Cycle A

Stephen P. McCutchan

CSS Publishing Company, Inc., Lima, Ohio

WATER FROM THE WELL

Copyright © 2007 by
CSS Publishing Company, Inc.
Lima, Ohio

The original purchaser may photocopy material in this publication for use as it was intended (worship material for worship use; educational material for classroom use; dramatic material for staging or production). No additional permission is required from the publisher for such copying by the original purchaser only. Inquiries should be addressed to: Permissions, CSS Publishing Company, Inc., 517 South Main Street, Lima, Ohio 45804.

Scripture quotations are from the New Revised Standard Version of the Bible, copyright 1989 by the Division of Christian Education of the National Council of the Churches of Christ in the USA. Used by permission.

Library of Congress Cataloging-in-Publication Data

McCutchan, Stephen P.
  Water from the well : Lectionary devotional for cycle A / Stephen P. McCutchan.
    p. cm.
  ISBN: 0-7880-2481-7 (perfect bound : alk. paper)
  1. Church year meditations. 2. Common lectionary (1992) I. Title.

BV30.M397 2007
242'.3—dc22
                                                                    2007015439

For more information about CSS Publishing Company resources, visit our website at www.csspub.com or email us at custserv@csspub.com or call (800) 241-4056.

Cover design by Barbara Spencer
ISBN-13: 978-0-7880-2481-8
ISBN-10: 0-7880-2481-7   PRINTED IN USA

*This book is dedicated
to my friend and colleague,
The Reverend Dr. Samuel Stevenson,
a pastor who has shared the joys and sorrows
with me as we have worked together
to proclaim the gospel to our people,*

and

*to the clergy of Salem Presbytery
who shared an earlier version
of these reflections
as we toiled together
in the vineyard of our Lord.*

*May God bless our ministry
in Salem Presbytery
as God has blessed our relationships.*

Table Of Contents

Introduction For Pastors	15
Introduction For Mainline Christians	19

Five Formats For Your Time Of Prayer

Praising God	25
Confession And Forgiveness	26
Offering Thanksgiving	27
Prayers Of Intercession	28
Benediction	29

Lectionary Meditations For Cycle A

Advent 1   33
Isaiah 2:1-5
Psalm 122
Romans 13:11-14
Matthew 24:36-44

Advent 2   37
Isaiah 11:1-10
Psalm 72:1-7, 18-19
Romans 15:4-13
Matthew 3:1-12

Advent 3   41
Isaiah 35:1-10
Luke 1:47-55
James 5:7-10
Matthew 11:2-11

Advent 4   45
Isaiah 7:10-16
Psalm 80:1-7, 17-19
Romans 1:1-7
Matthew 1:18-25

Christmas Eve/Christmas Day   49
Isaiah 9:2-7
Psalm 96
Titus 2:11-14
Luke 2:1-14 (15-20)

Christmas 1   53
Isaiah 63:7-9
Psalm 148
Hebrews 2:10-18
Matthew 2:13-23

Christmas 2   57
Jeremiah 31:7-14
Psalm 147:12-20
Ephesians 1:3-14
John 1:(1-9) 10-18

The Epiphany Of Our Lord   61
Isaiah 60:1-6
Psalm 72:1-7, 10-14
Ephesians 3:1-12
Matthew 2:1-12

The Baptism Of Our Lord/Epiphany 1/Ordinary Time 1   65
Isaiah 42:1-9
Psalm 29
Acts 10:34-43
Matthew 3:13-17

Epiphany 2/Ordinary Time 2   69
Isaiah 49:1-7
Psalm 40:1-11
1 Corinthians 1:1-9
John 1:29-42

Epiphany 3/Ordinary Time 3   73
Isaiah 9:1-4
Psalm 27:1, 4-9
1 Corinthians 1:10-18
Matthew 4:12-23

Epiphany 4/Ordinary Time 4   77
   Micah 6:1-8
   Psalm 15
   1 Corinthians 1:18-31
   Matthew 5:1-12

Epiphany 5/Ordinary Time 5   81
   Isaiah 58:1-9a (9b-12)
   Psalm 112:1-9 (10)
   1 Corinthians 2:1-12 (13-16)
   Matthew 5:13-20

Epiphany 6/Ordinary Time 6   85
   Deuteronomy 30:15-20
   Psalm 119:1-8
   1 Corinthians 3:1-9
   Matthew 5:21-37

Epiphany 7/Ordinary Time 7   89
   Leviticus 19:1-2, 9-18
   Psalm 119:33-40
   1 Corinthians 3:10-11, 16-23
   Matthew 5:38-48

Epiphany 8/Ordinary Time 8   93
   Isaiah 49:8-16a
   Psalm 131
   1 Corinthians 4:1-5
   Matthew 6:24-34

Epiphany 9/Ordinary Time 9   97
   Deuteronomy 11:18-21, 26-28
   Psalm 31:1-5, 19-24
   Romans 1:16-17; 3:22b-28 (29-31)
   Matthew 7:21-29

The Transfiguration Of Our Lord   101
(Last Sunday After Epiphany)
   Exodus 24:12-18
   Psalm 2
   2 Peter 1:16-21
   Matthew 17:1-9

Lent 1   105
   Genesis 2:15-17; 3:1-7
   Psalm 32
   Romans 5:12-19
   Matthew 4:1-11

Lent 2   109
   Genesis 12:1-4a
   Psalm 121
   Romans 4:1-5, 13-17
   John 3:1-17

Lent 3   113
   Exodus 17:1-7
   Psalm 95
   Romans 5:1-11
   John 4:5-42

Lent 4   118
   1 Samuel 16:1-13
   Psalm 23
   Ephesians 5:8-14
   John 9:1-41

Lent 5   122
   Ezekiel 37:1-14
   Psalm 130
   Romans 8:6-11
   John 11:1-45

Passion/Palm Sunday   127
   Isaiah 50:4-9a
   Psalm 118:1-2, 19-29
   Philippians 2:5-11
   Matthew 21:1-11

Easter Day   131
   Acts 10:34-43
   Psalm 118:1-2, 14-24
   Colossians 3:1-4
   John 20:1-18; Matthew 28:1-10

Easter 2   **136**
   Acts 2:14a, 22-32
   Psalm 16
   1 Peter 1:3-9
   John 20:19-31

Easter 3   **140**
   Acts 2:14a, 36-41
   Psalm 116:1-4, 12-19
   1 Peter 1:17-23
   Luke 24:13-35

Easter 4   **145**
   Acts 2:42-47
   Psalm 23
   1 Peter 2:19-25
   John 10:1-10

Easter 5   **149**
   Acts 7:55-60
   Psalm 31:1-5, 15-16
   1 Peter 2:2-10
   John 14:1-14

Easter 6   **154**
   Acts 17:22-31
   Psalm 66:8-20
   1 Peter 3:13-22
   John 14:15-21

Easter 7   **159**
   Acts 1:6-14
   Psalm 68:1-10, 32-35
   1 Peter 4:12-14; 5:6-11
   John 17:1-11

The Day Of Pentecost   **163**
   Numbers 11:24-30
   Psalm 104:24-34, 35b
   1 Corinthians 12:3b-13
   John 20:19-23

The Holy Trinity   167
    Genesis 1:1—2:4a
    Psalm 8
    2 Corinthians 13:11-13
    Matthew 28:16-20

Proper 4/Pentecost 2/Ordinary Time 9   171
    Genesis 6:9-22; 7:24; 8:14-19
    Psalm 46
    Romans 1:16-17; 3:22b-28 (29-31)
    Matthew 7:21-29

Proper 5/Pentecost 3/Ordinary Time 10   175
    Genesis 12:1-9
    Psalm 33:1-12
    Romans 4:13-25
    Matthew 9:9-13, 18-26

Proper 6/Pentecost 4/Ordinary Time 11   179
    Genesis 18:1-15 (21:1-7)
    Psalm 116:1-2, 12-19
    Romans 5:1-8
    Matthew 9:35—10:8 (9-23)

Proper 7/Pentecost 5/Ordinary Time 12   183
    Genesis 21:8-21
    Psalm 86:1-10, 16-17
    Romans 6:1b-11
    Matthew 10:24-39

Proper 8/Pentecost 6/Ordinary Time 13   187
    Genesis 22:1-14
    Psalm 13
    Romans 6:12-23
    Matthew 10:40-42

Proper 9/Pentecost 7/Ordinary Time 14   191
    Genesis 24:34-38, 42-49, 58-67
    Psalm 45:10-17; Song Of Solomon 2:8-13
    Romans 7:15-25a
    Matthew 11:16-19, 25-30

Proper 10/Pentecost 8/Ordinary Time 15   196
   Genesis 25:19-34
   Psalm 119:105-112
   Romans 8:1-11
   Matthew 13:1-9, 18-23

Proper 11/Pentecost 9/Ordinary Time 16   200
   Genesis 28:10-19a
   Psalm 139:1-12, 23-24
   Romans 8:12-25
   Matthew 13:24-30, 36-43

Proper 12/Pentecost 10/Ordinary Time 17   205
   Genesis 29:15-28
   Psalm 105:1-11, 45b
   Romans 8:26-39
   Matthew 13:31-33, 44-52

Proper 13/Pentecost 11/Ordinary Time 18   209
   Genesis 32:22-31
   Psalm 17:1-7, 15
   Romans 9:1-5
   Matthew 14:13-21

Proper 14/Pentecost 12/Ordinary Time 19   214
   Genesis 37:1-4, 12-28
   Psalm 105:1-6, 16-22, 45b
   Romans 10:5-15
   Matthew 14:22-33

Proper 15/Pentecost 13/Ordinary Time 20   218
   Genesis 45:1-15
   Psalm 133
   Romans 11:1-2a, 29-32
   Matthew 15:(10-20) 21-28

Proper 16/Pentecost 14/Ordinary Time 21   223
   Exodus 1:8—2:10
   Psalm 124
   Romans 12:1-8
   Matthew 16:13-20

Proper 17/Pentecost 15/Ordinary Time 22   228
   Exodus 3:1-15
   Psalm 105:1-6, 23-26, 45c
   Romans 12:9-21
   Matthew 16:21-28

Proper 18/Pentecost 16/Ordinary Time 23   232
   Exodus 12:1-14
   Psalm 149
   Romans 13:8-14
   Matthew 18:15-20

Proper 19/Pentecost 17/Ordinary Time 24   236
   Exodus 14:19-31
   Psalm 114
   Romans 14:1-12
   Matthew 18:21-35

Proper 20/Pentecost 18/Ordinary Time 25   241
   Exodus 16:2-15
   Psalm 105:1-6, 37-45
   Philippians 1:21-30
   Matthew 20:1-16

Proper 21/Pentecost 19/Ordinary Time 26   245
   Exodus 17:1-7
   Psalm 78:1-4, 12-16
   Philippians 2:1-13
   Matthew 21:23-32

Proper 22/Pentecost 20/Ordinary Time 27   249
   Exodus 20:1-4, 7-9, 12-20
   Psalm 19
   Philippians 3:4b-14
   Matthew 21:33-46

Proper 23/Pentecost 21/Ordinary Time 28   254
   Exodus 32:1-14
   Psalm 106:1-6, 19-23
   Philippians 4:1-9
   Matthew 22:1-14

Proper 24/Pentecost 22/Ordinary Time 29   258
Exodus 33:12-23
Psalm 99
1 Thessalonians 1:1-10
Matthew 22:15-22

Proper 25/Pentecost 23/Ordinary Time 30   262
Deuteronomy 34:1-12
Psalm 90:1-6, 13-17
1 Thessalonians 2:1-8
Matthew 22:34-46

Proper 26/Pentecost 24/Ordinary Time 31   266
Joshua 3:7-17
Psalm 107:1-7, 33-37
1 Thessalonians 2:9-13
Matthew 23:1-12

Proper 27/Pentecost 25/Ordinary Time 32   271
Joshua 24:1-3a, 14-25
Psalm 78:1-7
1 Thessalonians 4:13-18
Matthew 25:1-13

Proper 28/Pentecost 26/Ordinary Time 33   276
Judges 4:1-7
Psalm 123
1 Thessalonians 5:1-11
Matthew 25:14-30

Christ The King/Proper 29   280
Ezekiel 34:11-16, 20-24
Psalm 100
Ephesians 1:15-23
Matthew 25:31-46

Introduction
For Pastors

The danger of professional ministry is that we use all of the tools of grace in the exercise of our profession and often neglect to use them for our own nurture. We are asked frequently to pray in public and yet are often reluctant to claim time for our own prayer life. Scripture can be very inspiring, but it is endemic to our profession that we almost always read scripture with an eye to how it can be used for a sermon, a class, or to assist someone else with the trials of their life. As clergy we are so accustomed to having the responsibility for worship and to feeling as if we are being measured by how we conduct worship, that it is often difficult for us to simply sit and experience worship as a way to open ourselves to God.

It is not news that the stress of ministry has increased as the respect for the role of ministry has declined. The result is that fewer people are entering the ranks of clergy, and many who do become pastors find it so draining that they either leave the profession or retire early. This is all taking place during a period in which there is ample evidence of a vast spiritual hunger in our society. People are rapidly discovering that the gods of materialism, scientism, sex, spiritualism, and patriotism are unable to satisfy the deep longing in their souls.

Our society is in need of spiritually centered, well-balanced, committed pastors to guide this spiritually starving society. If we are going to feed this vast crowd with our meager resources of five loaves and two fish, we are going to need to discipline ourselves to stay connected with the well of living water that nurtures us.

This book is offered in support of your ministry. It is intended to support you in your profession by encouraging you to take time for regular prayer and devotions so that God might continually touch your life and speak to you through scripture.

The structure of the book builds on two features of our professional life — the structure of worship and the provision of the Revised Common Lectionary. The basic structure of most experiences of worship include the offering of praise, confession of sins, being nurtured by the word, offering prayers of thanksgiving and intercession, and experiencing the benediction or the blessing of God. The Revised Common Lectionary offers four readings normally drawn from the Hebrew scriptures, the psalms, the gospels, and the epistles.

You are offered five formats for your time of prayer beginning on page 23. The first one focuses on the praise of God. The second focuses on the confession of sins and assurance of forgiveness. The third is directed toward a time of thanksgiving. The fourth offers you the opportunity for offering prayers of intercession. Finally, there is a time to receive the blessing of God or the benediction. Following these formats for devotions, there is a series of brief meditations on each of the scriptures proposed by the lectionary for the following Sunday.

The intention is that you would find at least five times during the week to take time for prayer and meditation for one-half hour or more. You would begin the week with a time of praise. Next, you would have an opportunity to confess those burdens that are bothering you and experience the grace of a forgiving God. The third day would allow you to spend some time offering your thanksgiving for all that God provides you. On the fourth day, you would have an opportunity to focus on the needs of your congregation or the society around you. And on the fifth day, you can rest in the blessing of God who has called you to ministry. During this time, you will also be nurtured each day by the scriptures that form the basis of your worship on the following Sunday. I recognize that some may find it more helpful to alter the calendar and use the lectionary readings that will provide the basis of the worship several weeks in advance so that your meditation might also stimulate your thinking with respect to the sermon that you will need to prepare. You may find it helpful to have a pad of paper to capture the thoughts that occur to you.

The appropriate time to use this devotional will vary with the schedule of each individual. Many find that an early morning time can be set aside and is usually not disturbed, but for others it is an appropriate way to end the day. I also would suggest two other alternatives that have proved helpful to me. Most hospitals have chapels, and if you carry this devotional with you, you could often find a brief time after a hospital visit to nurture yourself in the chapel. Also, I have found a remarkable sanctuary in fast-food restaurants. I order a minimal meal, take it to the most remote corner in the restaurant, and allow the meal to be a spiritual experience that slows down my eating and feeds me with some bread of heaven. No pattern fits all personalities, and I encourage you to explore what time may best fit your pattern and personality. I have deliberately chosen to create just five formats for prayer under the assumption that there will be at least two days each week that do not fit into this rhythm. However, if you are fortunate enough to have a sixth or seventh time, you can simply choose to repeat any of the offered formats.

My hope is that the flexibility of the formats and the opportunity to reflect on the lectionary scriptures will encourage you to be good to yourself and strengthen that connection with God that has drawn you into your calling. God's call in your life was not a mistake, and the church needs your gifts in response to the hunger of God's people. May God strengthen you for the journey that lies ahead.

Introduction
For Mainline Christians

It is one of the sad realities of our modern times that many Christians feel guilty about their practice of the faith because it does not demonstrate the same intensity and confidence as some of the more fundamentalist groups that seem so certain about the answers to all questions. While God may use such fundamentalists to prod us in examining what we do believe, their certitude often leaves many faithful Christians feeling inadequate even as they are put off by what appears to them as self-righteousness. As modern Christians who attempt to weave our way through the complexities of our world, we are more attracted to the agony of the father in the gospel of Mark who cried out to Jesus, "I believe, help my unbelief" (Mark 9:24).

A very present danger in this tension between Christian believers is that we will expend our energy struggling with each other and forget that the real threat to our world is the secular, consumerist culture that is creating an almost unbearable stress in all of our lives. Many otherwise very good and sensitive people have, in the words of the prophet Jeremiah, lost contact with "the fountain of living water, and dug out cisterns for themselves, cracked cisterns that can hold no water" (Jeremiah 2:12). If, as the gospel of John reports, Jesus came "that we might have life, and have it abundantly" (John 10:10), many have lost touch with what Christ promises even in the practice of their faith.

This is all taking place during a period in which there is ample evidence of a vast spiritual hunger in our society. People are rapidly discovering that the gods of materialism, scientism, spiritualism, patriotism, and sex are unable to satisfy the deep longing in their souls. Many people who are active in their churches fail to experience God's activating Spirit continually refreshing their lives. You may remember your grandparents having augmented their Sunday worship experience with a daily devotional time in their homes. For most mainline Christian families, that is a practice that has been lost in the rush of time. Yet, I would suggest to you that in the same way that it was a source of spiritual strength for your ancestors, it can again be that source of refreshment for you. I would further suggest to you that rediscovering this more intimate connection with the Spirit of God might be vital as you seek to open yourselves to the full promise of your lives.

It is easy to feel lost and unimportant in the pressured society in which we live. Power and confidence come to those who feel like their life is filled with meaning and that their contribution is part of something greater than themselves. The Christian story is fundamentally about God who created everything that exists, who has become personally involved in the flow of time and history to accomplish a glorious purpose, and who calls you to be part of the unfolding of that story in this universe. Your life is not insignificant but is intended to be a paragraph in the divine story that God is unfolding. Even the mistakes and missteps you take do not need to be wasted but can be redeemed by God through Christ in the telling of this all-important story.

To feel our own connection with God's story, we need to reconnect with the Spirit that is animating the true meaning of our lives. We need to feel a personal connection with the God of our salvation. A major gift by which God invites us to stay connected with the divine purpose is that of prayer and scripture. For many Christians, those very practices have fallen into disuse or have become a routine that is devoid of power. This book is intended to provide you a means by which to reenergize your prayer life and to hear God speaking to you through scripture. It is intended to support you by encouraging you to take time for regular prayer and devotions so that God might continually touch your life and speak to you through scripture.

The structure of the book builds on two features common to many Christians in mainline churches — the structure of worship and the provision of the common lectionary. Whether your church uses the lectionary or not, the format can still be used. You will discover that it will help you feel connected with the wider body of the church that reaches across the world. The basic structure of most experiences of worship include the offering of praise, confessing of our sins, being nurtured by the word, offering prayers of thanksgiving and intercession, and experiencing the benediction or the blessing of God. The common lectionary offers four readings normally drawn from the Hebrew scriptures, the psalms, the gospels, and the epistles.

You are offered five formats for your time of prayer beginning on page 23. The first one focuses on the praise of God. The second focuses on the confession of sins and the assurance of forgiveness. The third is directed toward a time of thanksgiving. The fourth offers you the opportunity for offering prayers of intercession. Finally, there is a time to receive the blessing of God or the benediction. Following these formats for devotion, there is a series of brief meditations on each of the scriptures proposed by the lectionary for the following Sunday.

The intention is that you will find at least five times during the week to take time for prayer and meditation for one-half hour or more. You will begin the week with a time of praise. Next, you will have an opportunity to confess those burdens that are bothering you and experience the grace of a forgiving God. The third day will allow you to spend some time offering your thanksgiving for all that God provides you. On the fourth day, you will have an opportunity to focus on the needs of your congregation or the society around you. And on the fifth day, you can rest in the blessing of God who has called you to the faith. During this time you will also be nurtured each day by the scriptures that will likely form the basis of your worship on the following Sunday.

The appropriate time to use this devotional will vary with the schedule of each individual. Many find that an early morning time can be set aside and is usually not disturbed, but for others, especially those with children, other times will be more appropriate. It may be an appropriate way to end the day but there are some who feel so drained by the pressures of life that it is hard to focus when they are so tired. So, before you conclude that your life just does not allow for such a discipline, let me suggest a couple of other opportunities. First, many of you drive to work in your own car and often you can plan to arrive at your parking space in time to have some extra time alone before you enter your place of work. While it may seem shocking at first, let me further suggest that a perfect place to find alone time at many places of work is the stall in the restroom facilities. Also, I have found a remarkable sanctuary in fast-food restaurants. I order a minimal meal, take it to the most remote corner in the restaurant, and allow the meal to be a spiritual experience that slows down my eating and feeds me with some bread of heaven. No pattern fits all personalities, and I encourage you to explore what time may best fit your pattern and personality. I have deliberately chosen to create just five formats for prayer under the assumption that there will be at least two days each week that do not fit into this rhythm. However, if you are fortunate enough to have a sixth or seventh time, you can simply choose to repeat any of the offered formats.

My hope is that the flexibility of the formats and the opportunity to reflect on the lectionary scriptures will encourage you to be good to yourself and strengthen that connection with God which has drawn you into your faith. God's call in your life was not a mistake, and the church needs your gifts in response to the hunger of God's people. May God strengthen you for the journey that lies ahead.

Five Formats For Your Time Of Prayer

Praising God

Invocation
> *Praise the Lord! Praise God in his sanctuary; praise him in his mighty firmament! Praise him for his mighty deeds; praise him according to his surpassing greatness!* — Psalm 150:1-2

Personal Prayer
Spend ten minutes offering praise to God for the way in which God has called you, nurtured you, strengthened you, and worked miracles in your life.

Nurtured By The Word
Read the Hebrew scripture for the week.
Spend some time asking how God might be speaking to you through this lesson.
Read the meditation on the first lesson for the week.
If thoughts come to your mind as you muse on this passage, write them down.

Closing Prayer
Either sing or pray the doxology: Praise God from whom all blessings flow. Praise God all creatures here below. Praise God above you heavenly hosts. Praise Father, Son, and Holy Ghost.

Confession And Forgiveness

Invocation
Have mercy on me, O God, according to your steadfast love; according to your abundant mercy blot out my transgressions. Wash me thoroughly from my iniquity, and cleanse me from my sins. — Psalm 51:1-2

Personal Prayer
Take about ten minutes to confess to God those personal and relational sins that burden your soul. Also lay before God the feelings of anger, hurt, and disillusionment that are part of your ministry.

Assurance Of Forgiveness
Who is in a position to condemn? Only Christ, and Christ died for us, Christ rose for us, Christ reigns in power for us, Christ prays for us. I claim the good news of the gospel for myself. In Jesus Christ, I am forgiven.

Nurtured By The Word
Read the psalm for the week.

Spend some time asking how God might be speaking to you through this lesson.

Read the meditation on that psalm.

If thoughts come to mind as you muse on this passage, write them down.

Closing Prayer
Create in me a clean heart, O God, and put a new and right spirit within me ... Restore to me the joy of your salvation, and sustain in me a willing spirit (Psalm 51:10, 12). Amen.

Offering Thanksgiving

Invocation
> *It is good to give thanks to the Lord, to sing praises to your name, O Most high; to declare your steadfast love in the morning and your faithfulness by night.*
> — Psalm 92:1-2

Personal Prayer
Take about ten minutes to thank God for the many blessings in your life. Thank God for the ways God has been present in your ministry and your congregation. Thank God for how God has been present to you since birth.

Nurtured By The Word
Read the gospel lesson for the week.
Spend some time asking how God might be speaking to you through this lesson.
Read the meditation on the gospel lesson.
If any thoughts come to you while you are musing on the gospel, write them down.

Closing Prayer
The Lord is my shepherd, I shall not want. He makes me lie down in green pastures; he leads me beside still waters; he restores my soul. He leads me in right paths for his name's sake (Psalm 23:1-3). Amen.

Prayers Of Intercession

Invocation
> *Lord, you have been our dwelling place in all generations. Before the mountains were brought forth, or ever you had formed the earth and the world, from everlasting to everlasting you are God.* — Psalm 90:1-2

Personal Prayer
Take time to consider and offer in prayer all the needs within your congregation (within your life) of which you are aware. Take note of the spiritual and emotional needs as well as the physical needs. Lift up troubled relationships and career challenges as well as family and marital stresses. Do not neglect to lift up your own needs.

Nurtured By The Word
Read the epistle lesson for the week.

Spend some time asking how God might be speaking to you through this lesson.

Read the meditation on this lesson.

If there are thoughts that come to mind as you muse on this scripture, write them down.

Closing Prayer
Let the words of my mouth and the meditation of my heart be acceptable to you, O Lord, my rock and my redeemer (Psalm 19:14). Amen.

Benediction

Invocation
O Lord, you have searched me and known me. You know when I sit down and when I rise up; you discern my thoughts from far away. — Psalm 139:1-2

Personal Prayer
Take time to simply rest in the blessings of the Lord in your life. Review times in your life when you have felt the powerful presence of God lifting you up and times when you basked in the sheer joy of the life that God has provided you. Review some high moments in your ministry and allow them to be signs for you of God's continuing presence calling and guiding you.

Nurtured By The Word
Open the section of meditations at random and choose a particular scripture that is noted. Read it totally free of any agenda for its use.

Spend some time asking how God might be speaking to you through this passage.

Then read the meditation provided.

If there are thoughts that come to you during your musing, write them down.

Closing Prayer
Sing or pray the Gloria Patria: Glory be to the Father, and to the Son, and to the Holy Ghost; as it was in the beginning, is now, and ever shall be, world without end. Amen.

Lectionary Meditations For Cycle A

Advent 1

Isaiah 2:1-5

... nation shall not lift up sword against nation, neither shall they learn war any more. — Isaiah 2:4

The reading for the first Sunday in Advent lifts up the theme of peace. The dream of peace envisioned by Isaiah came as a response to what God would do. It did not begin with either a military victory or with a better proposal for peace. It began with the revelation of God's way. Peace would only come, suggested Isaiah, when the nations learned the way of God. In the meantime, as the world yearned for a peace that did not exist, Isaiah urged the people of faith to take those first steps toward peace. "Come," he said, "let us walk in the light of the Lord." When we seek personal peace, it is not the discovery of a new philosophy to conquer our anxiety but first a decision to respond to what God has already done. In many ways, our own lives reflect the very tensions and battles that beset our nations. Our world has tried to make peace by learning war and by converting the instruments of creativity into instruments of destruction. Look at the way that we try to handle domestic tension. We try to develop the better argument or exert our power over our competition. The very energies that should be directed toward nurturing love and creativity become the instruments by which we try to dominate each other. It is not that protecting the borders of our lives is unimportant, but our real security lies at the center of our lives. If you knew that your life had integrity and that your ultimate security was assured, could you not feel a greater sense of peace in yourself that could then flow out toward others? What if God has already provided the means of peace within your family or church and what was needed was your response of peace? How do you convert the weapons that you have been using into instruments of peace?

Psalm 122

> *Pray for the peace of Jerusalem: "May they prosper who love you."*
> — Psalm 122:6

Jerusalem contains within its name the word for peace. It is the city of peace, and yet for centuries it has been a city of contention. For humans, the city represents the failure of humanity to find the peace for which we long. Yet its very existence as a central focus of three major religions causes us to yearn for what we cannot achieve on our own. Therefore, we are driven to prayer as the only source of real peace. As we begin Advent, we know the tension between that for which we long and the reality of our violence-torn world. We are Jerusalem. "I was glad when they said to me, 'Let us go to the house of the Lord.' " Advent is our invitation to turn to the source of hope that only God can provide. Like the tribes of Israel, we turn to give thanks to the Lord as the only true source of peace. The reality is that we come to church and pray for peace but we continue to experience conflict even within the church. This harsh truth causes us, like the Israelites, to realize that we must trust not in our skills but in the grace of God. "For the sake of my relatives and friends, I will say, 'Peace be within you.' For the sake of the house of the Lord our God (church), I will seek your good." Advent is a good time to pray for the peace of God within the church for the sake of the world.

Romans 13:11-14

> *Instead, put on the Lord Jesus Christ, and make no provisions for the flesh, to gratify its desires.*
> — Romans 13:14

To "put on Jesus" is contrasted with gratifying the desire of the flesh. To live according to the flesh is to allow ourselves to be controlled by our feelings. Feelings are mercurial. In an instant, we can move from elation to despair, from confidence to fear. Paul spoke to the church in Rome. His image of the church living according to the flesh was very physical. He described it as "... reveling and drunkenness ... in debauchery and licentiousness ... in quarreling and jealousy." All of these images are based on a person responding to the feelings of the moment and not taking concern for those around them. Apply that image to the church. If the body of Christ is guided by the desires of the flesh, it makes its decisions according to what pleases its membership or, at least, what avoids the fears of the membership. The church that acts on its feelings will rarely act in a way that is controversial or that challenges the status quo. To put on Christ is to allow Christ to be the head of the body of Christ. To discern what we should do, we examine the life of Christ who challenged the accommodation that religion had made with society and emphasized the grace and forgiveness of God. Pray to imagine how your church would relate to each other and to the world if it were not guided by its feelings but rather by the mind of Christ. As we begin Advent, consider what your church needs to do to emphasize God's grace to those who feel excluded in your church or our world. "For salvation is nearer to us now than when we became believers; the night is gone, the day is near."

Matthew 24:36-44

> *But about that day and hour no one knows, neither the angels of heaven, nor the Son, but only the Father.*
> — Matthew 24:36

Each year we begin Advent caught in the tension between the expectations of our faith and the ordinariness of life. Because we have been here so often before, it is hard to escape the routine of the season and open ourselves to the real expectations of the coming of the Son of Man. We are like those in the days of Noah who "were eating and drinking, marrying and giving in marriage" without any awareness of the critical movements of God. The people in Noah's time knew the state of their society, like we do, but they did not expect anything new to happen. Matthew was clear that the people of faith were not given any special insight or clues to predict what would happen. The difference for believers is that we know that it could happen and therefore we live in hope. Advent invites us to live as if Christ might come again this year. The celebration of the birth of Jesus is an affirmation that God does enter time in order to alter the course of events. It is also a warning that most of the surrounding community will be unaware of the divine presence. Living with the expectation of divine visitation alters the way we perceive all events. If Christ were to come tomorrow, what would you want to be doing at the time of his coming? How would a church want to be behaving? "Keep awake, therefore, for you do not know on what day your Lord is coming."

Advent 2

Isaiah 11:1-10

On that day the root of Jesse shall stand as a signal to the peoples; the nations shall inquire of him, and his dwelling shall be glorious. — Isaiah 11:10

The Messiah that was awaited would be from the family line of Jesse. That Messiah would be of benefit to more than just his own Jewish people. He would be a symbol of hope for all the peoples. Now, for us, the Messiah has come, and we have been invited to share the hope he established. The messianic community, or Christians, continue Christ's mission. Advent is an appropriate time for the church to reflect on how it can be a signal of hope for others. Isaiah's picture of the peaceable kingdom was one of natural enemies living together in harmony and leadership coming from the most vulnerable members of society. Children were normally seen as investments for the future but hardly as leaders. When Jesus said, "Unless you change and become like children, you will never enter the kingdom of heaven" (Matthew 18:3), he was totally reversing the natural order. We wait for children to become like adults rather than the other way around. An adult would know better than to put his hand on the den of poisonous snakes, but a child might act out of innocent trust. Only a child could picture a wolf and a lamb lying down together or a cow and a bear grazing together. In our attempt to take control of our lives, we have grown suspicious and wary of all the dangers about us. We are skeptical and cautious about expecting anything unique coming out of Christmas. A child approaches Christmas with a sense of wonder and hope. Children believe in the impossible. Isaiah's vision is a vision of the impossible that stirs wonder and hope. It is only realistic if we trust in God who can offer us wonder and hope. If a Christian community lives in response to the hope of God, can they not become a signal of hope for the world?

Psalm 72:1-7, 18-19

Give the king your justice, O God, and your righteousness to a king's son. — Psalm 72:1

The psalmist yearned for a righteous king who would establish justice and bring peace to the world. For Israel, the king was the anointed one of God. The anointed one was the one who had been chosen by God as God's special servant. The Hebrew word that we translate "anointed" can also be translated "messiah." In Greek that same word is *christ*. Israel believed that it was God who chose their kings, and each king was to be the anointed one, or the messiah, or christ. In Isaiah 11, when the kingdom was failing, they recalled their glory days when David, the son of Jesse, was their king. This was the image Israelites used to form their hopes for the future. Projecting that vision into the future, they prayed that God would bring them a messiah, or christ, who would establish justice and equity on the earth. This christ would defend the cause of the poor, defeat the oppressors of the world, and allow righteousness to flourish and peace to abound. Jesus seemed to embody for his early disciples those very qualities. When he reached out to the excluded, healed the sick, fed the hungry, and chastised the rich and the powerful, they saw him establishing equity. The fact that he was crucified without God intervening to prevent it was a crisis of faith. It was only with the resurrection that they understood that Jesus was the Christ who would "judge your people with righteousness, and your poor with justice." The fact that he came and yet the world continues to display injustice and oppression becomes a crisis of faith for contemporary Christians. During Advent, we live in an "already but not yet" time frame. We believe that Jesus is the Christ and did embody the hope of Israel for the peace and justice for which we yearn, but each Advent season we are invited to believe that Christ will come again to complete his work. In the meantime, we are to live as if that might happen at any time.

Romans 15:4-13

> *May the God of steadfastness and encouragement grant you to live in harmony with one another, in accordance with Christ Jesus, so that together you may with one voice glorify the God and Father of our Lord Jesus Christ.* — Romans 15:5-6

When you consider how many churches there are across the world, or even in your own community, do you wonder at the power of our witness if we could commit to live in harmony with one another? What glory could be given to God if it was clear to the world that Christians in every nation and culture held a common commitment to live as Christ taught us. Can you imagine the impact if the members of your church would pledge for one year that they would put a moratorium on all gossip that divides; that they would cease complaining for one year; that they would "bear with the failings of the weak" and try to serve even our neighbors within the church according to their needs? Imagine every member of your church pledging to welcome one another as Christ has welcomed us. Could we, as Jesus did, commit ourselves and encourage our neighbors in the faith to worship God on a regular basis? Imagine what it says to nonbelievers that we say we accept Christ as our Lord but are not able to set aside time to worship God at least once a week. Consider the power of the voice we would have if we could at least agree that for one year we would with "one voice glorify the God and Father of our Lord Jesus Christ."

Matthew 3:1-12

> *Repent, for the kingdom of heaven has come near ... Prepare the way of the Lord, make his paths straight.* — Matthew 3:2-3

John's message was one of repentance or redirecting one's priorities if one was to recognize the kingdom of heaven or the power of God's rule in one's life. He quoted Isaiah 40:3 in telling people they must make preparation in order to receive God. John's dress drew obvious comparisons to Elijah (2 Kings 1:8). Tradition held that Elijah would come again and usher in the new age of God's presence in the world (Malachi 4:5). The popularity of John's call for repentance is seen in verses 5 and 6. When John saw the Pharisees and Sadducees coming for baptism, those whose practice of the faith had found its accommodation with the world, he challenged the sincerity of their repentance. He charged them with relying on their spiritual heritage (Abraham as our father) and challenged them to "bear fruit that befits repentance...." Like Jeremiah 11:16, John compared Israel to a barren olive tree whose leaders had failed to guide them in producing the expected fruit. John saw his baptism not as an end in itself but as a preparation for receiving the one who would come after him. For Matthew, the question was not whether God had entered the world in the birth of Jesus, but why the political and religious powers and the people failed to recognize and receive him. The encounter with God in this world can be one of both promise and peril. The Christ will baptize with the Holy Spirit, the power that enables a person to fulfill God's promise in life, and with fire, the judgment that falls on one's inability to receive God's gifts or to use them in the fulfillment of God's promise. God gives the church the freedom to reject the hope of God's presence or to receive it. The difference depends on our willingness to repent of the arrogance that blocks our receptivity to the entirely new thing being born into the world.

Advent 3

Isaiah 35:1-10

The wilderness and the dry land shall be glad, the desert shall rejoice and blossom ... and rejoice with joy and singing.... — Isaiah 35:1-2

Listen, for even now you can hear the faint sound of laughter bubbling up from deep within creation. It is not the laughter of the final celebration but rather the anticipatory laughter of one who has suddenly recognized the clue that unlocks the mystery. For the prophet Isaiah, and for us, there are still miles to go before the journey is complete, but there is an inner delight in having discovered the way. We can now "say to those who are of a fearful heart, 'Be strong, do not fear! Here is your God.' " The confidence of faith is expressed as, "Now faith is the assurance of things hoped for, the conviction of things not seen" (Hebrews 11:1). Is not a great deal of the pain in our lives, and particularly the stress of living, due to our loss of confidence in the why of life? If we knew that the weight we were carrying was for a worthy purpose, would it not be easier to bear? Is there any family tension, job demand, or frustration too difficult if we knew for certain that this is precisely what we need to be doing to accomplish the miracle of God's salvation? If we knew that God could use our efforts to accomplish God's purpose, that we were contributing to the larger story that God is unfolding, could we not "obtain joy and gladness, and sorrow and sighing" that would never flee away? Listen, for even now you can hear the sound of laughter.

Luke 1:47-55

His mercy is for those who fear him from generation to generation. — Luke 1:50

Mary's song of praise emerged out of her personal experience but had connections with both the past and the future. She had just experienced signs of God's activity in her own body and in that of her older cousin, Elizabeth. God had blessed this unknown teenager with the miracle of life and done the same for an elderly cousin who had previously been barren. As we continue the season of Advent, we are reminded that both the past and the future are full of life. The elderly in the body of Christ are never barren, and the young offer us repeated surprises of new life. God's generative presence in the church shatters our preconceptions of reality and our understanding of power and status. As we prepare for the birth of Christ, we are humbled and invited again to pay attention to the weak and the hungry among us for signs of God's birthing activity. As did Mary, we are invited to see this activity of God among us as both surprisingly new and in solid continuity with "the promise (God) made to our ancestors, to Abraham and to his descendents forever." The church reads the story of Mary as symbolic of its own history as a congregation. We are virgin territory for the miracle of God's impregnating us with unexpected and miraculous possibilities. We are never too old or too young to be bearers of God's word.

James 5:7-10

Be patient, therefore, beloved, until the coming of the Lord.... — James 5:7

Perhaps, in this third Sunday of Advent, it is particularly important to hear James' admonition to the church to be patient with one another. The hectic pace of Advent is but a microcosm of the challenge of church life in general. It is so easy to lose patience with the failure of the church to meet our expectations or the failure of the members to meet some mythical standard of faithfulness. "Do not grumble against one another so that you may not be judged," counseled James. He depicted the slow process of salvation in the church to be like farmers who waited for the crop. He had planted the seeds and cultivated the ground, but the true growth of faith among the members of the church was only partially dependent on what he did or the programs that were offered. It is hard to measure the impact of our being patient and not grumbling, but we all know of those who have left the church because someone acted impatiently or judgmentally toward them. James even went so far as to suggest the value of the suffering we endure. The clergy and lead members of a church are well aware of the extra burden they bear because many members do not actively participate. What we sometimes forget is that our very act of patience with them may be our strongest witness to our faith.

Matthew 11:2-11

> *... Are you the one who is to come or are we to wait for another?* — Matthew 11:3

John sat in prison and wondered whether Jesus was the Christ. Why should he wonder? Because the hope had been that when the Messiah came, the powers of injustice would no longer prevail, and yet John was continuing to experience that injustice in his own personal life. When Matthew wrote the gospel, that same haunting question plagued the early church. Despite their faith in the resurrected Christ, the problem was that the world continued to experience the injustice they had experienced prior to Jesus' coming. If it was Jesus who John's disciples questioned in Matthew, today it is the forms of the body of Christ. Many people have grown discouraged trying to find the true church and have tried to be Christian apart from the body of Christ. Many others float from church to church seeking the true church. Others grumble or seek changes within their church to try to make it more responsive to their expectations. All are asking: "Is this God's church or shall we look for another?" Jesus' response, "By their fruits you shall know them," is scary for a church that always feels inadequate in its response to its call. Jesus pointed to the fruits of his ministry — "the blind receive their sight ... and the poor have good news brought to them." Then he added, "Blessed is anyone who takes no offense at me." Why would anyone take offense at Jesus' good works? Was it because such good works were so other-directed that it called attention to their (our) selfishness? Do we demand that the body of Christ meet our expectation, or we will not follow? What is the faithful response when the body of Christ does not live up to our expectations?

Advent 4

Isaiah 7:10-16

Ask a sign of the Lord your God; let it be deep as Sheol or high as heaven. — Isaiah 7:11

Ahaz, king of Judah, and his capitol city of Jerusalem were under siege. The king of Israel in the North and the ruler of Syria had allied together to conquer Jerusalem. Ahaz also was seeking alliance with another nation that would help defend against this threat. Isaiah was urging an alternative action of trusting in God. "Take heed, be quiet, do not fear ..." (Isaiah 7:4). In what would, at first glance, appear to be a very pious act, Ahaz refused to "put the Lord to the test." The prophet then proclaimed, "The Lord himself will give you a sign." The sign that God gave to Ahaz was the very opposite of what one might expect. It was not a voice from the sky or a mountain suddenly moving from one spot to the other. In some ways it was a most ordinary event. It was the promise of the birth of a child. Rather than a display of divine power, God offered a symbol of vulnerability. A child is totally dependent on its mother for the first period of life. Rather than recognizing and seeking to trust his people's dependence on God, Ahaz sought a military alliance. In seeking such an alliance, it still offered the illusion that Ahaz was in control. The sign that God offered reminded Ahaz that someone else was in charge. In the face of the threat of violence, it is natural to use our energy to seek a counter-violence to ward off the threat. We buy a gun, get self-defense training, or hire a bodyguard. It is hard to focus our energies on listening to God in trust. The miracle of God's presence is that it is expressed through events we often see as ordinary but, when we look closer, are evidence of the miracle of life. The miracle of Christmas calls our attention to God's presence in the ordinary.

Psalm 80:1-7, 17-19

> *Restore us, O God; let your face shine, that we may be saved.* — Psalm 80:3

On this fourth Sunday of Advent, we approach the tension between romantic images celebrating an ancient birth and a troubled world that desperately yearns for restoration. For the cynic, Christmas easily can be seen as a frivolous extravagance that ignores the real pain in people's lives. Even believers struggle with the relevance of faith to the fragile state of the world. We read the stories of God's intervention in Israel's life and wonder if it can happen again. If God is the shepherd who led "Joseph like a flock," why does God not "stir up (his) might and come and save us"? We can join with the psalmist in wondering why God does not answer our prayers and do something about this violent world. "You have fed them with the bread of tears, and given them tears to drink in full measure." It is no wonder that people are cynical about the relevance of faith. "You make us the scorn of our neighbors, our enemies laugh among themselves." While the psalmist was thinking of Israel, as we near the Christmas season, we think of Jesus when we pray, "But let your hand be upon the one at your right hand, the one whom you made strong for yourself." Then, as Christians, we let that prayer be for the body of Christ that we might become God's healing presence in our troubled world. "Restore us, O Lord God of hosts; let your face shine, that we may be saved." We celebrate the birth of Christ and pray that the body of Christ might again give evidence of God's presence among us.

Romans 1:1-7

> *Grace to you and peace from God our Father and the Lord Jesus Christ.* — Romans 1:7

There is lots of information to be derived from this opening greeting from Paul to the Romans. Immediately, Paul described his life as centered on Jesus Christ. As an apostle, he had a particular mission to perform on behalf of Jesus. There is a certain freedom in knowing where your loyalties lie and what your purpose in life is. Paul believed that he had been set apart, or given the special assignment in life, as defined by the gospel of God. This is the good news that had been promised by the words of the prophets; while it is new, it also has continuity with the past. For the Jews, the prophetic writings include what we call the historical books. Unlike the later Marcionites, who would suggest that the God of Jesus is different from the God of the Hebrew scriptures, Paul was clear that the revelation of God was consistent throughout history. God does not contradict Godself. The new aspect of God's gospel was that it had now been revealed in God's Son "who was descended from David according to the flesh...."

Apparently, Paul had no knowledge of the concept of the virgin birth of Jesus. He assumed that Jesus was the child of Joseph and therefore a direct descendent of David. However, Jesus had more than human origins. Jesus "was declared to be Son of God with power according to the spirit of holiness by resurrection from the dead...." Our life is defined not only by our human origins, but also by the work of God's Spirit within us. In Mark, Jesus would also suggest that the family cannot be defined by bloodline alone but by our response to God in our lives (Mark 3:34-35). Paul defined two central aspects of God's presence in his life. The first was the experience of God's grace that laid claim to his life in a manner that transcended all criteria of human worth. The second was apostleship that gave Paul's life a sense of purpose and meaning. In Paul's life, that purpose was "to bring about the obedience of faith among all the Gentiles for the sake of his name...." As we approach the Christmas season, Paul's greeting can raise for us an awareness of the grace of God by which we have been invited into the faith. We are, after all, the Gentiles that were included into God's people through no merit on our part. It can also raise the question of apostleship. What is the purpose that connects us with God's purpose and therefore gives our lives meaning that has eternal significance?

Matthew 1:18-25

> *... do not be afraid to take Mary as your wife, for the child conceived in her is from the Holy Spirit.*
> — Matthew 1:20

This is a story told from the perspective of the privileged because Joseph and Mary lived in a clearly patriarchal world. For Mary to be betrothed to Joseph meant she was bound like property to him, and that betrothal could only be dissolved if Joseph gave Mary a writ of divorce and not vice versa. When Mary was found to be with child, Joseph would have been well within his rights to have her stoned to death. Matthew suggested that from the perspective of the privileged, "doing right" must be seen as a communal rather than an individual act. "Her husband, Joseph, being a righteous man and unwilling to expose her to public disgrace, planned to dismiss her quietly." It was because Joseph paused to consider the effect of his "doing right" on Mary, whom he had every reason to believe had wronged him, that he was open to God's revealing how the same events looked from the divine perspective. An angel asked him to recognize that the very action that seemed to have violated his "rights" might well contain birth pangs of the word of God. As will be true in the climax of the gospel, it was a woman who was able to bear the authentic message of God's word to a society of privileged men who were blinded by their positions. In both cases, their names were Mary, which in Hebrew is Miriam who was the sister of Moses. Joseph, by identifying with Mary rather than his "rights" contributed to the fulfillment of God's purposes.

Christmas Eve/Christmas Day

Isaiah 9:2-7

> *The people who walked in darkness have seen a great light; those who lived in a land of deep darkness — on them light has shined.* — Isaiah 9:2

The theme of God's light that splits the darkness is a constant in the Bible. Genesis tells us that "darkness covered the face of the deep," then God spoke a word and there was light (Genesis 1:2-3). The psalmist uses the same word as Isaiah in Psalm 23:3, "Even though I walk through the darkest valley." The gospel of John makes use of the same image when he speaks of the coming of the Word, "What has come into being in him was life, and the life was the light of all people. The light shines in darkness, and the darkness did not overcome it" (John 1:3b-5). From the chaos of the beginning, to the chaos of national disaster in Isaiah, to the chaos of oppression by the Romans, right up to the present-day chaos in many people's lives, the hope has always been that God would and will speak a word that will split the darkness. For the Israelites this had national implications in their current plight. As a nation, their very existence was at risk. As was common in their faith, the memory of how God had saved them previously gave them courage to face their future. This time, Isaiah recalls the time when the Midianites threatened their existence, and Gideon became their liberator (Judges 6-8). The connection Isaiah made between international peace and the birth of a child (Isaiah 9:5-6) reminds us as we celebrate Christmas that the birth of Christ has far larger implications for our world than just heartwarming stories about a birth in a stable. If we are to associate the birth the prophet speaks of with the birth of Christ, then we need to also explore the implications of that birth of which the prophet speaks, "His authority shall grow continually, and there shall be endless peace for the throne of David and his kingdom. He will establish and uphold it with justice and with righteousness from this time onward and forevermore." In what way has the birth of Jesus and our recognition of him as the Christ caused us to work for peace in the world?

Psalm 96

> ... *He will judge the world with righteousness, and the peoples with his truth.*   — Psalm 96:13

To read Psalm 96 as part of one's celebration of Christmas is again to be reminded of the emphasis on peace and the worldwide implications of the event. Psalm 96 is a proleptic celebration of the culmination of God's purpose for the world. It is in anticipation of the time when the whole earth will sing together a new song (v. 1) that will bless God's name and daily tell of God's salvation (v. 2). This is not a private message but one that has implications for the whole world: "Declare his glory among the nations, his marvelous works among all the people" (v. 3). When people recognize the contrast between what they have been worshiping or giving worth and value to (v. 5) and the source of true honor, majesty, strength, and glory (v. 6), they will understand the true source of peace. All peoples will be able to recognize what God does in life (v. 7) and want to respond with an appropriate offering (v. 8). It is in such unified worship that the world will come together (v. 9). It is when we all recognize that God's authority and justice provides the world with stability (v. 10) that true peace can be realized. Even the natural world, which has been suffering the consequence of human arrogance (Romans 8:18-25), will join in the celebration (vv. 11-12). The center of our ecological imbalance, as well as the violent divisiveness among nations, is our failure to recognize and give worship to God. It is our arrogance that denies God is the center of truth and justice. God's presence on earth is the fulfillment of righteousness and truth intended from the beginning (v. 13). Yet at Christmas time, we are again reminded that such truth is not imposed on others but is revealed as we become servants to the world.

Titus 2:11-14

For the grace of God has appeared, bringing salvation to all.... — Titus 2:11

If Christians are tempted to celebrate the birth of Christ as the advent of their own personal Savior, the early church's emphasis on the universal implications of this event is a helpful reminder. The birth of Jesus was the result of the grace of God for all humanity and not a reward for the better qualities of a few. First Timothy says it even more clearly in 2:3-6: "This is right and is acceptable in the sight of God our Savior, who desires everyone to be saved and to come to the knowledge of the truth. For there is one God; there is also one mediator between God and humankind, Christ Jesus, himself human, who gave himself a ransom for all...." As we are increasingly in relationship with other major faiths in the world, this emphasis would be a valuable idea to explore. The early church, which indeed lived in a pluralistic world, saw the universal implications of Christ not as a belief to be imposed on others but a truth that could be witnessed to by our behavior: "For the grace of God has appeared, bringing salvation to all, training us to renounce impiety and worldly passions, and in the present age to live lives that are self-controlled, upright, and godly ..." (Titus 2:11-12). As is true in most of Paul's letters, here the emphasis is on the unmerited grace of God that finds its manifestation in the fruits of the Spirit. The purpose of Jesus' sacrifice was to "redeem us from all iniquity and purify for himself a people of his own who are zealous for good deeds." While good deeds do not save us, they do become a strong witness to the rest of the world of the unmerited grace that we have received and which is available to all. We do not wait for others to come to an agreement with us as the to the nature of the faith but rather relate to them as ones that are already redeemed and worthy of our love and compassion.

Luke 2:1-14 (15-20)

In those days a decree went out from Emperor Augustus that all the world should be registered. — Luke 2:1

If you were in charge of determining which events were to be selected to be broadcast on the nightly news, would you select a decree by the Emperor Augustus, who ruled much of the known world, or what might be happening in the lives of a poor couple in one small village in a third-rate colony of the Roman empire? We are accustomed to believing that the decisions of the powerful are more significant than the events that take place in the lives of ordinary people. Yet 2,000 years later, even from a secular perspective, the event that most transformed the world was not the census that was taken in response to the decree of Emperor Augustus but the birth of a child that largely went unnoticed at the time. The ordinary person would hardly remember Augustus today. This same emphasis on God finding expression in the lives of ordinary people is continued in the event that is recorded next. It was neither through the wealthy nor the powerful that God chose to make the announcement of what had happened in Bethlehem. Rather it was to a group of shepherds who were working the night shift. We have romanticized shepherds in our telling of this story, but at the time shepherds were often considered a necessary but somewhat disreputable part of the society. Their invisibility might be compared to the garbage collectors or street sweepers of our time. Yet it was to them, as they toiled at night on behalf of someone else, that the angels of the Lord appeared. God's choice of a poor couple who had to make do with facilities found where animals are kept and shepherds who labored on behalf of others may have implications for where we look for the presence of God in our world. It might also make us more alert as observers of the ordinary events of life and less enthralled by what others might think of as the important events. God has a tendency to make his presence known in those areas of life that are often overlooked.

Christmas 1

Isaiah 63:7-9

> *For he said, "Surely they are my people, children who will not deal falsely; and he became their savior in all their distress."* — Isaiah 63:8

This passage is part of a lament that mourns the sad state of Israel. As Israel grieved its condition of poverty and powerlessness, in this passage it remembered its origin. When God graciously formed them as a people from a group of slaves in Egypt, "... he became their savior in all their distress." God did not do that as some distant force. "It was no messenger or angel but his presence that saved them...." As we celebrate the first Sunday after Christmas, we also experience the poverty and powerlessness of the church as the people of God. As we lament the sad condition of the church, it is important that we remember our origin, as well. It was God's gracious choice to dwell among us in the person of Jesus. "For he said, 'Surely they are my people, children who will not deal falsely; and he became their savior in all their distress.' " Whatever is true about the state of the church, our very existence is the result of God's gracious act. Like Israel, the church should be reminding ourselves that we are in the hands of God. As one continues to read the rest of Israel's lament, you hear Israel plead with God for God's renewed presence that they might be redeemed from their present state. To celebrate the incarnation of the Word of God in the community of faith is to remember our origin in the past but also to anticipate God's gracious work in our future.

Psalm 148

> *Let them praise the name of the Lord, for he commanded and they were created.* — Psalm 148:5

The book of Psalms, which has given expression to the total spectrum of emotions from despairing lament to ecstatic praise, culminates in six psalms of praise. If, as Calvin said, the psalms are an anatomy of the human soul, giving expression to every feeling humans have, then they also suggest that the culmination of life is in praise. Psalm 148 further suggests that the entire universe moves toward that same ecstatic expression of praise. From angels and heavenly hosts to sun, moon, and stars, the physical universe has structured into it the command to praise God. Such praise finds its expression in fire and hail, mountains and hills, wild and domestic animals, kings and princes, men and women, young and old. Our very existence finds its most authentic fulfillment in praising God. The most precious gift that God has given humanity, and has especially bestowed on the people of Israel, is the gift of worship that invites people to offer God praise. "He has raised up a horn for his people, praise for all his faithful, for the people of Israel who are close to him. Praise the Lord!" As the lectionary passage for this Sunday from Isaiah suggests, "It is God's presence that saves them." On this first Sunday after Christmas, after the rush of the season has begun to settle down, we can pause to reflect on the incredible gift of God's presence among us in the person of Jesus. In the face of such a stunning expression of love, we can only respond with praise. "Praise the Lord!"

Hebrews 2:10-18

Because he himself was tested by what he suffered, he is able to help those who are being tested.
— Hebrews 2:18

On this first Sunday after Christmas, we reflect on the amazing truth of the incarnation. The author was so sure that in Jesus, God was present to us, that he quoted Isaiah 8:17-18 from the Greek translation as if it were Jesus speaking: "I will put my trust in him ... Here am I and the children whom God has given me." Hebrews also saw the latter part of Psalm 22 as applying to Jesus: "I will proclaim your name...." While this might appear anachronistic to us because we see Jesus as having lived hundreds of years after these scriptures had been written, they reveal a very fluid sense of time that speaks of the church's understanding of the connection between eternity and time. The Word of God has been present in creation since the beginning and has been made fully manifest in the person of Jesus. The reality that seems to limit our existence is death. Hebrews declared that through Jesus' death and resurrection, he had broken the grip that death had over us and "set free those who all their lives were held in slavery through the fear of death." By Jesus' birth, eternity entered time, and by his death, he destroyed the tyranny of time over us. While this mixture of time and eternity has always been part of creation, it is through his suffering and death that it is made clear to us. Jesus' death was the final confirmation of what was made clear by his birth — God is for us.

Matthew 2:13-23

> *... an angel of the Lord appeared to Joseph in a dream and said, "Get up, take the child and his mother, and flee to Egypt...."* — Matthew 2:13

Joseph was warned in a dream to take the child and his mother and flee to Egypt. God communicated to an earlier Joseph through dreams (Genesis 37:5-11), and that Joseph was led into Egypt so that when starvation threatened the very existence of Israel, Egypt would be the place of their salvation (Genesis 37 and 39-45). Now again, when Jesus' life was threatened, it was by means of Joseph in Egypt that his life was preserved. Both Israel (Exodus 4:22) and Jesus are God's firstborn. Both are preserved by God in Egypt. Herod immediately ordered the killing of all the male children in Bethlehem and the surrounding region who were two years old or under. This is paralleled in Exodus 1:15—2:10 where the pharaoh was threatened by the growth in number of Israelites and ordered all male children killed at birth. The horrible events of the massacre, not God, fulfilled the prophecy of Jeremiah 31:15. Rachel was the favorite wife of Jacob but was barren, while her sister, Leah, and a couple of maids were very fertile (Genesis 29:31—30:21). Finally Rachel gave birth to Joseph and became pregnant a second time. The second birth was too strenuous for her, and as she was dying, she named her second son Benoni, or son of my sorrows. Rachel was buried at Rama, and the tradition grew that the spirit of Rachel, the ancestress of Israel, continued to mourn and protest the fate of chosen Israel whose sorrowful experience seemed to contradict the very promise of God. For Matthew, Jeremiah's promise of a new creation (Jeremiah 31:22) found fulfillment in the birth of Jesus that took place in the midst of the fratricidal tendencies of humanity. The world's violence needs to be protested by the Rachel in us that refuses to be consoled in the face of evil. But for Matthew, such violence did not end in protest. God was seen in Jesus reaching into that world of violence and giving birth to a new hope.

Christmas 2

Jeremiah 31:7-14

> *... for I have become a father to Israel, and Ephraim is my firstborn....* — Jeremiah 31:9

As we gather for worship on this second Sunday after Christmas, the echo of celebrating the birth of Jesus as God's Son is still fresh in our memories. We recognize that the term "firstborn" is used differently than is normally assumed. Jeremiah referred to Ephraim, a name used to refer to Israel, as God's firstborn. This reminds us that God told Moses in Exodus 4:22 to tell the pharaoh that Israel was God's firstborn Son. Exodus 13:1 spoke of the divine claim on the firstborn. To speak of Jesus as God's firstborn son is to see embodied in his person the life of all of Israel and to recognize God's special claim on the community of faith. In celebrating Jesus' birth, we do not forget the harshness of the world into which he was born. Like Israel, Jesus lived in a harsh world and suffered as a victim of the world's violence. But the violence of the world is not the final word. "He who scattered Israel will gather him, and will keep him as a shepherd a flock." Like Israel, Jesus also would go into Egypt, but God also would bring him out of Egypt. Hosea 11:1 also spoke of God's Son that God called out of Egypt, and Hosea foreshadowed the resurrection in Hosea 6:2, "... on the third day he will raise us up, that we may live before him." In Jesus we see incarnated the pattern of God's love that holds promise for a world embedded in violence. "Then shall young women rejoice ... gladness for sorrow." While violence nips at our heels, it is God who will lead us home.

Psalm 147:12-20

> *He declares his word to Jacob, his statutes and ordinances to Israel. He has not dealt thus with any other nation; they do not know his ordinances.*
>
> — Psalm 147:19-20

This psalm is part of a series of six psalms of praise that conclude the book of Psalms. This portion commands praise because of God's protective care of Israel. "He grants peace within your borders; he fills you with finest wheat." The care of God was felt in both the political and the natural realms of their lives. The forces of nature became an expression of God's care. "... He makes his wind blow, and the waters flow." Others, of course, also experienced these same forces of nature, but they were unaware of the divine presence. Much of our awareness of the presence of God is affected by our attentiveness. If we are attentive to God's presence, then we will notice it in even the most ordinary of events. What had helped Israel was that God had blessed them with his statutes and ordinances that instructed or taught them to be attentive. All of the people experienced the rhythms of both politics and nature, but Israel had been shown how to interpret these experiences. When we begin to pay attention to how God is at work in even the most ordinary of experiences, we gain strength from an awareness of his care. The church has also been given the privilege of the scriptures that teach us how and where to look for God. We gather to praise God and then depart with a heightened awareness of God's continual care. Praise the Lord.

Ephesians 1:3-14

... just as he chose us in Christ before the foundation of the world to be holy and blameless before him in love.
— Ephesians 1:4

The author of Ephesians, Paul, or a writer in his name, began his letter with some incredible claims. These themes were developed throughout his letter and became a major challenge for the church. What is the effect on the church of believing that we were chosen before the foundation of the world? When we are feeling inadequate to the task, what does it mean to suggest God has blessed us with every spiritual blessing in heavenly places? Can we afford to act toward the church as if it were simply a volunteer organization if God established its mission from the beginning of time? Since we are fully aware of the sins of the church, how are we to understand that we are to be "holy and blameless before him in love"? Does it not make "the riches of his grace which he lavished on us" all the more incredible? If the mystery of God's plan to bring together or reconcile everything in heaven and earth is revealed in the church, then do we need to view what is taking place in the church from a different perspective? Paul and the leaders of the early church were not naive people or blind to the human frailties that were evident in the church. We often become so focused on the human organization of the church, and whether it does or does not meet our expectations, that we lose sight of its divine dimension. In this clearly frail family of the people of God, the very mystery of the redemption of God is being revealed. God's glory is being revealed, and we are challenged to turn to the church with expectation of our redemption and the redemption of the world.

John 1:(1-9) 10-18

No one has ever seen God. It is God the only Son, who is close to the Father's heart, who has made him known.
— John 1:18

The other gospels begin with the humanness of Jesus and allow glimpses of God to shine through. John, with intentional reference to Genesis 1:1, makes the astonishing claim of the complete divinity of Jesus. "In the beginning was the Word, and the Word was with God, and the Word was God." The only similar claim was in Proverbs 8:22 ff where Sophia, the feminine spirit of wisdom, was said to be at the beginning with God and the partner in God's creation of the universe. Like wisdom, John claimed "all things came into being through him...." Jesus was the embodiment of God on earth. "No one has ever seen God," but Jesus made God known. In coming to live among us, Jesus laid claim to all of creation, but in a manner that offered them a free choice. "He came to what was his own, and his own people did not accept him." While John did not speak of Jesus' virgin birth, he described the possibility of a virgin birth for any who received him. "But to all who receive him ... he gave power to become children of God, who were born, not of blood or the will of the flesh ... but of God." If the other gospels give us a glimpse of God from below, John gives us a glimpse of God from above. Here we see that God began with Jesus Christ in order to provide creation with the hope of eternity. "From his fullness, we have all received, grace upon grace." This passage places the particulars of the Christmas story in a universal context.

The Epiphany Of Our Lord

Isaiah 60:1-6

> *For darkness shall cover the earth, and thick darkness the peoples; but the Lord will arise upon you, and his glory will appear over you.* — Isaiah 60:2

The image of light splitting the darkness is a continuing theme of scripture. In Genesis 1, God speaks the word, "Let there be light," and light splits the darkness. In Isaiah 9:2, "The people who walked in darkness have seen a great light." In John 1:5, light again becomes a central image. "The light shines in darkness, and the darkness did not overcome it." So now, for Epiphany Sunday, we draw on the same theme from Isaiah. Traditionally, Epiphany celebrates the world's recognition of the Christ. It was the pagan wise men from the East who knelt before the infant Jesus. In a world that confines Jesus to the religious sphere of one among many religions, the prophet speaks of, and Matthew will confirm, the universal nature of the truth of God toward which the world moves. It is not a truth that needs to be imposed on the world. It is a light that will shine in the darkness of the world and illuminate a path that will invite the world's recognition. "Lift up your eyes and look around; they all gather together...." The light of God will ultimately overcome the economic divisions that plague the world. Instead of being the source of division, the wealth of the world will manifest the glory of God. "They shall bring gold and frankincense and shall proclaim the praise of the Lord." Epiphany is a proleptic celebration of that which God will yet accomplish. Christians are invited to live within that light in a way that invites the world to see God's truth made visible among them.

Psalm 72:1-7, 10-14

May he judge your people with righteousness, and your poor with justice. — Psalm 72:2

This is a royal psalm. It is a prayer for the king. It asks God to enable the king to rule as God would intend. "Give the king your justice, O God, and your righteousness to a king's son." By slightly altering the subject, we can hear ourselves praying for our leaders. "Give the [president] your justice, O God, and your righteousness to [his administration]. May [the courts] judge your people with righteousness, and your poor with justice." We affirm that the purpose of a good government is to release the prosperity of the land. "May the mountains yield prosperity for the people, and the hills, in righteousness." We recognize the proper role of government to provide security. "May [our government] defend the cause of the poor of the people, and give deliverance to the needy, and crush the oppressor." There is an appropriate prayer for the well-being of those who govern well. "In [this administration] may righteousness flourish and peace abound, until the moon is no more." Of course from a Christian perspective, the image of the proper way for a government to rule is reflected in the way in which Christ ruled. This psalm can also be amended in a way that recognizes the reign of Christ in our lives. "For [Christ] redeems their life; and precious is their blood in his sight." On Epiphany, when we hear the story of the kings bringing their gifts and bowing before Christ, we learn to pray for a government that will recognize its responsibility to utilize its wealth and power to serve the justice and compassion we see reflected in Christ.

Ephesians 3:1-12

> *... so that through the church the wisdom of God in its rich variety might be made known....*
> — Ephesians 3:1-12

Ephesians lifts up an understanding of the role of the church in God's plan. The mystery of Christ was made visible in Paul's own story. Here was a Zealot violently pursuing a mission to destroy the early group of Christians. God took this enemy of the church and transformed him into its chief champion. "Although I am least of all the saints, this grace was given to me...." This movement of God in Paul's life became a parable of God's work in Christ. God was, in Christ, transforming the Gentile outsider into a member of the people of God. The mystery that had been hidden that "the Gentiles have become fellow heirs, members of the same body ..." was now revealed. The mystery of "the boundless riches of Christ" was revealed in Paul's life. In turn, he was made "a prisoner of Christ Jesus for the sake of you Gentiles." Paul was captured by this parable of grace in his own life and commissioned to "bring to the Gentiles the news of the boundless riches of Christ." This limitless grace in Christ is the secret to God's plan "hidden for ages in God who created all things." This truth that the grace of God has no boundaries and reaches out to include the most disparate of peoples is now the commission of the church. The church is to carry this message of grace to all authorities in heaven and earth. The church's commission is to boldly proclaim that everyone can have "access to God in boldness and confidence." The incredible task of the church is to become that parable of grace to the world and break through the walls of exclusive membership that is so common in human groups.

Matthew 2:1-12

> *... and they knelt down and paid him homage. Then, opening their treasure chests, they offered him gifts of gold, frankincense, and myrrh.* — Matthew 2:11

Jesus, as the son of Abraham (Matthew 1:1), by whom the whole world is blessed (Genesis 12:3), was first recognized by pagans from the East. Two great rival powers ruled the world. There was Rome in the West and Parthia in the East. Mark Anthony, ruler of Rome, had named Herod "king of the Jews" so that Rome might have a puppet in this buffer state between these two great powers. The Magi were people who, through wisdom and observation, had made themselves valuable advisors to kings. These Parthian priests, men of wealth and status from the East, were willing to risk their lives by standing in Herod's court and announcing knowledge of a potential rival to Herod and their intention of paying homage to him. These pagan truth-seekers recognized via signs of nature that God had broken into history in a new way. The religious community had failed to see the signs of what God was doing, and the seekers lacked the scriptures to confirm the place.

Unlike those in political power, here symbolized by Herod, the religious community at least knew where to look to discover the truth when they were asked the right question. Herod, the keeper of political power, feigned interest in the birth of Christ, but only so he could regain control by crushing this new hope that had emerged in the world. The Magi, still pursuing the signs that God had provided them through their pursuit of astrology, discovered the birthplace of Jesus. They fell on their knees to worship Jesus and offer him the wealth that formed the basis of their status. The message to Matthew's hearers, who might be tempted to protect their status, was that by protecting their positions they might fail to recognize the presence of God in their lives. Matthew's story about Jesus began, as it will end (Matthew 27:54), with pagans recognizing the truth of Jesus while the religious community sought to do him harm.

The Baptism Of Our Lord
Epiphany 1
Ordinary Time 1

Isaiah 42:1-9

> *Here is my servant, whom I uphold, my chosen, in whom my soul delights; I have put my spirit upon him; he will bring forth justice to the nations.* — Isaiah 42:1

While Christians hear this passage in connection with the Spirit of God resting on Jesus at his baptism, it is important to first hear it as it relates to Israel. Isaiah spoke to a people who had lost all power in the world. Israel had been defeated, and their people had been carried into exile. Yet Isaiah continued to speak of the significant role that Israel would play on behalf of the world. The Israelite people were still the chosen people of God. "Here is my servant, whom I uphold, my chosen, in whom my soul delights." They were not chosen for themselves but because God had a mission for them to carry out on behalf of the world. "I have put my spirit upon him; he will bring forth justice to the nations." (See also Isaiah 49:6.) Since Israel was looked upon as a defeated nation, it was understandable that the prophet did not see them advancing the cause of justice through preaching (Isaiah 42:2) or by means of force (Isaiah 42:3), "but he will faithfully bring forth justice." There was recognition that this mission would involve hardships and require endurance. "He will not grow faint or be crushed until he has established justice in the earth...." This would be made more explicit in later servant songs (Isaiah 52:13—53:12).

Under these conditions, there was only one way that this vision could be anything other than pure delusion. The power to accomplish the mission rested on God, "who created the heavens and stretched them out, who spread out the earth and what comes from it...." Isaiah spoke to a dispirited people and reminded them that their existence depended on the God who created the universe and said, "I have taken you by the hand and kept you; I have given you as a covenant to the people, a light to the nations...." This vision that God revealed to them gave their lives purpose for the future. It was the same vision that was embodied by Jesus when the gospels reported that the Spirit rested upon him at his baptism. His mission would not be carried out by great displays of power but by faith in God. When the church grows dispirited because of its lack of power and influence to shape the world, we need to hear again that the success of our mission rests not on our strength and wisdom but on the Spirit of God that infuses us with hope. "See, the former things have come to pass and new things I now declare; before they spring forth, I tell you of them."

Psalm 29

> *The voice of the Lord is over the waters; the God of glory thunders, the Lord, over mighty waters.*
> — Psalm 29:3

Particularly in response to Isaiah 42:1-9, with which this psalm is paired in the lectionary, we hear the echo of the creation story in Genesis 1. In Genesis, the Spirit of God moved over the face of the waters, and God spoke with the result of creation emerging out of the formless void of chaos. The prophet Isaiah spoke of God making all things new. The psalmist saw this "voice of the Lord" shattering all the structures and preconceptions like a violent thunderstorm that treated the mighty cedars of Lebanon like toothpicks that snapped and are tossed about in the wind. For the Israelites, who were a land-based people, the waters were the perfect symbol of chaos, and a raging flood was an image of a return to chaos. When they said, "The Lord sits enthroned over the flood, the Lord sits enthroned as king forever," they were affirming two things. First, they recognized that life was filled with interminable floods where the chaos of evil seemed to predominate. Second, no matter how threatening the chaos appeared in their life, the creator God was always more powerful. Therefore, to sing of the mighty power of God is to trust God in the midst of the chaotic tumbles of our lives and to look for signs of new creation. All chaos is an experience that upsets the boundaries of the past and opens us to the possibility of the new thing that God is creating. For Christians who believe that in Christ God is reconciling the world, we face the chaos dependent on God and hear the prayer of the psalmist, "May the Lord give strength to his people! May the Lord bless his people with peace!"

Acts 10:34-43

> *I truly understand that God shows no partiality, but in every nation anyone who fears him and does what is right is acceptable to him.* — Acts 10:34-35

What if it was really true that anyone who fears (has reverence for) God and does what is right is acceptable to God? You do not have to belong to the proper race, nationality, or religion to be saved. In Acts, Peter spoke of this new understanding having begun "after the baptism that John announced." This was truly the baptism that rocked the world and broke open our preconceptions. In a sense, it was a return to the covenant with Noah (Genesis 9:1-7), which Jewish understanding suggests is the basic covenant that God requires of all humanity. To fear God and do what is right is to have a reverent care for all of life and to recognize that every living human is a reflection of the image of God. This basic covenant was embodied in the life of Jesus who was anointed by God "with the Holy Spirit and with power (and) went about doing good and healing all who were oppressed by the devil...." In this way, Jesus' baptism shattered the power of religion to offer or deny salvation. The grace of God transcended the narrowness of all religion. What then is the role of Christianity in such a world? In the same way that Jesus gave up power over others and became their servant, so Christians are invited to become servants of all humanity and seek to release in all individuals the image of God within them. "He commanded us to preach to the people and to testify that [Christ] is the one ordained by God as judge of the living and the dead." And that judgment is based on humans demonstrating a "love of God and neighbor." In one sense it is quite simple, but it is also frighteningly radical. The church, historically, has never been very good at using power and judgment. It is invited to try servanthood and grace.

Matthew 3:13-17

> *... Let it be so for now; for it is proper for us in this way to fulfill all righteousness....* — Matthew 3:15

John was offering a baptism of repentance for sins. Jesus came to him and asked to be baptized. Why would Jesus need to experience a baptism of repentance? Being chosen did not set him above others but rather caused him to identify with people's struggle with the sin in their lives. Jesus entered into the water because that was where the people were. God, in Jesus Christ, came to us first so that we might come to him. He did it to "fulfill all righteousness." Righteousness carries the sense of right relationships. If we are in right relationship with God and neighbor, then the whole intention of the law and the prophets is fulfilled. Being in right relationship requires us to be willing to be vulnerable to the struggle of our neighbor. In Isaiah 42:1-9, where the prophet described the servant of God as filled with God's Spirit, he said of that servant, "A bruised reed he will not break, and a dimly burning wick he will not quench; he will faithfully bring forth justice." If someone stands outside the struggle and tells others what they should do, the result is a division rather than reconciliation. When Jesus acted to fulfill righteousness by entering into the struggle with the people, the Spirit of God alighted on him, and God affirmed him as God's Son. This is the one who pleased God.

Epiphany 2
Ordinary Time 2

Isaiah 49:1-7

> ... *The Lord called me before I was born, while I was in my mother's womb he named me.* — Isaiah 49:1

It is clear that the prophet was speaking about the corporate community of faith, even though he used the image of an individual. In verse 3 he said, "You are my servant, Israel, in whom I will be glorified." For Christians, however, who see the life of Israel reembodied in the person of Jesus, we hear the words of the prophet on at least three levels. The prophet's words speak to us about Israel as a community, Jesus as a person, and the church as a community. In all three instances, they remind us that the call of God that sets our path has its origin in the eternity of God. "The Lord called me before I was born." There is a meaning and purpose in our lives that transcends any immediate experience. Even our dark moments have a larger significance. "But I said, 'I have labored in vain, I have spent my strength for nothing and vanity; yet surely my cause is with the Lord, and my reward with my God.'" As Israel has repeatedly had to remind itself, and as Jesus affirmed in his prayer in the Garden of Gethsemane (Matthew 26:39), the church would do well to remind itself that it has a purpose that is greater than its individual success and survival. "It is too light a thing that you should be my servant ... I will give you as a light to the nations, that my salvation may reach to the end of the earth." Like Israel, the church has frequently displayed a weakness for the temptation to disobedience and fractious fighting among ourselves. By our internal quarreling, we, also, have become "deeply despised, abhorred by the nations, the slave of rulers...." but God keeps advancing the divine purpose through us "because of the Lord, who is faithful, the holy one of Israel, who has chosen you."

Psalm 40:1-11

He drew me up from the desolate pit, out of the miry bog, and set my feet upon a rock, making my steps secure. — Psalm 40:2

You can listen to this story with the life of David in mind, as the superscription suggests. You can hear David praying these words after he had escaped the exile that Saul had driven him into and had been hailed king by the people. Or you could hear the words as David's prayer after he had escaped the coup attempt by his own son and had his kingdom restored. "I have told the glad news of deliverance in the great congregation." But with that memory in mind, you can also hear Jesus praying these words as he prayed right before his arrest. In the moment of great anguish (Luke 22:44), you can hear Jesus pray, "Do not, O Lord, withhold your mercy from me; let your steadfast love and your faithfulness keep me safe forever." In that same prayer, Jesus could recognize that his life had a greater purpose than whether he survived that immediate challenge. So he prayed, "Then I said, 'Here I am; in the scroll of the book it is written of me I delight to do your will, O my God, your law is within my heart.' " As the church hears this prayer with both David and Jesus in mind, it can gain strength to resist the seduction of the society around her. "Happy are those who make the Lord their trust, who do not turn to the proud, to those who go astray after false gods." All churches go through crises in which their very survival seems to be threatened. At such times, they need to remember again the one who sets their feet upon a rock, making their steps secure.

1 Corinthians 1:1-9

> *He will also strengthen you to the end, so that you may be blameless on the day of our Lord Jesus Christ.*
> — 1 Corinthians 1:8

It should jar our ears to hear Paul speak of the church of Corinth appearing blameless. This was a church that existed in the port city of Corinth with its low morals and a higher than normal prosperity. The city was controlled by the few at the expense of the many. The church itself clearly had experienced the strain of arrogance on the part of some toward others. Economic division, sexual problems, and marital difficulties, to name just a few, as well as some serious theological misunderstandings, plagued the church. In one form or another, we see in Corinth many of the problems that threaten the integrity of the church today. Picture writing any of numerous conflicted churches today and saying: "I give thanks to my God always for you because of the grace of God that has been given to you ... so that you are not lacking in any spiritual gift...." Read this passage slowly and insert the name of your church or a neighboring church of which you have felt critical. Hear yourself praying (and believing?) God "will also strengthen [the church you named], so that the church may be blameless on the day of our Lord Jesus Christ." As you read on in Corinthians, it is clear that Paul was not hesitant to criticize and challenge behavior in the church. Yet underneath his criticism was a core belief that "God is faithful; by him you were called into the fellowship of his Son, Jesus Christ our Lord." Picture how the debates in our churches would be different if they were undergirded by this core belief.

John 1:29-42

> *I myself did not know him, but the one who sent me to baptize with water said to me, "He on whom you see the Spirit descend and remain is the one who baptizes with the Holy Spirit."* — John 1:33

If the first three gospels emphasized the human side of Jesus in whom the divine was slowly revealed, John approached Jesus from the divine perspective. Yet, in doing so, he clearly drew upon the tradition of Israel provided in the Hebrew scriptures. John declared, "Here is the lamb of God who takes away the sins of the world." The image of the Passover Lamb (Exodus 12:1-13), by which the Hebrews were delivered from the plague of death in Egypt, was transformed into the Lamb of God that delivered the world from sin that led to death. Later, Andrew would speak of Jesus as the Messiah and quickly translated the word so that we would understand that it meant "the anointed" — or God's chosen one. While this was God's chosen one, he clearly was connected with what God had been doing with Israel all along. John also made clear that he knew this not because of his own knowledge but from God's revelation. Further, he declared that God revealed this in the midst of John's being obedient to his call. "I myself did not know him but the one who sent me to baptize with water said to me...." The journey of faith does not begin with revelation. It begins with being obedient to God's call, and God provides us with understanding as we go along.

Epiphany 3
Ordinary Time 3

Isaiah 9:1-4

But there will be no gloom for those who were in anguish.... — Isaiah 9:1

We often hear this as an Advent passage building up our expectation for the coming birth of Christ. It is perhaps helpful to also reflect on this passage apart from Advent. Isaiah was anticipating God raising up a new king that would restore Israel and take away its shame. The tribal regions of Zebulum and Naphtali and the region of Galilee had been conquered by Tiglath-Pilser in 733 BCE. As was the custom of a conqueror, he had exiled some of the leading citizens of those areas to live elsewhere and transplanted people from other lands to live in that area. The result, through intermarriage, was a mixed population. To the people of Judea, this population was polluted and hopelessly lost in darkness. Now, declared Isaiah, a new transformation was about to take place. "The people who walked in darkness have seen a great light...." Like in earlier days when Midian had oppressed Israel (Judges 6:1—8:28) and a judge was raised up to set them free, so Isaiah saw God about to shape historical forces in a way to regain hope and healing for Israel. Even before we read Isaiah's speech about a new king being born (Isaiah 9:6-7), we already hear that God was at work in life's events to shatter people's gloom and enable them to again celebrate the joy intended for their lives. "They rejoice before you as with joy at the harvest." Far too often, we give in to the despair of our situation as if the succession of events is inevitable. It is precisely at such times that we should anticipate a word from God that shatters our darkness.

Psalm 27:1, 4-9

> *The Lord is my light and my salvation; whom shall I fear?*
> — Psalm 27:1

This psalm celebrates the power of worship in the face of personally devastating circumstances. It is attributed to David, and one can imagine several incidents in David's life when he would have exulted in God's deliverance from his enemies. If we translate evildoers and adversaries into the negative circumstances of our lives, we can easily hear our name in the psalm. Whether it is David, or ourselves, we can recognize that it is in the act of worship that we gain strength. "One thing I asked of the Lord ... to live in the house of the Lord all the days of my life." As we rehearse God's faithfulness to us in the past, we gain strength for the future. "... I will offer in his tent sacrifices with shouts of joy. I will sing and make melody to the Lord." We lift our voices in praise, not because God's presence is obvious to us, but because we retain the memory of his saving grace, and so we seek to experience it anew. Scripture repeatedly speaks of God as one who hears the cry of those in distress. So, despite the seeming absence of God in a given moment in our lives, we lay claim to the faithfulness of God that we have heard about. "Hear, O Lord, when I cry aloud, be gracious to me and answer me!" Our very act of crying out evokes something deep within us. " 'Come,' my heart says, 'seek his face!' Your face, O Lord, do I seek. Do not hide your face from me." Even when tragedy has shattered our faith, it is worth participating in the act of worship because it is in worship that our faith can be restored.

1 Corinthians 1:10-18

> *Now I appeal to you ... that there be no divisions among you, but that you be united in the same mind and the same purpose.* — 1 Corinthians 1:10

Can one possibly read this passage without a deep sense of shame at the continuing divisions within the body of Christ? Paul satirized the division by naming several key leaders as possible claimants to loyalty. "What I mean is that each of you says, 'I belong to Paul ... Apollos ... Cephas' or 'I belong to Christ,' " as if such claims could set you above other believers. Can you not hear, "I belong to Calvin, John Wesley, or the true church" as if such claims do anything but shame us? Or, today, would such a claim be in the form of "I am born again, speak in tongues, am a liberal, a conservative, or an evangelical"? Should we not also tremble in response to Paul's rhetorical question, "Is Christ divided?" Given all of the foolish attempts throughout history, and in our current day, to establish the "pure" church, should we not step back from all human attempts to structure perfection through human wisdom and recognize with Paul that we are seeking to empty the cross of Christ of its power? If the crucifixion and resurrection of Christ "destroy(s) the wisdom of the wise," then perhaps we need to reflect deeply on how we have been behaving as Christians. If we are to be united in the same mind and the same purpose, then have our very divisions reflected our stubborn unwillingness to have "the same mind (in us) that was in Christ Jesus" (Philippians 2:5)? Until we are at least willing to strive to do that, can any of us claim to be faithful disciples of Christ?

Matthew 4:12-23

From that time Jesus began to proclaim, "Repent, for the kingdom of heaven has come near."
— Matthew 4:17

John was arrested. No protest by Jerusalem's leaders was heard. The politics of power, as seen in Herod and the religious leaders, allied together to silence John's call to repentance. Repentance was necessary if people were to be open to the presence and activity of God in their lives. Jesus withdrew to the fringe province known as "Galilee of the Gentiles." Normally, people would have expected that any word from God would come from Jerusalem and the temple. But when the religious center that is called to be a "light to the nations" (Isaiah 49:6), allows the call to repentance to be silenced, the "word of God" will move elsewhere. Since they had refused to listen in the center, it would be at the edge that the light would shine and bring joy to the nations (Isaiah 9:3).

The message of repentance was not silenced by John's arrest but now was spoken through Jesus. For Matthew, when we become so conditioned by our culture that we arrest the call to repentance and shut God out of the center of our lives, then the foreign element, that which disrupts our normal life, creates a crack in our impregnable fortress that allows new light to shine through. When Jesus began to call his disciples, he began with Peter and Andrew, who were seen by Jesus "casting a net into the sea," which would suggest that they were economically poor since they have to fish from the shore. Then he called James and John, who were fishing from a boat owned by their father and had more than one net. The kingdom would be made up of rich and poor, and the poor would be the first to be called. The call took place, not in a religious setting, but in the midst of people practicing their professions. The challenge for the church is to bring the call of Christ to the center of people's lives.

Epiphany 4
Ordinary Time 4

Micah 6:1-8

> *He has told you, O mortal, what is good; and what does the Lord require of you but to do justice, and to love kindness, and to walk humbly with your God.*
>
> — Micah 6:8

Micah pictured God arguing his case in a court in which nature was the jury. God served as both judge and defendant against a humanity that accused God of not doing enough. "Rise, plead your case before the mountains, and let the hills hear your voice ... for the Lord has a controversy with his people and he will contend with Israel." First, God asked the people to defend why they had wearied of being a faithful people. Christians can hear God asking the church why are they growing weary of being faithful. "O my people, what have I done to you? In what have I wearied you? Answer me!" You can hear the respondents complaining that their prayers and worship have not seemed to benefit them in any measurable way.

God then summarized the many ways that God had rescued the Israelites beginning with Egypt and proceeding forward. The people responded by asking in exaggerated terms what God wanted from them. "Will the Lord be pleased with thousands of rams, with ten thousands of rivers of oil? Shall I give my firstborn for my transgression, the fruit of my body for the sin of my soul?" God responded through Micah with classic simplicity. "[God] has told you, O mortal, what is good; and what does the Lord require of you but to do justice, and to love kindness, and to walk humbly with your God." All of our religious practices are designed to bring us into a state of reverence for God and compassion for our neighbor. In the supreme court of the universe, we are finally judged by how our lives have reflected love for God and love for our neighbor. I once saw a cartoon in which the petitioner said to God, "How can you allow so much hunger to exist in the world?" to which God responded, "I've been meaning to ask you the same question."

Psalm 15

Who may dwell on your holy hill? — Psalm 15:1

Despite our repeated attempts to complicate the truth of God, both in the Old and New Testaments, there is a core set of truths that reflect a universal yearning for reconciliation of the divisions among humanity. Jesus summed up the law in terms of the two basic relationships of love of God and love of neighbor. Micah summed it up in three parts — to do justice, love mercy, and walk humbly with your God. The psalmist also spoke against those acts that divided human from human. These are people who do not do what is right and speak the truth from their heart; people who do slander with their tongue and do evil to their friends and take up a reproach against their neighbors. In addition, the psalmist recognized the power of economics to divide and added, "who do not lend money at interest, and do not take a bribe against the innocent." Try to picture such admonitions becoming an ethic for nations in their foreign policy. If nations chose to live in this way with other nations, would we not be taking giant strides toward peace? Since Jesus commanded his disciples to go and teach the nations what he has taught us (Matthew 28:19-20), do we not have a responsibility to first reflect such behavior among ourselves and then to commend such behavior as practical politics for the nation?

1 Corinthians 1:18-31

> *For Jews demand signs and Greeks desire wisdom, but we proclaim Christ crucified, a stumbling block to Jews and foolishness to Gentiles....*
> — 1 Corinthians 1:23-24

In many ways, Christians are divided into two camps. There are those who want to base their faith on signs. The proof of their faith is contained in the miraculous stories of the unexplainable. A young man is filled with cancer, and with prayers of the faithful, he is suddenly free of cancer. A woman is overwhelmed with economic problems, and suddenly a check arrives in the mail for the exact amount she needs. No wonder Jesus was tempted to throw himself off of the temple and demonstrate a miraculous rescue. The dramatic has drawing power. Another camp wants their faith to be fully rational. God must obey the laws of the universe to be acceptable. Miracles are but primitive descriptions that, with sufficient wisdom, can be explained. The demons Jesus exorcised were really psychological blocks that, with deft insight, Jesus overcame. The resurrection was but a metaphor for hope. In between those camps, Paul preached Christ crucified, which is neither a miracle nor a logical way to overcome evil. There are events in our lives that defy rational explanation. We can give thanks for such events but clearly cannot control when they occur. Our faith operates largely in a rational world. Yet in this world, when evil occurs, we know that God is not powerless to defeat such evil. Because of the cross, we know that God can take that which is evil and transform it into redemptive possibilities. "For God's foolishness is wiser than human wisdom, and God's weakness is stronger than human strength."

Matthew 5:1-12

Then he began to speak, and taught them, saying....
— Matthew 5:2

Paul said in 1 Corinthians 1:25, "For God's foolishness is wiser than human wisdom, and God's weakness is stronger than human strength." The beatitudes have stood as a challenge to human wisdom for 2,000 years. They tend to stand our values, or at least our accepted wisdom, on their head. They call blessed, or happy, those who are needy — blessed are the poor in spirit, those who mourn, who are meek, and hunger for righteousness. They also call blessed those who seek to respond to that need — blessed are the merciful, the pure in heart, the peacemakers, the persecuted and reviled. Human wisdom seeks to understand so that it can gain a measure of control over the chaos that threatens our lives. Human wisdom is motivated by seeking to control that which we have come to fear. There is no room for a fearful response in the beatitudes. Instead of seeing our neediness as a condition to be feared, it is seen as a path to blessing. Instead of weighing the costs of opening ourselves to the needs of others, the beatitudes proclaim such vulnerability as a path to blessing. Even the negative consequence of taking a stand for what is right is redeemed as a blessing. The beatitudes are clearly an invitation to the way of the cross. The way of the cross challenges the wisdom of life that suggests that we must secure all our needs before we can respond to our neighbor. It is an absolute commitment to trust in God who we cannot manipulate or control. Fear can easily become the determining factor in shaping our lives. Jesus offered faith as an alternative that can set us free for the blessings of God.

Epiphany 5
Ordinary Time 5

Isaiah 58:1-9a (9b-12)

> *Yet day after day they seek me and delight to know my ways, as if they were a nation that practiced righteousness and did not forsake the ordinance of their God....*
> — Isaiah 58:2

Christians assume that this may have been the passage that Jesus read in the synagogue as recorded in Luke 4:18-19. If so, one can see why it caused anger among his listeners. Here were the people who had returned from exile to their homeland. Daily they engaged in acts of worship. "Yet day after day they seek me and delight to know my way...." But they remain a troubled society far from the ideal community that they dreamed of having. As a nation, we could substitute the United States, and the words of Isaiah would challenge any illusion of comfort for us as a people. There are many churches that seem to prosper, and people flock to courses on spiritual disciplines and discipleship. Yet God seems strangely distant from our national life. "Why do we fast but you do not see? Why humble ourselves, but you do not take notice?" Did Israel also have such a private faith that it was separated from social responsibility? "Look, you serve your own interests on your fast day and oppress all your workers. Look you fast only to quarrel and to fight and to strike with a wicked fist." Do not our church quarrels reveal a missing dimension to the practice of our faith? "Is not this the fast I choose: to loose the bonds of injustice ... to let the oppressed go free ... Is it not to share your bread with the hungry and bring the homeless poor into your house...?" There is a frightening parallel between what Isaiah saw in his society and the emptiness we find in our society. All of the exciting worship experiences, the well-developed educational programs, and the profound spiritual retreats that we can offer will be empty unless they result in our responding to the iniquities of our society. "... If you offer your food to the hungry and satisfy the needs of the afflicted, then your light shall rise in the darkness and your gloom be like the noonday." As Jesus discovered, it is not a truth that many people want to hear, but it is critical for our spiritual health.

Psalm 112:1-9 (10)

> *It is well with those who deal generously and lend, who conduct their affairs with justice.* — Psalm 112:5

Something within us rebels against what appears to be naive optimism in this psalm. We can point to too many people who seem to belong to "the generation of the upright" but who do not seem to be blessed. It does not seem to be true that "wealth and riches are in their houses, and their righteousness endures forever." Jesus was certainly upright and look at what happened to him. Is that not a more realistic picture of the nature of the world? Yet, Jesus prayed the psalms. Picture Jesus praying this psalm after his betrayal, arrest, and abandonment by his disciples. He was certainly one who feared the Lord and delighted in God's commandments. The Romans arrested him, stripped him of his few possessions, and sentenced him to death by crucifixion. Jesus was fully aware of the stark realities of the injustice of life. In that condition, picture Jesus praying, "[the righteous] are not afraid of evil tidings; their hearts are firm, secure in the Lord. Their hearts are steady, they will not be afraid; in the end they will look in triumph on their foes." It is not that the righteous are protected from suffering, but that at the core of their being they know a deeper truth allowing their hearts to be steady; beneath their fear, they are not afraid. It is not unusual for the poorest of the faithful to feel that "wealth and riches are in their houses" while the insatiable desire of the greedy come to nothing.

1 Corinthians 2:1-12 (13-16)

So that your faith might rest not on human wisdom but on the power of God.   — 1 Corinthians 2:5

Paul offered some very unsettling advice for all of us who read all the books on programs for making our churches successful. He refused to depend on the pragmatic and rational wisdom that the world admires. "My speech and my proclamations were not with plausible words of wisdom...." He contrasted such worldly wisdom with a spiritual wisdom that transcends our temporal understanding. "... These things God has revealed to us through the Spirit; for the Spirit searches everything, even the depth of God." If one reads this in isolation from the exceedingly practical advice that Paul offered on many church issues, one could slip into a spiritual self-righteousness. Yet all practical wisdom must be filtered through an understanding of the guidance of the Spirit. Paul began with a core belief. "For I decided to know nothing among you except Jesus Christ, and him crucified." Our dependence on practical wisdom for success and survival was nailed to the cross. No matter how successful we are in church building, it is empty unless we are guided by God's Spirit. "Those who are unspiritual do not receive the gifts of God's Spirit, for such gifts are foolishness to them, and they are unable to understand them because they are spiritually discerned." So how are we to pierce the cultural wisdom that surrounds us and listen to God's Spirit? Paul built on Isaiah 40:13 but interpreted it as referring to Christ. "For who has known the mind of the Lord so as to instruct him? But we have the mind of Christ." It is as if we continually ask that if our decisions are patterned after the mind of Christ, we will discern the spiritual wisdom to guide us (Philippians 2:1-5). Sometimes this will lead us into taking apparently foolish actions like Jesus did in going to the cross.

Matthew 5:13-20

> *You are the salt of the earth; but if salt has lost its taste, how can its saltiness be restored ... You are the light of the world. A city built on a hill cannot be hid.*
> — Matthew 5:13-14

Actually, salt cannot lose its saltiness, but it can be polluted by other elements so that it is no longer effective. Perhaps that makes an even more challenging metaphor for the church. If the church is to be the salt of the earth, then our challenge is to prevent it from being so polluted by other elements that it is no longer effective. The challenge is to let the church be the church. If you were to remove those aspects of church life that you believe might be polluting the saltiness of the church, what would they be? What is it in our life as a community of faith that causes people to dismiss the church as "no longer good for anything, but is thrown out and trampled under foot"? Even when people do not feel able to live up to the high calling of Christ, they still are attracted to such teachings. Yet when they see the church quarreling among itself or enriching itself at the expense of the needy, they grow cynical about the church. "You are the light of the world." Light cannot be turned into darkness although it can be hidden under a bushel. The church does not lose its capacity to be salt or light. Sometimes, however, we overwhelm it with other activities or forget to lift it to its proper priority where it can shine so that others will see its good works and give glory to God. "For I tell you, unless your righteousness exceeds that of the scribes and Pharisees, you will never enter the kingdom of heaven."

Epiphany 6
Ordinary Time 6

Deuteronomy 30:15-20

> ... *I have set before you life and death, blessings and curses. Choose life so that you and your descendents may live.* — Deuteronomy 30:19

There is something within us that rebels against the ambiguity of life and is attracted to simple "either-or" choices. Deuteronomy suggested that God has set before us the basic choice between life and death, blessings and curses. While, at first, it might seem a simple choice of choosing the positive over the negative, the implication of the choice is a lot more complex. Deuteronomy declared that choosing life meant "loving the Lord your God, obeying him, and holding fast to him...." Choosing to love and obey God required a fundamental choice of faith over appearances. The risks that lead to death seem so real that we tend to live our lives in response to the power that death holds over us. The story of Israel, beginning with Abram in Genesis 12:1ff, was a struggle to be obedient to the mysterious promises made by an invisible God. The temptations to build one's own security through greed and hating one's enemies versus obeying God who asks us to take risks of loving our enemy are overwhelming. Churches will often decide to protect their own future rather than risk some behavior in faith. To protect oneself, rather than make oneself vulnerable in love, especially toward those who have not been loving toward us, seems natural. It is hard for us to comprehend that in the Garden of Gethsemane Jesus chose life as he headed for the cross. Choosing life is not as simple as it seems.

Psalm 119:1-8

Happy are those whose way is blameless, who walk in the law of the Lord. — Psalm 119:1

This is the longest psalm in the book of Psalms. Built on an acrostic framework using each letter of the Hebrew alphabet to begin a set of eight line couplets, it is a work of art. Each couplet reflects on an aspect of God's law as one would look at different facets of a diamond. Because Christian tradition has sometimes reduced our understanding of law to a series of regulations, we miss the beauty of the Torah. For the Jew, the law is not a burden but more like a rudder of a boat. Without the rudder, a boat has no capacity to choose a direction and is simply buffeted about by the wind and current. The law, or Torah, is much more than a series of regulations. It includes all of the stories and commandments in the first five books of the Bible. It is an attempt to make visible the character and will of God. The life of Israel, as depicted in those books, was the incarnation of God. One could substitute Christ for law in this psalm and have an extended meditation of the meaning of Christ in our lives. "Happy are those whose way is blameless, who walk in the [way] of the Lord." Jesus becomes, in one person, the embodiment of Israel when the people are guided by the will of God. "Happy are those who keep [Christ's] decrees, who seek him with their whole heart, who also do no wrong, but walk in his ways."

1 Corinthians 3:1-9

And so, brothers and sisters, I could not speak to you as spiritual people, but rather as people of the flesh, as infants in Christ. I fed you with milk, not solid food, for you were not ready for solid food.
— 1 Corinthians 3:1-2

It would be interesting for a church to try to decide whether they were still infants in the faith and so should be fed milk, or whether they had matured enough to be fed solid food. The milk of the gospel is the basic nutrient by which our lives are sustained. Just as milk is the first food a baby receives and consumes nothing solid until the digestive tract matures, so it is for the infant Christian. The first nutrient, the first essential food of the faith, is the belief that Jesus Christ died for us and took our sins upon him. It is only as the body matures that we are able to chew on more solid food, the more complex and challenging issues of our faith. Paul suggested the flesh factor as a measure of the church's maturity. A leading barometer of the flesh factor was whether there was jealousy, quarreling, and factionalism within the church. "For as long as there is jealousy and quarreling among you, are you not of the flesh, and behaving according to human inclinations?" It is very easy for any of us, using such a criteria, to pronounce judgment on a current church or denomination from the outside. Certainly there is sufficient evidence of quarreling to give rise to a question about the maturity of many churches and denominations. It is more difficult for a church community to discuss their level of maturity among themselves and whether they were ready to tackle more solid food. That might be a good foundation to lay as the church proceeds to tackle some of the difficult issues before it. Paul reminded the quarreling Corinthian church, "For we are God's servants, working together; you are God's field, God's building." During times of heated debate, it is difficult to remember that we are all God's servants, working together. Being people of the flesh, we are often primarily concerned with our individual egos and desires. To be spiritual people is to engage in the issues confronting us with an openness that anticipates that through the Spirit, God has new things to reveal to us (John 16:13). We need not be afraid of solid food even though, at times, it is hard to digest.

Matthew 5:21-37

> *So when you are offering your gift at the altar, if you remember that your brother or sister has something against you, leave your gift there before the altar and go; first be reconciled to your brother or sister, and then come and offer your gift.* — Matthew 5:23-24

Who has not been angry? Did not even Jesus show anger? If you, in offering worship, remember that someone is angry with you, go and be reconciled; then come to offer your worship. Notice that the question is not whether you are angry but whether someone else is angry with you. The issue is not whether you did something wrong that caused someone to be angry. If a person is angry with you for all the wrong reasons, still you are asked to take the initiative to be reconciled. That act of seeking reconciliation takes precedence even over the act of worship. What a massive, continuous challenge this reconciliation business is. One could devote an entire life, every minute of the day to it, and still the job would not be finished. Is this what it means "to present your bodies as a living sacrifice, holy and acceptable to God, which is your spiritual worship"? (Romans 12:1b). Is our entire life an attempt to make our worship a worthy praise of God? And, in the meantime, is our worship only acceptable on a contingency basis? Does our worship depend on the reconciling work of Christ and our commitment continue to the reconciliation God, in Christ? If the Christian community took this admonition seriously, would our churches be empty on Sunday morning or would there be a massive healing within our communities that could only be expressed in praise of God? "Blessed are the peacemakers, for they shall be called the children of God" (Matthew 5:9).

Epiphany 7
Ordinary Time 7

Leviticus 19:1-2, 9-18

> *... You shall be holy, for I the Lord your God am holy.*
> — Leviticus 19:2

It is important to listen to this scripture on at least three levels. First, it was written to describe the distinctive quality of the people of God. To be holy was to be different, and the people of God were called to be different from the rest of humanity in a similar way to the fact that God was different from the world. On a second level, remember that the priestly writers wrote this during the time of exile. Israel had been destroyed as a nation, and the question of how they might be restored as a people of God haunted them. This part of Leviticus was called the holiness code, and it was put forth as a vigorous reform proposal of how the people could again live as God's people. Third, this particular passage was given added emphasis because it was from here that Jesus drew the second great commandment that we should love our neighbors as ourselves. If the church agonizes over its weakened condition in the world and worries that it has become corrupted by the society around it, it could do well to reflect on this holiness code for its own life. If the church wants to restore the strength of its witness to society, to be holy as God is holy, here is a vision that it could focus on. We are invited to make provisions for the poor and the stranger. We are called to live with absolute integrity and to never take advantage of the weak and never revile the physically disadvantaged. We should advocate a sense of justice that is evenhanded and refuse to take part in vengeance. In sum, for the church to be a holy witness, we need to demonstrate to the world how to love our neighbors as ourselves.

Psalm 119:33-40

> *Give me understanding, that I may keep your law and observe it with my whole heart.*   — Psalm 119:34

This reflection on the law was based on the fifth letter of the Hebrew alphabet — "He." The theme of the reflection is prayer for divine guidance in living faithfully. There are frequent attempts to provide a program or discipline that can renew the church. Many of them flounder after a time because they focus on external behavior and fail to involve an inner transformation. The psalmist recognized that such transformation is only possible if it is directed by God (v. 35). Even a vigorous dedication to a disciplined life of faith can cause people to fall victim to self-centeredness (v. 36), or people will fall victim to the continual pressure to please those around them (v. 39). As the psalmist made clear, God has offered, to the people of faith, guidance for how they should live their lives in relation to each other and to the world around them. We cannot deny the importance of ethics in making our testimony to the world. However, as history repeatedly demonstrates, it is easy for such efforts to become displays of self-righteous legalism. It is only God who is able to infuse such efforts with the grace that transforms us. "See, I have longed for your precepts; in your righteousness give me life."

1 Corinthians 3:10-11, 16-23

> *... all belong to you, and you belong to Christ, and Christ belongs to God.*   — 1 Corinthians 3:22-23

This passage can provide an excellent reflection concerning the transition of leadership within a given church. It is a reminder that the church does not belong to Paul, Apollos, Cephas, the latest pastor, or the strongest lay leader. God has already been at work in your church. The foundation is Jesus Christ, and the pillars of your church are reflected by the themes that were emphasized through the history of your church. Now you must choose how you are going to build upon that which has been prepared for you. Paul warns us about being deceived by our own cleverness into thinking that we are in charge of the church. It is the cleverness of God's Spirit, not our foolishness, that shapes the church. Church history is an important resource for understanding what God has been doing in your church.

Paul spoke to the church about everything being part of what God was doing in the church. Included in the "all" that belonged to the church were the world, life, death, the present, and the future. Such a claim makes the world, which sometimes looks hostile, appear to be friendlier and death and the future less frightening. All of this belongs to us through Christ who belongs to God. When Jesus was in the garden about to be arrested, the only way to see the world, the future, and life and death as full of promise, was to understand that it all came from God and that God could be trusted. If God is absolutely in charge, then all that is fearful becomes transformed. If we belong to Christ, then all of what we have is subject to the love that reconciles the world to God. While Christ opposed that which was evil, he did not accept that it was capable of defeating God. Therefore, even when evil's craft and power seemed great, Jesus trusted that God had not lost control. This gave him the freedom to not let his life be shaped by fear.

Matthew 5:38-48

> *You have heard that it was said, "An eye for an eye and a tooth for a tooth."* — Matthew 5:38

The law, "an eye for an eye and a tooth for a tooth," had the effect of limiting retribution. Endless blood feuds, which often plagued the society, were prohibited. But Jesus saw God's will as going beyond retaliation and seeking reconciliation. "Do not resist an evildoer." The cycle of violence had to be interrupted. Jesus gave four examples in ascending order of conflict. The first was a response to personal conflict. To be struck on the right cheek would be especially vicious because it would mean the violator struck you with the back of the hand rather than the palm. By offering the other cheek, one interrupted the violator's expectation and left room for new possibilities. Next, Jesus posed a legal conflict in which one would be sued for one's coat and would voluntarily offer one's cloak, which was beyond all legal expectations (Exodus 22:26). In the third example, we see institutional conflict. By the laws of occupation, a Roman soldier could conscript a citizen to carry his pack. But for a citizen to go voluntarily an extra distance was not grudging compliance but a genuine act of kindness. The fourth example raised an economic conflict that separated citizen from citizen. The beggar, who fits into the lowest class of an agrarian society, and the borrower, who has fallen on hard times, were both to be responded to with an openness that contradicted the normal possessiveness of society. Jesus' vision was not that of just passively absorbing violence but of choosing to act in ways that offered the violator a future. We are to love our enemy because that is how God acts toward even those who choose to be enemies of God.

Epiphany 8
Ordinary Time 8

Isaiah 49:8-16a

> *Can a woman forget her nursing child, or show no compassion for the child of her womb?* — Isaiah 49:15

When you live in the depth of despair, perhaps the most important fact to grasp is that you have not been forgotten. "See, I have inscribed you on the palm of my hand." Israel had been defeated as a nation and the people scattered among other nations. The possibility of them coming together again could only happen by the power of God. "Lo, these shall come from far away ... north ... west ... For the Lord has comforted his people, and will have compassion on his suffering ones." Hope requires a memory of God's past faithfulness, so the prophet recalled the early miracle of the Exodus. "... for he who has pity on them shall lead them ..." only this time would be even better than the last time. "They shall feed along the way, on all the bare heights shall be their pasture, they shall not hunger or thirst...." The primary question for a community of faith that suffers despair is always whether God might abandon them. The prophet broke the mold of a patriarchal faith and drew upon feminine imagery to speak of God's faithfulness. The most powerful image of human bonding was that of mother and infant. "Can a woman forget her nursing child or show no compassion for the child of her womb?" Even stronger, the prophet asserted, was God's bonding to his people. "Even these may forget, yet I will not forget you." The essential core of our faith is not the outward appearance of prosperity but the key reality that God is so connected to us that all of reality can be reshaped for our sake. For Israel, that was experienced in the return from exile. For Christians, who see the life of Israel in the person of Jesus, the love of God reshapes our reality in the resurrection.

Psalm 131

> *... my soul is like the weaned child that is with me.*
> — Psalm 131:2

Patrick Miller, professor of Old Testament, has suggested that this is one psalm that we can be certain was written by a woman. She speaks of the firm, quiet confidence of her relationship with God as being like that of a small infant child that is with its mother. After all the philosophical debates are over and all the doctrinal disputes have subsided, the essence of our faith rests on the core of our relationship with God. "I do not occupy myself with things too great and too marvelous for me." Without that innocent level of trust in God's love, much of what we believe can be challenged by the mysteries that are beyond our comprehension. A recently weaned child is beginning to venture out into the larger world. Having emerged from the womb and been fed at her mother's breast, now she begins to venture forth. The world can appear frightening unless she can occasionally return and be held by the mother who has birthed her. It is in that reassurance that she again gains confidence to venture back out into the world. For the believers, prayer and worship can be experiences of reconnection with God. For a moment, we leave all of the debates and challenges behind and simply rest in the joy and peace of the primary relationship that gives us strength. "But I have calmed and quieted my soul, like a weaned child with its mother...."

1 Corinthians 4:1-5

> *Therefore do not pronounce judgment before the time, before the Lord comes, who will bring to light the things now hidden in darkness and will disclose the purposes of the heart....*
> — 1 Corinthians 4:5

Paul's encounter with the overpowering grace of God that triumphed over his own zealously righteous and violent past shaped his understanding of the faith. By that experience, Paul had been entrusted with the care of, or stewardship of, this mystery of God. How is it possible for God to overcome sin in the world through grace? The human community had always assumed that bringing order to life required the exercise of an authority that could make judgments in disputes and punish wrongdoing. Paul challenged this perspective. "But for me it is a very small thing that I should be judged by you or by any human court." This was not the first step toward anarchy and irresponsible freedom. Paul recognized that we are all responsible to a higher authority. "... I am not thereby acquitted. It is the Lord who judges me." What Paul was recognizing was the impossibility of making such judgments because of our limited perspective. "Do not pronounce judgment before the time, before the Lord comes, who will bring to light the things now hidden in darkness and will disclose the purposes of the heart."

Picture a church that accepts their stewardship responsibility of the mystery of God's grace. Such a church resists the type of self-righteous judgmentalism that continuously leads to splits and divisions. Because it knows of the transforming grace of God and its own limited perspective, the church is optimistic that each person and situation has redeeming possibilities. The church does not advocate an irresponsible freedom but is united in its conviction that each of us is accountable to God. It is this God who sees the best in us. "Then each one will receive commendation from God."

Matthew 6:24-34

So do not worry about tomorrow, for tomorrow will bring worries of its own. Today's trouble is enough for today.   — Matthew 6:34

This whole passage is a counsel against allowing anxiety to rob you of the joy of life. In days of high blood pressure, heartburn, and ulcers, there could hardly be a more important message than this. We spend so much energy and anxiety on what we cannot control about the future that we destroy ourselves without experiencing the joy of the gifts of God for today. To pray "Give us this day our daily bread" is a radical prayer. It is praying just for food for today. The Hebrews had to learn in their journey across the wilderness that God could be trusted to provide manna for each day, and if they tried to hoard it, it would spoil. As we pray this prayer, we are trying to learn to trust God for today and not be anxious about tomorrow. Life is more than food and the body more than clothing, Jesus declared. He pointed to the traditional male role of sowing and reaping and the female role of toiling and spinning and suggested that life did not depend on these. He didn't disparage work, but he suggested both men and women could become so consumed by their toil that they were eaten alive by the very acts that were meant to enrich their lives. What is life about? It is experienced in right relationships as reflected in the kingdom of God and God's righteousness. It is not that wealth gained by labor is bad, but when it is so much the focus of life that it produces anxiety about tomorrow, it harms right relationships and becomes a false path.

Epiphany 9
Ordinary Time 9

Deuteronomy 11:18-21, 26-28

> *You shall put these words of mine in your heart and soul, and you shall bind them as a sign on your hand, and fix them as an emblem on your forehead.*
> — Deuteronomy 11:18

In the story life of Deuteronomy, Israel was about to make the transition from nomadic life to a settled agricultural life. Times of major transition make one vulnerable in faith as well. The god of Canaan was an agricultural god who could look very attractive to the Israelites that were trying to adjust to the rhythms of planting and harvest. In this time of transition, the Israelites were told to keep the word of God always before them. While the orthodox Jews have tried to obey this literally, its symbolic meaning is also very powerful. The word of God was to be part of the hand that worked, the head that thought, and the soul that directed their lives. The word of God was to be taught continually to their children. They were to make it part of their conversation at home and when they traveled, at night and in the morning. It was to be a visible part of entering their house — at the doorpost — and as they left — at the gate. All of this was to remind the Israelites that the life they lived was both a blessing and a curse. We will always be faced with decisions and choices. It is the intention of God that, by being instructed by God's word, we can be filled with the blessings of life. We, too, live in a very transitional time in which all of the familiar patterns of life seem to be changing. It may be critical to discover ways that we can keep God's word always before us so that we might make good choices in response to our changing future. "See, I am setting before you today a blessing and a curse...."

Psalm 31:1-5, 19-24

You are indeed my rock and my fortress; for your name's sake lead me and guide me. — Psalm 31:3

Because the lectionary suggests we read this psalm in light of the Deuteronomy passage that prepared Israel to live in a changing future, we can also hear this as a prayer for us as we live in a time of constant change. Whether it be the challenge of science, communication, economics, or church, it is clear that we are experiencing changes that confront us with totally new choices. Our prayer to God is that we might discover blessings and avoid the curses of this new territory that is before us. The constant for us is God. "In you, O Lord, I seek refuge; do not let me be put to shame; in your righteousness deliver me." The prayer is for guidance in unfamiliar territory. We know that the choices we face because of advances in DNA are like a minefield full of explosive possibilities, so we pray, "Take me out of the net that is hidden for me...." We know that our world is confronted with difficult political changes, so we pray, "hide [us] from human plots...." It is easy to allow the challenges of our new world to cause us to neglect the practice of the presence of God. "I had said in my alarm, 'I am driven far from your sight,' but you heard my supplications when I cried to you for help." The church itself is going through a period of transformation that can be very confusing to its members. It is critical for its members to hear in the midst of our changing reality, "Be strong, and let your heart take courage, all you who wait for the Lord." We need to be reminded of the constancy of God in the midst of the changes we are experiencing.

Romans 1:16-17; 3:22b-28 (29-31)

> *For there is no distinction, since all have sinned and fall short of the glory of God; they are now justified by his grace as a gift....* — Romans 3:22b-24

Given the intense focus that Romans 1:18-32 has received in recent years in the debate over homosexuality, it is interesting that the lectionary selection provides us with the larger context of Paul's argument on either side of those verses. It begins with Paul's declaration: "For I am not ashamed of the gospel; it is the power of God for salvation to everyone who has faith...." The lectionary selection then passes over the now much discussed passages (Romans 1:18-32) in which Paul described the condition of humanity as evidenced by their focus on lust. It also skips the infrequently noted passes in which Paul warned against judging each other. "You say, 'We knew that God's judgment on those who do such things is in accordance with truth.' Do you imagine ... that when you judge those who do such things and yet do them yourself, you will escape the judgment of God?" (Romans 2:2-3). The lectionary reading begins again with a passage that should leave us all shaking our heads in wonder. "For there is no distinction, since all have sinned and fall short of the glory of God; they are now justified by his grace as a gift...." God spoke to the church through the sacrifice of Christ and told them to share God's righteousness "because in his divine forbearance, he had passed over the sins previously committed...." If God did not respond with wrathful anger in judgment of a world that cruelly tortured and killed his Son, but rather took that dark act of rebellion and transformed it into the instrument of the world's salvation, then should we not be ashamed as a church to use far less distinctions of right and wrong to split the church? The problem with accepting that we are saved by grace is that it leaves no room for boasting that we are any better than the person with whom we disagree.

Matthew 7:21-29

Not everyone who says to me, "Lord, Lord," will enter the kingdom of heaven, but only the one who does the will of my Father in heaven. — Matthew 7:21

It is easy to read this passage with a sort of reverse self-righteousness. Most of us have experienced the religiously self-confident who arrogantly assume that they are among God's favored. One might read this passage as an assertion that they may well be in for a surprise at the time of God's judgment. However, it is important to recognize that this passage should raise cautions for us as well. Clearly those about whom Jesus spoke had been very involved in practicing the faith. He quoted them as saying, "... did we not prophesy in your name, and cast out demons in your name, and do many deeds of power in your name?" That list could cover almost anyone who actively tried to live the faith. The danger for all of us is that we treat faith as an abstract set of ideas that form our philosophy of life. "Everyone then who hears these words of mine and acts on them will be like a wise man who built his house on rock." While we cannot avoid the storms of life, we yearn for a solid anchor that will enable us to weather the storms. Jesus had been providing a framework for faith in the Sermon on the Mount. He concluded by declaring that faith could not be just a set of ideas. For our life to be well grounded, we must live our faith as an integral part of all of our relationships. It is only as we consciously integrate our beliefs into the actions of our relationships, that we will discover the strength to weather the storms. As we live out our faith, we discover our beliefs themselves becoming stronger. Jesus had focused on a series of practical implications of loving God and neighbor. In the abstract, these two commandments are attractive. As they are fleshed out in the practical situations in life, we realize how challenging they are. As we meet those challenges in our everyday lives, we discover they are the foundation that gives us courage.

The Transfiguration Of Our Lord
(Last Sunday After Epiphany)

Exodus 24:12-18

> *The glory of the Lord settled on Mount Sinai, and the cloud covered it for six days; on the seventh day he called to Moses out of the cloud.* — Exodus 24:16

Particularly because this passage is offered on Transfiguration Sunday, it is important to see the parallels and echoes in the passage. Frequently in the Bible, ascending a mountain is part of drawing closer to God. Jesus also ascended a mountain for his transfiguration. A cloud led the Hebrews through the wilderness and was the source of God's voice both at Mount Sinai and also in the transfiguration. God gave the law and commandment from a cloud and later told the disciples to listen to his Son in the transfiguration. In both cases the principle human figure — Moses or Jesus — took companions with him and told others to wait for them. In an echo of the creation story, in both stories, we have the reference of six days and on the seventh day God spoke.

The sabbath was lifted up as separate from other days. It was that thin moment when the eternal was made manifest in the finite lives of humans. In both stories, the glory of God was made manifest. In this passage it was like a devouring fire, where in the transfiguration it was seen in Jesus' face that shown like the sun. In both stories, there was mention of disputes among the believers. In this passage, Aaron and Hur are appointed as mediators. The result of both of these stories was the formation of a people set aside and given special instructions for their unique life as servants of God. While it is common for the church to experience disputes among themselves and while it is common to find ourselves waiting for, rather than possessing, God's instructions, God does draw near in those unique sabbath moments to sustain us with experiences of God's glory. We are not left alone.

Psalm 2

Why do the nations conspire, and the peoples plot in vain? — Psalm 2:1

This passage is provided on Transfiguration Sunday because of the reference that is picked up in the transfiguration stories: "He said to me, 'You are my son; today I have begotten you.'" It should not be forgotten that the psalmist saw this declaration as a direct challenge to the arrogance of nations and peoples who assumed that they were the measure of all things. "The kings of the earth set themselves ... against the Lord and his anointed, saying 'Let us burst their bonds asunder, and cast their cords from us.'" While the church has proven no better at handling power than any other group, it is important that we remember that we do have a message that speaks to the powerful of the world. No nation or group has a lasting hold on their power and all are accountable for how they exercise it. "Now therefore, O Kings, be wise; be warned O rulers of the earth. Serve the Lord with fear...." The model by which all governments are to utilize their power is the servant ministry of Christ. The psalmist said, "You are my son; today I have begotten you." This same affirmation was spoken from the cloud in Matthew's telling of the transfiguration. It was joined with the admonition that we should "Listen to him." At the conclusion of Matthew, Jesus instructed the disciples, and therefore the church, "Go therefore and make disciples of all nations ... and teaching them to obey everything that I have commanded you" (Matthew 28:19).

2 Peter 1:16-21

This is my Son, my Beloved, with whom I am well pleased. — 2 Peter 1:17

Second Peter is not read frequently, although lately it has been used by some in supporting their end-of-the-world theories. Note especially 3:1-12. While many scholars doubt its claim to have been written by Peter, it was clearly written to address some of the issues of the early church. As in our contemporary church, there was apparently much dissension and theological debate about the way to understand the truth. This passage makes particular reference to the disciples' experience of Jesus' transfiguration. The author reemphasized a traditional biblical claim that faith was based on the historical experience of the divine being present. "For we did not follow cleverly devised myths ... but we had eyewitnesses of his majesty." The transfiguration challenges the purely rational orientation of our culture that suggests that all truth must fit within the categories of our finite universe and its natural laws. The transfiguration claims that God entered time and conveyed to us eternal truth expressed in historically experienced reality. "We ourselves heard the voice come from heaven, while we were with him on the holy mountain." This passage further claims that scripture can continue to be experienced as an intersection of the divine with the human. "... No prophecy ever came by human will, but men and women moved by the Holy Spirit spoke from God." In our current church struggles, we would do well to revisit our understanding of how God enters our experience as a church to speak God's truth that transforms our lives.

Matthew 17:1-9

Lord, it is good for us to be here; if you wish, I will make three dwellings here, one for you, one for Moses, and one for Elijah. — Matthew 17:4

The concept of hospitality in the Middle East is essential for understanding Peter's response to this vision of Moses and Elijah talking to Jesus. Rabbinic tradition said Moses did not die, and scripture said Elijah was taken into heaven via a flaming chariot. In this passage these two representatives of the best of Israel's faith, symbolic of the law and the prophets, were seen talking with Jesus. By offering to erect tents for them, Peter was demonstrating hospitality. When Abraham showed hospitality to three strangers by the oaks of Mamre, he encountered God (Genesis 18:1 ff). The same thing happened for Peter. The bright cloud that overshadowed them was a reference to the bright cloud of Exodus 40:34-38, which marked the presence of God in the newly constructed tabernacle. Jesus was the tabernacle of God's abode. Echoing Psalm 2:7 and the voice from heaven that confirmed him at baptism (3:17), a voice from the cloud of God's presence confirmed Jesus to be the true reflection of the divine as a faithful son reflects the father.

Though attested to by the law and the prophets, it was Jesus of whom God said, "Listen to him." The divine authority was not to be constrained by the traditional interpretations of the law and the prophets but was to be represented in all its radicalness by a living presence. In contrast to Moses, Exodus 33:23, and Elijah, 1 Kings 19:9, each of whom found shelter in a cave or cleft, Jesus found no need for a shelter (Matthew 17:4). In this brief moment, Jesus moved from being a teacher and companion to being the Christ, the beloved Son of God. Sometimes we think of Jesus as a moral teacher or a companion who supports us on our life's journey. In that moment the disciples heard the voice of God saying, "This is my son ... listen to him." What would it mean in your life if Jesus moved from being your personal support in the life you were living to being the Christ whose commands shaped your life? For Jesus to be transfigured is for us to see that in Jesus we see God.

Lent 1

Genesis 2:15-17; 3:1-7

> *"Did God say, 'You shall not eat from any tree in the garden'?" The woman said to the serpent, "We may eat of the fruit of the trees in the garden; but God said, 'You shall not eat of the fruit of the tree that is in the middle of the garden nor shall you touch it, or you shall die.'"*
> — Genesis 3:1-3

The subtlest of corrosions that eats away at the bonds of trust in any relationship begins with a question. Where there had been absolute trust before, which allowed the couple to be naked, or vulnerable, before God and each other, now the question drove the smallest of wedges into all of the relationships. The question began to make distant, and an object for evaluation and judgment, a relationship that before had been a subjective experience. Now the couple stood back and weighed the possibilities where, before, trust had been an integral part of the experience. Note that even as the woman evaluated the situation, it began to be distorted. God prohibited their eating of the fruit of the tree of knowledge of good and evil, but now the woman interpreted the prohibition as including not touching it either. Prior to the question, the couple knew what God wanted and trusted that that was what they wanted as well. To have the knowledge of good and evil is to assume that you have the platform from which you can objectively evaluate the situation. This automatically distances you from the relationship. "Did God say ..." places you in the position of evaluating God. That same sense of distancing and judging drives a wedge into all our relationships. Sin results in that sense of distance, even alienation, from the love that allows us to be naked and not afraid in our relationships. As we begin the season of Lent, we are offered the opportunity to reflect on all of our relationships and seek to extend ourselves in love that overcomes that distance.

Psalm 32

> *... and in whose spirit there is no deceit.*
> — Psalm 32:2

The ultimate weapon of the enemy for the psalmist was a deceitful tongue. Recall how often it is the tongue that drives a wedge into a relationship. When the psalmist tried to imagine what a person who was truly blessed by God would be like, there was an ascending litany that began with deeds: "Blessed is the one whose transgression is forgiven." Our actions often cause separation. The litany then moved to the effect of the deeds: "Whose sin is covered." In addition to the actual deed, the effect of that deed lingered. Then the psalmist spoke of the condition of the person: "To whom the Lord imputes no iniquity." Even if the other person gets past our deed, we carry its effect in us. You could have a transgression forgiven, a sin covered, and not be found guilty of iniquity, but you would still not be whole until your spirit was free of deceit. When your spirit was free from deceit, there would be no need to cover up your life from others. You would be free to be vulnerable and therefore loved by God and neighbor. The opposite of that is to allow your sins to make you guarded in your relationships. Deceit distances you from others to protect yourself from being exposed. Deceit requires an elaborate structure of rationalization that absorbs your energy and eats away at your vitals. By God's forgiveness, we can be healed of the urge to deceive and restored to the wholeness of relationships. Lent provides us an opportunity to examine our relationships and open ourselves to the forgiveness of God that can offer us a fresh beginning.

Romans 5:12-19

Yet death exercised dominion from Adam to Moses, even for those whose sins were not like the transgression of Adam....   — Romans 5:14

As a child, I wondered how God could be so mean as to punish all of us for the sin of Adam. Paul tied the sin of Adam and the power of death together. The sin of Adam was disobedience to God's clear command not to eat of the fruit of the tree of knowledge of good and evil. By breaking trust with God, humanity — the basic definition of the word "adam" — felt the loneliness of the universe. Death and its avoidance became the primary focus. As Paul stated, this was true even for those whose transgressions differed from that of Adam. When we assume that death, not God, has the final word, then death claims our ultimate loyalty. Whether it manifests itself in lust for power, wealth, reputation, and the like, we seek that which will ward off the inevitability of death. Even our practice of religion can become a form of worshiping death. We accept Jesus as our Savior because we want eternal life. Paul countered this distortion of faith with "the grace of God and the free gift in the grace of one man, Jesus Christ...." If we seek to escape the power of death by meeting a criteria of faith by which we must be saved, we are bound by the laws of religion and still under the power of death. If, however, we are saved by grace, and not by works, then the power of death is broken. Now we live, not to escape death, which has already been defeated in Christ, but to glorify God. Life is now lived not in fear but in thanksgiving. "Therefore just as one man's trespass led to condemnation for all, so one man's act of righteousness leads to justification and life for all."

Matthew 4:1-11

Then Jesus was led up by the Spirit into the wilderness to be tempted by the devil. — Matthew 4:1

It is striking that immediately after the high moment of Jesus' affirmation by God at his baptism, he faced temptation. God's Spirit led Jesus into this temptation. The blessing and power of God that enables us to do good and the temptation to do evil are not opposites but often are part of the same experience. Satan, the adversary of God, became God's servant to prepare Jesus for ministry. It is not the avoidance of evil but confronting it in faith that prepares us for ministry. The first two temptations derived from the very confirmation Jesus received at his baptism. Both begin with the phrase "If you are the Son of God...." In the Hebrew scriptures, Israel was called the Son of God (Exodus 4:22). Matthew saw Jesus' life as a reliving of the experience of Israel. Like Israel, Jesus, too, experienced hunger in the wilderness. As God's Son, he was tempted to manipulate the gift of divine favor into self-controlled security and display one's divinity by becoming the source of bread for the world. In the first temptation, he could win the world's favor by providing for their needs. In the second temptation, he was invited to win people's loyalty by demonstrating his access to divine power. He was taken to the holiest of cities, Jerusalem, and placed on the holiest of places, the temple, and quoted to from the holiest of books, scripture. If God was present anywhere, then God should be there.

The temptation of ministry is to claim God's protection as a right in return for one's faithfulness. The third temptation was a more naked temptation to power that exposed the subtle message behind the other two. This would be the obvious answer to the question, "If God is good, why does God allow evil to flourish?" God, in Christ, could simply exercise divine power and eradicate evil from the world. In resisting this temptation, Jesus set the pattern of a ministry of servanthood. In these temptations, Jesus recapitulated the wilderness journey of Israel who was called the Son of God, as well (Exodus 4:22-23), and Matthew prepared the church for facing similar temptations in her ministry as the children of God (John 1:12-13).

Lent 2

Genesis 12:1-4a

> *I will make of you a great nation ... and in you all the families of the earth shall be blessed.*
> — Genesis 12:2-3

If you remember that this was before God made a covenant with Abram, renamed him Abraham, and made circumcision a mark of identity (Genesis 15 and 17), then in a sense this took place before Abram was a Jew. Abram was still the father of all nations, and all nations would be blessed by him. Humanity gets a fresh start by being invited to once again enter into a relationship of total trust with God. Only this time, unlike in the story of Adam and Eve, the fulfillment of God's promise did not depend on the faithfulness of humanity (Genesis 15:17 — only the firepot, the symbol of God, passes between the cut pieces). Abram had to leave behind the security of the familiar — country, kindred, and father's house — and go on a journey in which God was his only security. Abram's responsibility was not perfect morality but a discovery of the faithfulness of God. It would be the same lesson that his descendents would have to learn in their journey across the wilderness. It is the same lesson that the church has to learn over and over again. One can see in the call of Abram that he was chosen not for his own sake but for the sake of the world. The church, also, has to keep learning that lesson. As Jesus commanded his disciples right before he departed from them, they were to go into all the world and teach the nations what he had taught them (Matthew 28:19-20). As Jesus demonstrated in his own temptation, that which they were to teach the nations could not be imposed on the world through displays of divine power but must be demonstrated in servanthood.

Psalm 121

> *The Lord will keep your going out and your coming in from this time on and forevermore.* — Psalm 121:8

Paired with the call of Abram in Genesis 12:1-4a, the psalm reminds us of God's protection in the mysterious journey of life into the future. Most people find some measure of comfort in the familiar trappings of life. While we would say that God is not restricted to a particular place, or even a set of doctrines, when the familiar is ripped from under us, it often throws us into disorientation. The psalmist reminds us that God is creator of all time and space and so can accompany us wherever we go. "My help comes from the Lord who made heaven and earth." Like Abram, many of our comfortable assumptions about life and faith seem to be challenged by the events around us. It is as if we, like Abram, are being asked to "go from your country, your kindred, and your father's house to a land that I will show you." As Paul reminded us in the passage from Romans, faith existed before the law or the religious rituals that comfort us. If both our church and our society seem to be changing around us, it is important to be reminded of the real center of our trust. When we look to the hills, the familiar place where people reach out to God, and we cry out for help in confusing times, it is important to recall again that the God behind all of creation is in charge of that changing future. We are called to trust that God knows where God is leading us.

Romans 4:1-5, 13-17

> ... *"Abraham believed in God and it was reckoned to him as righteousness."* — Romans 4:3

The name of Abraham is used by Paul more frequently than any other person except Jesus. Paul saw Abraham as epitomizing the essence of faith. This man trusted God before there was the support of scripture, law, traditions, or a supportive community.

According to our scriptural records, Abraham even trusted God before God had performed any acts for Abraham to experience. According to Genesis 12:1-4a, Abraham's first encounter with God was in response to God's call and promise. Abraham's relationship with God was founded on trust in God's promise. Here, Paul saw, was the essence of faith. The first act between God and Abraham was not based on a deed performed, on God's part or Abraham's, but on trust. "Abraham believed God and it was reckoned to him as righteousness." Paul went on to build his case for the inclusion of the Gentiles as God's people by showing that this right relationship between God and Abraham not only preceded God's having given the commandments on Mount Sinai but also before circumcision. Building on the promise in Genesis 17:5-6 that God would make Abraham the father of many nations, Paul concluded that all humanity was included in God's promise. We are all heirs of a promise made before anyone had done anything to earn it. Since the vast majority of Christians are beneficiaries of Paul's understanding of God's grace, it might suggest that we ought to be exceedingly gracious in our reception of those outside the church who have yet to act in ways that demonstrate their faith.

John 3:1-17

> *What is born of the flesh is flesh, what is born of the Spirit is spirit.* — John 3:6

Nicodemus would have made the perfect Presbyterian. He came with a genuine intellectual curiosity and yet a cautious enthusiasm. He came at night because night provided some cover from public scrutiny. His was a private quest not a public commitment. Perhaps he believed that religion should be a private, personal decision. He affirmed Jesus in a general way — "We know that you are a teacher that has come from God...." He never made clear who "we" were. In phrasing his inquiry this way, he skillfully skirted the issue of personal involvement. He did not begin with a question. He led with a statement. Jesus' response was ambiguous. The

Greek phrase that Jesus used could either mean "born from above" or "born again." Nicodemus chose to explore the more literal meaning. "How can anyone be born after having grown old?"

Mystified, Nicodemus maintained a cautious skepticism. He was concerned about the mystery of faith but wanted to explore it from a safe distance. Jesus clarified that he was speaking of a different kind of birth. This was a birth that "comes from above." If you can only see God's kingdom by being "born from above," then salvation is in God's hands, not ours. Like the wind, you can experience it, even develop an intellectual appreciation of its characteristics, but you cannot control it. Nicodemus, like many good Presbyterians, preferred to keep his options open. "How can these things be?" Nicodemus wanted to understand an issue of personal faith. Jesus was speaking of a worldly faith. "Indeed, God did not send the Son into the world to condemn the world, but in order that the world might be saved through him." Faith in Jesus Christ was too significant for the world to keep it a private affair.

Lent 3

Exodus 17:1-7

> ... *"Is the Lord among us or not?"* — Exodus 17:7

This is a critical passage in both the Jewish and Christian journey. Many key passages describing Israel's relationship with God were cast in the form of a court lawsuit. This passage described the people's lawsuit against God. It accused God of not being present to them, as God had promised. The wilderness journey was described as God's test of the people (Deuteronomy 8:2), and now the people have filed a countersuit against God. Moses, the defense attorney for God, needed more evidence to prove his case. As with most of the biblical stories, the evidence of God's presence was seen in the practical challenges of living. In this case, the issue was water to drink in the wilderness. Since one of the descriptive names Israel used for God was "rock," it is significant that it was a rock that produced the life-giving water that proved God's presence. "I will be standing there in front of you on the rock at Horeb." This was not a visible presence (Deuteronomy 4:15 f), but an experiential presence. Paul, in 1 Corinthians 10:4, later referred to this rock in the wilderness as Christ. Thus, for Paul, Christ was present long before Jesus was born. This incident, as reported in Numbers 20:1-13, also became the reason why Moses could not accompany the people into the promised land. While the charge against Moses in Numbers was rather vague, it seemed to center on Moses' failure to demonstrate God's holiness as he struck the rock to bring forth the life-giving water. For Christians, following Paul's identification of the presence of God as Christ, perhaps there is an invitation to trust that the presence of God accompanies us and a warning not to be casual as to how we respond to that presence.

Psalm 95

Do not harden your hearts, as at Meribah....
— Psalm 95:8

In the midst of a strong call to praise God, there was this prophetic reminder of the human failure to trust God. For Israel the wilderness experience was the paradigm for their entire relationship with God. Both in the wilderness and in the act of creation itself (Psalm 95:4-5), God had provided ample evidence of God's faithful and generous support of Israel. The natural response was one of praise, "O come, let us worship and bow down, let us kneel before the Lord, our Maker." Life itself summons us to praise God. For Christians and Jews, there is the recognition of the privilege of our relationship, "For he is our God, and we are the people of his pasture, and the sheep of his hand." Yet worship can become "like a noisy gong or a clanging cymbal" (1 Corinthians 13:1) if it does not result in our response of trust in the difficult challenges of our life. Again, the wilderness was a paradigm for how people learned to trust God. "... your ancestors tested me, and put me to the proof, though they had seen my work." The need to respond to God in trust is what is required for the completion of creation and the enjoyment of sabbath rest. Our failure to trust God denies us the ability to fully experience the sabbath. "Therefore, in my anger, I swore, 'They shall not enter my rest.' " If our worship is but a hasty interruption of our drive to work, our lives will fail to experience the sabbath joy that God invites us to on the seventh day of creation. The sabbath is an invitation to trust God. Our failure to trust God results in unending stress for our weary souls.

Romans 5:1-11

But God proves his love for us in that while we still were sinners Christ died for us. — Romans 5:8

Some in the Christian community approach the task of evangelism by asking people to identify the date when they were saved. Paul's answer to such a question would be that we were saved by God through Christ's death and resurrection almost 2,000 years ago. Paul does not speak of salvation as a conditional event dependent on our action but as a completed event accomplished by God. We were justified by faith, have peace with God, and already stand in the grace of God. For Paul, recognizing this incredible truth set him free to experience all of life from the perspective of that new reality. When many people experience tragedy and suffering, they ask "why?" The assumption is that their suffering must be the result of some action on their part for which they are being punished. Paul, knowing that he had already been justified, viewed it differently. "... We also boast in our suffering, knowing that suffering produces endurance, and endurance produces character, and character produces hope...." To be saved is to view all of life as an opportunity to mature in our relationship with God. Even our suffering becomes an opportunity to share in the suffering of God. The love of God has been demonstrated "... in that while we still were sinners Christ died for us." God, in Christ, suffered for us while we were still sinners, so we can surely trust that God stands with us now that we have been justified. Picture your church being fully confident that God had removed their guilt and facing the challenges of their lives was an opportunity to build endurance, character, and hope. All of life's challenges now become opportunities to praise God.

John 4:5-42

> *A Samaritan woman came to draw water, and Jesus said to her, "Give me a drink..." The Samaritan woman said to him, "How is it that you, a Jew, ask a drink of me, a woman of Samaria?"* — John 4:7, 9

When listening to a passage of scripture, it is often helpful to make a conscious decision to identify with one of the characters in the story. For example, you might identify with one of Jesus' disciples "who were astonished that he was speaking with a woman...." From that perspective, you would want to choose who it was that the Samaritan woman represented in your world. We know that the Jewish community disdained Samaritans. While the Samaritans practiced a faith that had the same roots as those who lived in Judea, it was considered an inferior faith that had been polluted by outside influences. Who in your community might serve as a parallel to the Samaritans? Jesus had chosen to take a shortcut between Galilee and Jerusalem and pass through Samaritan territory. Where are the shortcuts in your community that bring you into contact with people who are outside your faith? Jesus took the initiative to ask the Samaritan woman for a drink. Instead of acting in a superior manner, Jesus approached her with a humble request for help. Can you picture yourself approaching a member of a different religious tradition with a genuine openness to what they have to offer you?

Knowing the prejudices of the Jews toward Samaritans, the woman was puzzled that he would make such a request. She immediately identified the prejudice that normally separates Jew from Samaritan. Since you have identified with one of Jesus' disciples, can you admit to your own astonishment that you might find Jesus present and interacting with people from a different religious tradition? As the story developed, it was clear that the disciples were focused on feeding those within their own community. Jesus admonished them that there were "fields (that) are ripe for harvesting" as a result of seeds of faith that have been planted by others. Are you and your church alert to the plantings of faith that are emerging outside the Christian tradition to which we are called to attend to their growth? We are told "many Samaritans from that city believed in him because of the woman's testimony...." Is it possible that Jesus has been working in the lives of people outside the faith, but we have overlooked them because they do not match the profile of what we assume believers look like? It is questions like these that emerge when you view this passage from the perspective of the disciple.

Lent 4

1 Samuel 16:1-13

> *...for the Lord does not see as mortals see; they look on outward appearance, but the Lord looks on the heart.*
> — 1 Samuel 16:7

We have plenty of disastrous examples of how easily we are seduced by appearances in making wrong choices. Even with the sophisticated tools of modern personnel committees, companies are continually frustrated with the ease which they can choose the wrong person for the job. The difficulty of making the right choice is explored in scripture around the contrast between how humans make choices and how God makes choices. There is a mystery in how God chose and called people in the Bible. God often seemed to turn the "way of the world" upside down. The rules of biblical society favored the eldest son. The further you got from being the eldest son, the less you received in inheritance. It was a way of preserving the family land and preventing the land from being divided into insignificant parcels. The same format of favoritism in that society seemed to apply to other choices as well. Yet, God's way of choosing people almost always went against such conventions. In 1 Samuel, it was not the eldest but the youngest that God chose. God reminded Samuel that God did not base God's choices on criteria that are often used by the world, such as outward appearances. God looked for an inward quality symbolized by the heart. This theme of how God made God's choices would continue throughout scripture. Jesus was not born of nobility but of a homeless peasant couple. The disciples were not drawn from the ranks of the learned or wealthy but were fishermen and tax collectors. The character of God's leaders seemed to be an attitude of the heart that recognized dependence on God and reminded the world of the true source of our power. This is a lesson that might cause a church to reflect on how often they are swayed by appearances in their choice of leaders and how frequently it is the one almost overlooked that becomes the true servant leader in the church.

Psalm 23

> *The Lord is my shepherd, I shall not want.*
> — Psalm 23:1

In a world that suffers from all sorts of needs from hunger to disease, from violence to agonizing loneliness, it seems unreal to say that I would not want for anything when the Lord is my shepherd. Much of the antagonism of our world is generated by the fear that someone will deprive us of something we need. However, if you absolutely knew that you would never want for material goods, would you spend so much energy on gathering more? If you knew for certain that the people you cared about would always love you, would you be as subject to jealousy? If it were clear that you would always have time enough to do what you want, would you feel the pressure of the clock? Try to imagine the full impact of the declaration of faith that, as long as God cares for you like a shepherd cares for his sheep, you will never want for anything. We cannot deny that there are people who are deprived in this world even though they pray fervently to God. Yet some people who seem to have great needs in this world and have faith seem to be more content than many who have all the advantages but are cut off from God. The psalmist saw his needs fulfilled by one who provided nourishment for body and soul (v. 2) and right relationships (v. 3). He did not deny that there were threats to his life (v. 4) and enemies that threatened (v. 5), but he had learned to trust that in the midst of a turbulent world, there was a faithful provider who had met his needs and such experiences gave him hope and confidence for the future (v. 6). Perhaps to be freed from want is not an absence of need but to be sustained in whatever condition we find ourselves.

Ephesians 5:8-14

For once you were darkness, but now in the Lord you are light. Live as children of light.... — Ephesians 5:8

To be Christian does not mean you have all the answers. Paul urged Christians whom he declared already to be the light to "try to learn what is pleasing to the Lord." Sometimes this is called sanctification or the continual path of maturing in the faith. Christians are on a journey just like the children of Israel who journeyed across the wilderness were on a journey. The compass by which Christians chart their course is Jesus who is their Lord. Jesus once provided the criteria by which one determined a true prophet from a false one — by their fruits you will know them. The authority of the church is not in their doctrine but in the fruits of their lives. The fruit of the children of light "is found in all that is good and right and true." What was good, right, and true in Jesus was not his ability to impose answers on society but his ability to demonstrate compassion, communicate forgiveness, and invite people to be reconciled. Such fruits could be exposed to the light because there was no shame in them. While the church should be concerned about right doctrine, because our beliefs shape our behavior, the authority of such doctrines will not be in their abstract truth but in the fruits of their compassionate, forgiving, and reconciling love as experienced by those who walk in darkness.

John 9:1-41

... One thing I do know, that though I was blind, now I see. — John 9:25

Sometimes our experience is so powerful that it supersedes all rational thought. A major theme in this passage is the difficulty that everyone had with the experience of this blind man. It began with the disciples trying to answer the theological question of whether the man's blindness was the result of his own sinfulness or that of his parents. Since they knew he was born blind, if his blindness was the result of his own sins, that would have raised other questions. Jesus refused to attribute the man's physical condition to either his sins or those of his parents. All such deprivation was an opportunity for the compassion of God to be displayed. The challenge for the church is not in providing a rationale for human suffering but to respond to it with a compassion that reveals the love of God. This powerful experience of the power of God to heal the blind man occurred outside the framework of the traditional religious understanding. The Pharisees were offended and challenged the source of the man's healing. Because the healing took place on the sabbath, they said, "This man is not from God, for he does not observe the sabbath." It raises the question of how we react when our experience of God challenges the orthodox standards of our faith.

The Pharisees brought the parents in on the dispute, but his parents refused to be triangled in the argument. "He is of age; ask him." The Pharisees returned to dispute with the man who rested his case on his own personal experience. "I do not know whether he is a sinner. One thing I do know, that though I was blind, now I see." Then, as an example of John's love of irony, the formerly blind man proceeded to instruct the Pharisees in theology. "Here is an astonishing thing! You do not know where he comes from, and yet he opened my eyes. We know that God does not listen to sinners, but he does listen to one who worships him and obeys his will ... If the man were not from God, he could do nothing." The Pharisees were as offended as many theologians would be today if a lay person tried to instruct them in their discipline. "You were born entirely in sins, and you are trying to teach us?" The entire story is a lesson in the dangers of arrogance in the religious community and the power of God to reach beyond our traditional framework and challenge our assumptions.

Lent 5

Ezekiel 37:1-14

> *... They say, "Our bones are dried up, and our hope is lost; we are cut off completely."* — Ezekiel 37:11

The imagery of the valley of the dry bones is so powerful that people often miss the message. The message is of a people who were of the living dead. They were entirely devoid of hope. They were cut off from the Spirit that gave them life. Even the form and shape of the people had begun to dry up like bones of an animal in which the flesh had disintegrated, and the wind and elements had even separated the bones one from the other. It is totally beyond their control to save themselves or even imagine how it could be possible. All sense of community and connectedness had been fractured beyond repair. This was not a comatose situation in which, somehow, they could be miraculously revived. This was the total disintegration and dispersal of a people. This was three days in the grave when the body had begun to decay. In such a situation, which was beyond despair, the prophet told of what God would do. God would raise them from the grave and put God's Spirit in them.

Recall that in Genesis 2:7, when God had formed Adam from the clay, he still did not live until God breathed the breath of life into him. Ezekiel was speaking of resurrection on a corporate level. In the same way that Jesus would embody the corporate Israel in his person, so he also would embody their being raised to new life in his person. (One should note the reference in Matthew 27:52-53, which suggests fulfillment of this vision in the resurrection of Jesus.) When the cynical predictions of the death of the church or of the denomination overwhelm one, one needs to turn to this passage. Hear the death rattles of people who are tinkering with the bones of the church trying to rearrange them and give them new life. Then hear the prophet: "Come from the four winds, O breath, and breathe upon these slain that they may live." Perhaps what the church needs today is fewer tinkerers and more prophets.

Psalm 130

> *Out of the depths I cry to you, O Lord ... O Israel, hope in the Lord! For with the Lord there is steadfast love, and with him is great power to redeem.*
>
> — Psalm 130:1, 7

On the fifth Sunday of Lent, when we have examined our lives and our distance from God as we approach Easter and in response to the passage from Ezekiel that offered the image of the valley of the dry bones, this psalm speaks to us of the true source of hope in the world. A continual theme throughout the scriptures is that God is one who hears the cry of the people. It was most poignantly described in God's hearing the cry of the oppressed slaves in Egypt and initiating a plan that would set them free (Exodus 3:7-9). Ezekiel expanded on that theme to suggest that God remembered his covenant with Israel even when every human imagination of hope had been destroyed. Even when the Spirit of God had departed and the bones or structures that gave meaning to life had been totally dried up and scattered by the winds, God had the power to reconstitute them. It is at the very depth of despair, the psalmist declared, that we can cry out and be heard by God. "Out of the depths I cry to you, O Lord."

The psalmist further declared that our hope in God is not dependent on our faithfulness. "If you, O Lord, should mark iniquities, Lord, who could stand? But there is forgiveness with you, so that you may be revered." The lesson that needs to be repeatedly learned is that we are not in charge of God's agenda. Yet we can depend on it and therefore have the task of waiting. "I wait for the Lord, my soul waits, and in his word I hope...." Waiting seems so beyond our control. There is no way to measure it. As we come to the end of the Lenten season, if we should feel a sense of despair about the condition of life or the condition of the church, it is important to be reminded again of the value of waiting on the Lord. Like Christ, the body of Christ is totally dependent on God, and our hope is that God "will redeem Israel from all its iniquities" and, in doing so, will redeem the church as well.

Romans 8:6-11

To set the mind on the flesh is death, but to set the mind on the Spirit is life and peace. — Romans 8:6

Paul's contrast between flesh and spirit might be illuminated by thinking of flesh as an earthly, strictly material perspective and spirit as a more godlike perspective. If your mind is focused on the finite framework of the earthly life, then much of your energy is directed toward the power that death has over your decisions. The phrase "where there is life there is hope" is a very pragmatic, materialist perspective. If that is true, then one must avoid death at all costs because unless there is a physical life, there is no hope. Death becomes people's god to whom they give full attention and obedience. In contrast, the Spirit opens the parameters in which hope can be experienced. If God, not death, has the final word, then the faithfulness of God, revealed in the death and resurrection of Christ, can provide a deep peace.

When the Spirit of God dwells in you (recall Genesis 2:7), your perspective enlarges. Measuring your life from God's viewpoint, as Jesus did in his life, brings you into conflict with the strictly pragmatic perspective of the materialist. "For this reason, the mind that is set on the flesh is hostile to God...." Your reason for living is not confined to what is best or immediately most rewarding for you personally. Rather you see your life in terms of the way in which it corresponds to God's purpose for the whole world. Since Paul was addressing the church, and not just individuals, the challenge for the church is to make decisions not according to the survival mentality of the flesh but according to what is most in accord with Christ who dwells within us.

John 11:1-45

> *Accordingly, though Jesus loved Martha and her sister and Lazarus, after having heard that Lazarus was ill, he stayed two days longer in the place where he was.*
> — John 11:5-6

Lazarus was ill. Jesus loved the entire family. When he heard that Lazarus was ill, he delayed going to him. What was going on? If, as John believed, Jesus was the Word of God incarnate, then are we not dealing with the seeming paradox of God's love for us? If God loves us, why is God not present to us when we are suffering? Jesus said of this illness, "This illness does not lead to death; rather it is for God's glory, so that the Son of God may be glorified through it." Yet, from a purely human perspective, it clearly did lead to death. So we must look at it from the divine perspective that death does not have the final authority. Sometimes God allows us to experience tragedy, even death, for a higher purpose. It is important to recognize that, in time, Jesus did journey to Judea. God may delay in responding to our need for a greater purpose, but God does not forget us. God did respond. God permitted Lazarus' death for the purpose of helping his disciples believe in Jesus more fully.

When Jesus arrived, Martha met him on the way and told him of Lazarus' death. Martha proclaimed her faith in Jesus, and Jesus told her that death did not have the final say. "I am the resurrection and the life. Those who believe in me, even though they die, will live and everyone who lives and believes in me will never die." Mary came to meet Jesus and expressed the depth of sorrow that her brother's death has caused her. Jesus was deeply moved by her sorrow. "Jesus began to weep." In Jesus we see the sorrow of God that is created by human suffering. Some skeptics said, "Could not he who opened the eyes of the blind man have kept this man from dying?"

Jesus saw this incident as having a higher purpose than simply avoiding personal pain. Jesus came to the tomb and told them to remove the stone at the entrance. Martha, recognizing that dead people began to decay after three days in the tomb, protested, but

Jesus insisted on the removal of the stone. Then Jesus cried out with a loud voice, "Lazarus, come out!" Lazarus came out of the tomb still wrapped in his grave cloths. God was not constrained by the power of death, and Jesus was the Son of God. While many came to believe because of what they had seen, this very demonstration of God's power working through Jesus convinced some of the religious leadership that he must be killed. The power of the presence of God does not always result in a response of faith. Sometimes it engenders fear.

Passion/Psalm Sunday

Isaiah 50:4-9a

> *The Lord God has opened my ear, and I was not rebellious, I did not turn backward. I gave my back to those who struck me, and my cheeks to those who pulled out the beard; I did not hide my face from insult and spitting.* — Isaiah 50:5-6

When we recall the passion of Christ, we are reminded that all suffering is not meaningless. The importance of remembering that this is Passion Sunday, as well as Palm Sunday, is that we need to realize that the victory of God comes with a price. Given the state of the world, responding to God's call often is accompanied by a struggle and some pain. All clergy who take seriously the call of God in their lives recognize that faithfulness includes absorbing a measure of insult and sometimes injury in the pursuit of their call. "I gave my back to those who struck me, and my cheeks to those who pulled out the beard; I did not hide my face from insult and spitting." Suffering is endurable if it is for a higher purpose. "The Lord God helps me; therefore I have not been disgraced...." The prophet Isaiah, in seeking to understand the apparent insult to God's people of having been destroyed as a nation and carried off into exile, recognized that God was working through their suffering for a higher purpose. Jesus recognized the same truth in enduring his own suffering. All Christians, and especially those called to be pastors, must keep this truth firmly in mind. Our faith does not invite suffering, but it recognizes that our suffering does not defeat God. We are confident in God that "all things works together for good for those who love God, who are called according to his purpose" (Romans 8:28).

Psalm 118:1-2, 19-29

Open to me the gates of righteousness, that I may enter through them and give thanks to the Lord.
— Psalm 118:19

This is traditionally known as one of the "praise psalms" that was sung at Passover time. It is assumed that this may have been the psalm that Jesus and his disciples sang as they concluded their meal and went to the Mount of Olives. As such, one can picture how this psalm would have given Jesus strength as he began this final journey. Listen to several of the verses while recalling events in Jesus' life. Jesus' central message was the steadfast love of God. "O give thanks to the Lord, for he is good; his steadfast love endures forever!" His wilderness experience had confirmed for him that in all circumstances he needed to depend on the faithfulness of God (vv. 5-9). His faith was severely tested by the behavior of other humans. "It is better to take refuge in the Lord than to put confidence in mortals" (v. 8). When he experienced the assistance of Simon of Cyrene, did he remember the words of the psalm, "I was pushed hard, so that I was falling, but the Lord helped me" (v. 13)? Jesus' willingness to enter through the gates of righteousness even through suffering (vv. 19-20) permitted him to hear God's response of salvation to the stone that the builders were rejecting (vv. 21-22). Because he trusted in God's ultimate saving power even in the face of death, he could join the psalmist in saying, "This is the day that the Lord has made; let us rejoice and be glad in it." Even the earlier palm-strewn path of his entry into Jerusalem could have reminded him of the psalmist's words, "Bind the festal procession with branches, up to the horns of the altar. You are my God, and I will give thanks to you; you are my God, I will extol you." It is a worthy psalm for Christians to sing on Palm Sunday.

Philippians 2:5-11

Let the same mind be in you that was in Christ Jesus....
— Philippians 2:5

In this early Christian hymn is captured the theological center of the message of Christ. Here Christians are confronted with the vision of faith by which we are invited to live. "Though he was in the form of God, (he) did not regard equality with God as something to be exploited...." The invitation for the church is to live the same type of servant-ministry that their Lord lived. A church that draws upon its status and power within society to achieve its own goals falls short of the mind of Christ through which it is to view its ministry. The servant-ministry of Jesus was depicted as one who voluntarily became a slave of others. His whole life was shaped in response to the needs of and service to humanity. Even his own survival was not more important than what his death might do on behalf of humanity. The church, as the body of Christ, is never to seek the advantage of their relationship with God to benefit themselves but is to seek how the power of God working through them might be of service to their neighbors. The challenge for the church to overcome their fears and their desires and allow their ministry to be entirely shaped by the mind of Christ is daunting. Yet, each time a decision is made or an act taken in the Spirit of Christ, the name of Jesus is exalted. We often lift up such stories in celebration.

Matthew 21:1-11

The crowds that went ahead of him and that followed were shouting, "Hosanna to the Son of David! Blessed is the one who comes in the name of the Lord!" ...
— Matthew 21:9

The triumphal entry was a moment in time when some in the world recognized and proclaimed a greater truth than they fully understood. There are moments in time when only praise can speak to a truth that is greater than we fully understand. In entering Jerusalem from the Mount of Olives riding on a donkey, Jesus was fulfilling the words of Zechariah 9:9, "Lo our king comes to you; triumphant and victorious is he, humble and riding on a donkey, on a colt, the foal of a donkey." The fact that the journey began from the Mount of Olives also recalled the vision of God's judgment in Zechariah 14:4. Jesus' very entry was a challenge to the authority of Jerusalem under the reign of Rome. Palm Sunday is a political challenge, as well as a religious celebration. It recalls that it is finally God who reigns and that judgment belongs to God. While others may hold power temporarily, they are accountable to a higher power. The challenge for churches is how to proclaim the lordship of God in the form of the servanthood of Christ. Too often the church has pronounced the rule of God in a triumphalistic manner that suggests more arrogance than faithfulness. It is part of the mission of the church to lift up the accountability of the nations to the lordship of God. Our model for doing so, however, is made visible in the Christ who entered Jerusalem to challenge the powers of the world "humble and riding on a donkey...." The theology of the cross is a continuing challenge for the church.

Easter Day

Acts 10:34-43

> *... I truly understand that God shows no partiality, but in every nation anyone who fears him and does what is right is acceptable to him.* — Acts 10:34-35

This comes at the conclusion of Peter's encounter with the Roman centurion, Cornelius. Reading it on Easter day makes clear the worldwide impact of the resurrection. This was not an event that only had significance for the Jewish community. In raising Jesus from the dead, God was acting on behalf of all humanity. It began in Judea when "God anointed Jesus of Nazareth with the Holy Spirit and with power ... (and he) went about doing good and healing all who were oppressed by the devil, for God was with him." This verse is a helpful reminder that we do not celebrate Easter as merely a personal affirmation of faith. Rather, we celebrate a critical event for the whole world. In addition, as Peter learned, God is already at work well beyond our religious traditions. "In every nation anyone who fears (God) and does what is right is acceptable to him." The bonds of exclusivity are shattered.

Because of the resurrection, we can no longer keep our attention only on those who believe like us. God calls us out into the larger world where he is already at work. This is not to suggest that all religions are equal or that we do not have something special to offer the world. God has called us into the Christian community for a purpose. "God raised him on the third day and allowed him to appear, not to all the people but to us who were chosen by God as witnesses...." Our particular vocation as Christians is to carry the message of God's love as seen in Christ out into the world. As Peter discovered, however, we need to be aware that as we bring our message out into the world, we will discover that God is there ahead of us working the miracle of faith in the lives of others.

Psalm 118:1-2, 14-24

> *The Lord has punished me severely, but he did not give me over to death. Open to me the gates of righteousness, that I may enter through them and give thanks to the Lord.* — Psalm 118:18-19

Portions of this same psalm were read for last Sunday. The emphasis in these selected verses is the celebration of the triumph of Jesus over death. The difficulty for many Protestant churches is that we move directly from the celebration of Palm Sunday and the triumphal entry to the celebration of the resurrection on Easter. The reason the Protestant church displays an empty cross is to emphasize the victory of God over death. However, sometimes in our rush to celebrate, we neglect to recognize the suffering of Christ that preceded this event. This is more clearly depicted in the crucifix that the Catholic church uses that shows Jesus still on the cross. When the psalmist said, "This is the gate of the Lord; the righteous shall enter through it," it is important for us to remember that Jesus entered that gate by way of the cross. One of the difficult struggles that the early Christians had to confront was accepting the fact that the Son of God had to suffer and die on the cross. If he were the beloved Son of God, why did God not intervene and protect him from such evil suffering? It is the parallel question to that of other believers who wonder why, if they were faithful, God permitted them to suffer. If God is good, why does God permit the good to suffer? It seems to contradict common sense. The cross is God's challenge to that worldly reasoning. "The stone that the builders rejected has become the chief cornerstone." Jesus' experience of the cross transformed the human understanding of the way God works to effect God's purpose. "This is the Lord's doing; it is marvelous in our eyes. This is the day that the Lord has made; let us rejoice and be glad in it."

Colossians 3:1-4

Set your minds on things that are above....
— Colossians 3:2

Living the resurrected life as Easter people is the promise of Christianity. Life is often shaped by what is attractive to us. The mind's eye focuses on that which is beautiful because it pulls us ahead. When Paul spoke of setting our minds on things that are above, he was suggesting that we could lift our heads and see a vision of eternity. We do not turn our backs on the physical realities of life. Rather, our physical realities now serve a higher master. It is not wrong to be successful, but we need to be conscious of who our success serves. It is very easy to allow success to become an end in itself. It is not wrong to be wealthy, but we need to be careful not to allow wealth to become our master. This same reorientation of our perspective applies to all dimensions of our life. Because of the resurrection, we are free to allow compassion, kindness, patience, forgiveness, and most of all, love to unleash the peace of Christ in our relationships. We are liberated from the petty competition that divides and separates us. To be raised with Christ is not to be instantaneously perfect. It is to grow toward this vision of loveliness. It is to choose each day to "put to death that which is earthly" because we are no longer afraid of death. Because each day we strive to view life from the perspective of eternity, each day can become a taste of eternity.

John 20:1-18

... she turned around and saw Jesus standing there, but she did not know it was Jesus. — John 20:14

The resurrection is a confusing story and apparently was equally confusing for those who were present at the time. Mary Magdalene, whose very life had been transformed by Jesus, came to the tomb early in the morning. Despite what Jesus may have said about the future resurrection, it is clear that Mary had come to see the dead. She believed that death was final. When she saw the empty tomb, she assumed that someone had stolen the body. What other explanation could there be? She reported this bad news to two of Jesus' closest disciples, and they ran to the tomb. They also saw the empty tomb, but the story continues to be confusing. "Then the other disciple ... also went in and he saw and believed; for as yet they did not understand the scripture, that he must rise from the dead." So what was it that the disciple believed? Their belief, apparently, was weakened by misunderstanding. What was their response to this earth-shattering event? "Then the disciples returned to their homes." It was Mary who stayed around. Seeing is not believing, because we often interpret what we see by what we already believe. Because Mary believed that death was final, she did not recognize Jesus when she saw him. Even being addressed by two angels did not change for her the cold reality of death. It was only when Jesus addressed her personally that the prison of her mind was opened to believe that Christ had been raised from the dead. When she believed, she was able to see. Despite her confusion, she did not leave, and, in her staying, she became the first evangelist. Sometimes, in our confusion, we have to continue to stick around until we can be addressed in a way that alters our beliefs so that we can see with new eyes.

Matthew 28:1-10

So they left the tomb quickly with fear and great joy, and ran to tell his disciples. — Matthew 28:8

Imagine yourself living in a world of great uncertainty. The faith that had once seemed so important to you has been arrested somewhere along the way. It is no longer a living, vital faith for you. You still believe, or want to believe, so you stumble to your church, that structure of brick and mortar that once offered you the practices that nurtured your faith. This is the body that once had told you how to live and given you hope. Here was where you had heard scriptures read, hymns sung, and prayed prayers that had nurtured you in your faith. In recent years, however, there have been conflicts that have challenged your faith. The church has done and said things that have caused anger among both religious and nonreligious people. Because of those conflicts, or maybe just because you got too busy, you found yourself running away from the church. You have not wished it harm, and you are saddened when you see life go out of the body that had once meant so much to you. A part of you even feels that you have betrayed Christ's body. Although another part of you mocks it and says, "If you're so good, save yourself." And now people are saying that the church is dead. You wander back on Easter morning to this tomb of brick and mortar so that you might be near this body that once gave you your faith. As you enter the church, you hear the words, "Do not be afraid ... he is risen." In those words you begin to recognize hope being renewed within you. The body of Christ is not dead. You feel this powerful urgency to go and tell other disciples who have also drifted away, "The body of Christ is not dead. God has raised it from the dead." So you depart this day with fear and great joy to tell of the resurrected Christ.

Easter 2

Acts 2:14a, 22-32

> *But God raised him up, having freed him from death, because it was impossible for him to be held in its power.*
> — Acts 2:24

Luke, the author of Acts, found support in scripture for his belief that God had not lost control. The most compelling evidence that our universe is out of control, or at least not under the control of a loving God, has always been the suffering of the innocent. We continue to hear the question today of how a good God can allow such a tragedy to take place. Luke took the critical tragedy of the cross where Jesus was "killed by the hands of those outside the law" as the point of his reflection on this issue. Here was the Son of God, the most innocent of all, and he was crucified by those who rejected his message of God's love. If God did not intervene to prevent such a tragic event, how could one say that God is good and loving? Luke, through Peter's sermon, did not deny that the deed was evil. What he did claim was that God was aware of the depth of evil in human nature ahead of that time and had taken it into account as God worked out his purpose in the universe. He found evidence for that belief in the scriptural account of how God worked in the life of David. He quoted Psalm 16 as it had been translated in the Septuagint, or Greek translation of the Hebrew scriptures. "I saw the Lord always before me, for he is at my right hand so that I will not be shaken ... For you will not abandon my soul to Hades, or let your Holy one experience corruption."

Since everyone knew that David had died and been buried, Luke suggested that there was a larger meaning to David's words that applied to God's Messiah. "Foreseeing this, David spoke of the resurrection of the Messiah, saying, 'He was not abandoned to Hades, nor did his flesh experience corruption.'" In the same way that God had been faithful to David during his life, so now God was continuing to be faithful to his promise by raising up Jesus.

This was not a violation of God's plan, or even a desperate act in response to the unexpected events, but a continuing working out of God's purpose in the context of an imperfect but beloved humanity. God had planned to take the evil of the cross and make it a redemptive event. It is by faith that we allow tragedy to be redeemed by a loving God.

Psalm 16

> *I keep the Lord always before me; because he is at my right hand, I shall not be moved.* — Psalm 16:8

The author of Acts quoted this psalm extensively (Acts 2:25-28) and declared that David was speaking of Christ in this psalm. This is an audacious claim that throws our concept of time into confusion. Yet it was similar to the assertion of Paul, in 1 Corinthians 10:4, that the "rock" that provided the children of Israel with water in the wilderness was Christ. It was also the claim of John 1:1 ff that the Word that became flesh was also at the beginning of time. In all of these examples, no one was suggesting that Jesus appeared like some astronaut from outer space. Rather, they were saying that God was present in Christ before God was manifest in the body of Jesus. What the New Testament writers seemed to be suggesting was that in Jesus they had recognized the Spirit of God that had been manifest in less concrete, but no less real, ways in their past. In Jesus' being raised from the dead, it became clear that the boundaries of death and time could not contain Christ. Therefore the psalmist could say, "I keep the Lord before me; because he is at my right hand, I shall not be moved," and later generations, who had experienced God's power in Jesus, could also believe that the Lord of the psalmist was their Lord who could not be defeated by death nor contained by time.

1 Peter 1:3-9

> *... By his great mercy he has given us a new birth into a living hope through the resurrection of Jesus Christ from the dead.*   — 1 Peter 1:3

First Peter is a letter to the early church. The daunting challenge of this new faith was to entrust their lives to this new revelation. "Although you have not seen him, you love him; and even though you do not see him now, you believe in him...." The challenge for all believers is to trust in that which they cannot see. Christianity is not a formula for a protected life or a secret for worldly success. From the beginning of the church, believing in Christ often increased rather than reduced the challenges of life. "In this you rejoice, even if now for a little while you have to suffer various trials...." This was not a philosophy for comfort but a reinterpretation of the experience of living. In a way, it was similar to how Israel interpreted the wilderness experience as a way that God refined them as a people, so early Christians saw the trials of life as God preparing them for something better. Their suffering was "... so that the genuineness of your faith — being more precious than gold that, though perishable, is tested by fire...." It may be one of the significant challenges of the contemporary church to confront the cultural seduction of avoiding all discomfort and to recognize that a genuine faith not only experiences trials but is strengthened by them. Churches that do not shy from such challenges seek to receive "the outcome of your faith, the salvation of your souls."

John 20:19-31

> *If you forgive the sins of any, they are forgiven them; if you retain the sins of any, they are retained.*
>   — John 20:23

What an awesome and frightening task to be responsible for the sins of the world. Whether the world's sins be forgiven or retained depends upon our response. How does the church respond to the sins of the world? What is the effect of our condemning a situation rather than offering forgiveness? Immediately upon hearing of this responsibility for the sins of the world, we hear the story of doubting Thomas. If sin is that act or condition of life that separates us from God or neighbor, then death becomes the principle tool to effect that separation. We can only believe that Christ overcame the sins of the world if we believe that in him God has conquered death. Thomas expressed the doubt that exists in most of us. We doubt that God can conquer the power of sin in us. The reason we retain the sins of others is that we fear that God has not conquered sin in us. We pray, "Forgive us our debts as we forgive our debtors," and then we can only pray that God is more gracious to us than we often are to others. In our world, the sins of racism, sexuality, and greed, among others, separate us from our neighbor. It is the awesome responsibility of the church to determine how to convey the forgiveness of Christ to the world.

Easter 3

Acts 2:14a, 36-41

> *So those who welcomed his message were baptized, and that day about three thousand persons were added.*
> — Acts 2:41

Acts recorded this as the report of the first converts to Christianity in response to the preaching of Peter following the Pentecost experience. The Spirit of God had found a channel to the world through the preaching of these disciples. Throughout scripture, the Spirit of God was a power that enabled a person or group to accomplish far more than they would have thought possible. The Spirit had been released, and those once fearful apostles were ready to take on the world. Peter's sermon not only had drawn upon ancient texts to demonstrate continuity with the earlier revelation of God but also had revealed the new thing that God was doing in Jesus Christ. "God has made him both Lord and messiah, this Jesus whom you crucified." If people repented, or shifted their focus from living in response to their human desires to living their life in response to the will of God, and if they were baptized in Christ's name, they would be forgiven of their sins and would receive the gift of the Holy Spirit.

The church is called to carry this message of Christ to the world, advancing the purpose of God to reconcile the world to himself. Receiving the Spirit is their first step in that direction. The overwhelming response of 3,000 converts on the first day set the tone of Acts for the growth of the church. For contemporary Christians, many of whom are participating in churches that are not growing, it is an intimidating story. What are we missing that we cannot get that type of response from the community around us? A central message of Acts was that a critical element in such growth was the presence of the Holy Spirit. In other stories of the early church, it was clear that this growth did not always come smoothly. Even in

Jesus' own ministry, there were times of growth and times of falling away. It may be, however, that the churches need to reexamine the manner in which they can open themselves to the power of the Spirit working among them.

Psalm 116:1-4, 12-19

> *The snares of death encompassed me; the pangs of Sheol laid hold on me; I suffered distress and anguish. Then I called on the name of the Lord....* — Psalm 116:3-4

This is a psalm of a people who were almost stunned in their thanksgiving for having been delivered from a desperate situation. It is not clear whether the desperate situation from which the person was saved was that of death, illness, or some major social crisis. It is only clear that the petitioner was once in a state of desperation and turned and cried out to God. "I love the Lord, because he has heard my voice and my supplications." The crisis had been resolved and the psalmist felt a deep need to "lift up the cup of salvation and call on the name of the Lord." When we have experienced a deliverance from what we saw as a hopeless situation, there is a need to offer praise. To fail to offer praise at such a time would rob the experience of its importance. It is also a reminder of our dependence on a power outside of us. "O Lord, I am your servant; I am your servant, the child of your serving girl. You have loosed my bonds." For believers, there is a need to perform acts of worship making visible our thanksgiving. "I will offer to you a thanksgiving sacrifice and call on the name of the Lord." While this psalm is paired with the story of the first conversions following Pentecost, it also reminds us of the importance of the church offering rituals of thanksgiving by which we can all acknowledge the providential care of God in our lives.

1 Peter 1:17-23

> *Now that you have purified your souls by your obedience to the truth so that you have genuine mutual love, love one another deeply from the heart.*
> — 1 Peter 1:22

The people to whom Peter wrote were living as resident aliens in a foreign land. There was an uneasiness in such a situation. You were always on edge because you knew that you were different from the dominant culture and could be the object of prejudice at any given moment. Peter reminded them that though they were living in a culture that was foreign to them, that culture was not outside of the awareness of God. "If you invoke as Father the one who judges all people impartially according to their deeds, live in reverent fear during the time of your exile." In one sense, all Christians live as resident aliens regardless of our situation. Because our loyalty is finally with Christ, there is always a certain tension between what we believe and the values of the culture around us. Within that tension, we are to live with a certain respect for others around us because they will judge us according to how they see us living.

Peter tells us that God "judges all people impartially according to their deeds." The paradox of faith is that we are saved by grace but judged by our deeds. While our deeds do not save us, they are important as part of our testimony for God. If it is through Christ that "we have come to trust in God," it is also through Christ that we discover how important our deeds really are. Peter suggested that Christ purified our soul through obedience to the truth that enables us to have genuine, mutual love. Through Christ we experience God's love for us that heals us and sets us free to love one another. We are urged to "love one another deeply from the heart." The heart, as the Bible speaks of it, is not just the seat of our feelings but the very center of our character and decision-making process. We are saved by grace, but we live that salvation by demonstrating a character of love in our relationships with others.

Luke 24:13-35

> *When he was at the table with them, he took bread, blessed and broke it, and gave it to them. Then their eyes were opened, and they recognized him....*
> — Luke 24:30-31

In this very familiar post-resurrection story, we learn some significant points about our faith. First, we hear that Cleopas and his companion had had the experience and knew the story but were without understanding. They were able to relate the whole story of the crucifixion and even the story of those who went to the tomb and found it empty, but they were still caught in their despair. It is not enough to know the story or even to have had an experience. There is something more that has to put it all together and give us new eyes. According to the story, it is not even enough to walk with Jesus. Is there the suggestion here that many may walk with Jesus and not recognize with whom they are walking? Jesus took the same stories that they knew, "beginning with Moses and all the prophets" and interpreted them for these disciples in a way that broke open their minds to a new understanding.

Yet even a powerful scripture study, inspirationally taught, was not enough. When they arrived at their destiny, while they were moved by Jesus' interpretation, they still did not recognize him. Two acts had to come together before they came to a full understanding. First, they offered hospitality to a stranger. "But they urged him strongly, saying, 'Stay with us, because it is almost evening and the day is now nearly over.' " There is an echo of the story of Abraham offering hospitality to strangers at the oak of Mamre (Genesis 18:1-15) and discovering that he was welcoming God. By offering hospitality to a stranger, they were opening themselves to the possibility of the presence of God (Hebrews 13:2). But still there was no recognition until "he was at the table with them, (and) took bread, blessed and broke it, and gave it to them." It was that combination of their having offered hospitality and participating in the familiar act of breaking bread with Jesus that they finally understood who was in their midst. The lesson for the contemporary church may be that if we truly want to encounter Christ in our midst, we need to understand the scriptures, offer hospitality to strangers, and break bread together. It is the combination of study, ethics, and ritual that is critical for our faith.

Easter 4

Acts 2:42-47

> *All who believed were together and had all things in common; they would sell their possessions and goods and distribute the proceeds to all, as any had need.*
> — Acts 2:44-45

There has been a lot of energy spent on trying to understand this statement about the life of the early church. Some try to explain it in terms of the early church's belief that Christ would come again soon and that their whole lives needed to be directed in preparation for receiving him. When Christ did not return, they explain, the church soon realized that such an ethic was hopelessly impractical. Others suggest that it is the ideal toward which the church should continue to try to move. Certainly it is a story intended to place material goods in their proper perspective. "You cannot serve God and wealth" (Matthew 6:24). It is instructive that far more commentary has been focused on this verse than the other verses describing the early church's activity. "They devoted themselves to the apostles' teaching and fellowship, to the breaking of bread and prayers."

The economic decisions were a direct outgrowth of their emphasis on fellowship, scripture, and prayer. In that intense devotion to loving God and neighbor, as experienced in the fellowship of these new believers, all their economic possessions became merely materials to be used for a greater good. The question to be addressed is whether a church could be so devoted to each other and to God and not be willing to share whatever material blessings they had with each other as each had need. For these believers, the church was family and that is just how you act in a family. The testimony to the power of that loving community is seen in the reaction of outsiders: "And day by day the Lord added to their number those who were being saved."

Psalm 23

> *You prepare a table before me in the presence of my enemies; you anoint my head with oil; my cup overflows.* — Psalm 23:5

This is probably one of the most famous passages in the whole Bible. For thousands of years, people have drawn strength from these words. Because the words are so familiar, we may overlook the powerful analysis of the human condition that is depicted here. The psalm begins with a recognition of the power that need plays in our psyche. While it manifests itself in many ways — food, love, security, and such — our sense of neediness reflects the self-centeredness of our lives. This neediness, and the drive to fulfill it, leads to a continuing experience of stress that gnaws at our very soul. Recognizing this, God provides experiences that interrupt this stress and "restores my soul." Need also causes us to act in ways that distort the right relationships that we could have with each other. Again, it is God who leads us "in right paths for his name sake." Our neediness makes us aware of our vulnerability, which in turn leads us to live life in fear. Only by trusting God can we rise above that fear. "Even though I walk through the darkest valley, I fear no evil; for you are with me; your rod and your staff — they comfort me."

Enemies, in some form or another, personal or circumstantial, are a normal part of our lives. It is easy to become too focused on their presence and forget the lovelier qualities of our lives. So God provides us with experiences that remind us of the joy of life. "You prepare a table before me in the presence of my enemies...." It is in those repeated experiences of God's caring presence that we gain confidence: "Surely goodness and mercy shall follow me all the days of my life...." While the power of neediness continues to accompany us in life, it is when we recognize the faithfulness of God that we learn the freedom to say, "The Lord is my shepherd, I shall not want."

1 Peter 2:19-25

> *When he was abused, he did not return abuse; when he suffered, he did not threaten; but he entrusted himself to the one who judges justly.* — 1 Peter 2:23

The lectionary, understandably, begins this reading with verse 19 and, thus, avoids the explicit reference to slaves. Verse 18 may well have been used in America as part of Christian justification for slavery. In that context, it is important to recognize that the letter is addressed to the slaves and not the slave owners. It is recognizing that in the real world there is injustice, and the powerful will mistreat the powerless. Given that reality, how should a Christian victim of such injustice live? While the victim of injustice may feel powerless to resist, he or she gains dignity in identifying with Christ in the experience of suffering. The danger to such advice is that it can be used to encourage passivity in the face of injustice. The intent of the writer was the opposite. By relating the suffering from injustice to the suffering of Christ, there is the possibility of redemptive suffering. One no longer becomes simply a victim; one is a participant in a larger story that God is unfolding for the redemption of the world. Now one no longer suffers needlessly; we suffer for a larger purpose. Christ's suffering did not give approval to those who treated him unjustly but neither did Jesus passively accept the role of victim.

John 10:1-10

> *... I came that they may have life, and have it abundantly."* — John 10:10

In Ezekiel 34:1-10, the prophet Ezekiel indicted the leaders of Israel for not caring for the sheep entrusted to them and, instead, used their positions to enrich themselves. Jesus had just accused the Pharisees of spiritual blindness, and then he developed this image of a good and a false shepherd to enlarge on this indictment.

The focus of the word image is on the gate that allows people to enter the sheepfold legitimately. Building on the image in Ezekiel, Jesus suggested that there were true and false shepherds. False shepherds were those who manipulated the situation for their own benefit. The true shepherd was recognized by the gatekeeper and by the sheep as one who truly cared for the sheep. At that point, it appeared that Jesus was contrasting his own ministry with that of the Pharisees.

The image gets confused because Jesus proceeded to speak of himself as the gate rather than the shepherd. Now we recall that, in Ezekiel, God had become the true shepherd (Ezekiel 34:11-16) because of the failure of the false shepherds. Since the gate was both the way into the sheepfold where there was safety and the way out to the pasture where there was nourishment, we can expand our image of what God has provided us through Jesus. "Whoever enters by me will be saved, and will come in and go out and find pasture." Here is the pictorial image of what John would later say in 14:6, "I am the way, and the truth, and the life. No one comes to the Father except through me." As pastors read this passage, we are cautioned of the danger of becoming false shepherds who enrich themselves at the expense of the true needs of the sheep. As congregations read this passage, we are reminded of the responsibility of the body of Christ to be the way through which people find both safety and nourishment.

Easter 5

Acts 7:55-60

While they were stoning Stephen, he prayed, "Lord Jesus, receive my spirit." — Acts 7:59

The stoning of Stephen marked a critical transition in the story of the church. Stephen was the first of Jesus' disciples to die on behalf of the gospel. Acts made the parallel with Jesus' life and death explicit, thus making clear what it means for Christians to be Jesus' disciples. The faith Stephen proclaimed was a challenge to the orthodox faith of his day (7:1-53). The negative reaction, even fury, to what he said matched the reaction to Jesus' sermon at Nazareth (Luke 4:25-29). Stephen's final prayer, offering his spirit to God, paralleled Jesus' prayer in Luke 23:46, and his prayer that God would forgive his executioners also echoed Jesus' prayer in Luke 23:34. The challenge for Jesus' disciples in the current church is tremendous.

The purpose of our witness is to reveal the glory of God. According to Luke/Acts, the glory of God, which signifies God's active presence in the world, began with Abraham even before he came to Haran (Acts 7:2). It was manifest at Jesus' transfiguration (Luke 9:32) and the resurrection (Luke 24:26). It could be anticipated in Jesus' return (Luke 9:26 and 21:27). According to the model of Stephen, the glory of God could be seen prior to Jesus' return at significant moments of faithfulness (7:55). Stephen was seen as the model of the ideal Christian disciple. He was bold in his interpretation of scripture, fearless in his obedience to God in the face of opposition, confident of God's faithfulness even in the face of death, and loving toward his enemies.

The glory of God was made visible in Stephen's act of praying for the forgiveness of those who were stoning him. This demonstration of the grace of God in Stephen's story also provided the context for introducing Saul into the Christian story. God's grace would transform this enemy of the church into its greatest advocate. The capacity of God to overcome our sins is infinite and challenges the church to proclaim this transforming grace to the world.

Psalm 31:1-5, 15-16

> *Into your hand I commit my spirit; you have redeemed me, O Lord, faithful God.* — Psalm 31:5

This verse is most remembered as part of Jesus' prayer from the cross at the end of his life. It is less well known as part of Stephen's prayer at the time of his stoning. The context of the psalmist's words, which were used not only by Jesus and Stephen but also by countless other believers down through the ages, is the firm belief in the covenant relationship between God and God's people. God made a covenant with a particular people beginning with Abraham and reconfirmed this covenant many times with other believers throughout scripture. An aspect of that covenant that is repeatedly made was that God's reputation is affected by the way in which God responds to the needs of God's people. "He leads me in right paths for his name's sake" (Psalm 23:3b). Therefore, throughout their history, the people of God have felt confident that they could cry out to God in times of need as the Israelites did when they were slaves in Egypt. God had made a commitment to hear the people's cry, and God would not fail to be faithful. "Incline your ear to me; rescue me speedily. Be a rock of refuge for me, a strong fortress to save me."

The experience of Israel, however, which was repeated in the lives of Jesus and Stephen, was that God's timing was different from that of humans. The faithful could be confident that God would deliver them but not when or under what conditions God would deliver them. "My times are in your hand; deliver me from the hand of my enemies and persecutors" was a prayer of trust and a recognition that the believer was not in charge of God's behavior. There were times when all the believers could do was trust in God's faithfulness and commit their spirit to God's care. "Into your hand

I commit my spirit...." This was the prayer of both Jesus and Stephen at the point of their deaths when it became clear that God would not intervene to prevent their dying. This becomes the ultimate prayer of trust for all Christians when they are in a desperate situation that offers no obvious solution.

1 Peter 2:2-10

> *Come to him, a living stone, though rejected by mortals yet chosen and precious in God's sight, and like living stones, let yourselves be built into a spiritual house....* — 1 Peter 2:4

Each of the lectionary passages for this Sunday seeks to prepare the church for conflict. Conflict is a normal part of church life, and, far too often, it is an internal conflict among Christians rather than a conflict with the world's values. These passages assume that if the church is faithful, it will experience conflict with the larger community in which it exists. As was made clear in the life and death of Jesus, the faith that he proclaimed was an offense to many who prospered in the world: "A stone that makes them stumble, and a rock that makes them fall." While this does not preclude Christians being successful in life, scripture does suggest that we need to be careful that we have not become too accommodating to the values of the world in our pursuit of that success. Since the book of Peter was written to the early church, this should be of particular concern as a church seeks to plan its mission. "But you are a chosen race, a royal priesthood, a holy nation, God's own people, in order that you may proclaim the mighty acts of him who called you out of darkness into his marvelous light."

Using this variety of Old Testament images, the author reminded the church that they were called for a purpose. They were meant to be different from other organizations in the world. Priests were called to interface between God and the world. To be holy was to be different from those around you. The mission of the church is not to "fit in" but to respond to a call from God who speaks from outside of the values in which our world exists. God seeks to reveal to the world a better way and calls the church to expose the world to that alternative to the darkness in which they have found themselves. This is not because the church consists of people who are superior to others who live in the world. The church has no claim to being better than others. "Once you were not a people, but now you are God's people; once you had not received mercy, but now you have received mercy." The quality of life that the church is called upon to proclaim to the world is the life of forgiven sinners that offer hope to others who recognize their need for forgiveness.

John 14:1-14

> *... I am the way, and the truth, and the life. No one comes to the Father except through me.* — John 14:6

In many ways, we want to argue with this passage. In an age where we have seen the suffering caused by religious intolerance, we want to believe there are many paths to God and that we are all on a common journey. Then we read that Jesus made this exclusive claim to being the way, the truth, and the life. Further, he claimed a common identity with God. This is the challenge of the incarnation. We are not allowed the easy escape of believing Jesus is one among many prophets. But what are we to do with the other prophets and other religions? Philip responded for us when he said to Jesus, "Lord, show us the Father, and we will be satisfied." Jesus responded, "Believe me that I am in the Father and the Father is in me; but if you do not, then believe me because of the works themselves." Seen through the lens of Jesus' works, the statement that Jesus is the way, the truth, and the life, take on a different meaning.

Jesus' life was that of a servant to the needy. Nothing he did was determined by how it would benefit him personally. He demonstrated an accepting love that included even his enemy. He was critical of those attitudes and possessions that resulted in excluding the needy and separating others into classes. To say that Jesus was the way, the truth, and the life was to say that the path to God was through serving those in need, offering forgiveness even to your enemy, and not letting either your religious belief or your possessions become a barrier to including those who hunger for the healing love of God. If Christians lived the life of their Lord, no one would think of them as being exclusive in their faith.

Easter 6

Acts 17:22-31

> *For as I went through the city and looked carefully at your objects of worship, I found among them an altar with the inscription, "To an unknown God."*
> — Acts 17:23

Consider doing what Paul did. Walk through a major city and notice the objects that we appear to worship. Perhaps you will see a tall skyscraper reaching for the sky, brilliantly flooded with lights, reflecting our longing for economic security. Or maybe as you are walking along, you will be passed by a bright red convertible sports car that is speeding past a gleaming Mercedes Benz. Do they reflect our drive for personal recognition or even personal satisfaction? In that same traffic pattern, you might see a young professional with a full beard and flowing hair weaving between the cars on his motorcycle signaling his freedom or perhaps disdain of such status symbols. Each of the drivers uses one of a vast network of highways to which we cling in order to preserve our freedom. Perhaps one of them will be headed to a nearby university where he or she will find our hunger for knowledge. That person might also find a professor and a group of students chanting a mantra as they reach for inner peace. Paul responded to this worldly hunger by saying, "What therefore you worship as unknown, this I proclaim to you." Christianity has shown a remarkable adaptability in framing its message in the context of its environment.

The major Christian seasons were transformations of pagan rituals into Christian expressions. The festival of Saturnalia was transformed into a celebration of Christ's birth. Easter was an adaptation of a spring goddess festival. The cross was intended to be a sign of shame but was transformed into a sign of hope. Like Paul, these Christians knew that the false gods were "not gods" and therefore felt free to transform them into vehicles of faith. The danger for us, however, is that the reverse process is also possible. Crosses can become merely jewelry. Christmas can again become simply a self-indulgence, and Easter a spring festival. It is only through the eyes of faith that we can look through the symbols of the world and see God.

Psalm 66:8-20

> *... we went through fire and through water, yet you have brought us to a spacious place.* — Psalm 66:12

We are living in an almost schizophrenic time. On the one hand, we are experiencing a prosperity that has never been matched in history. Medical science is conquering many fearful diseases and extending the length of life to undreamed of proportions. On the other hand, the children of our culture are revealing the horrible violence that lies just below the surface of our civilization. Violence seems to be the prime stimulant that young people seek in video games and movies, and the horror of young people expressing their alienation through the shooting of their fellow students is far too frequent. The adult world fails to offer many alternatives to this violence. We easily can be overwhelmed by such insanity. It is as if we are engaged in a battle for our souls. As the Israelites reflected on their often violent history, they interpreted their experience as God using such experiences to refine them. "For you, O God, have tested us; you have tried us as silver is tried." They accepted that such experiences were part of their reality and tried to understand what God could say to them through such experiences. They never doubted that God was accompanying them through the rough experiences. "You brought us into the net; you laid burdens on our backs; you let people ride over our heads; we went through fire and through water; yet you have brought us out to a spacious place."

It is important, in this chaotic time in which we live, that we are both realistic about our conditions and confident in God's ability to speak through these events and bring us into a better place. We live in a society that reacts to the violence of our society with a desire for harsh punishment. The people of faith know that such vengeful thinking is destructive for the whole community. "If I had cherished iniquity in my heart, the Lord would not have listened." We live in a time when there is a powerful witness in demonstrating a confidence in the steadfast love of God and an openness to the hope that God offers us.

1 Peter 3:13-22

> *Always be ready to make your defense to anyone who demands from you an accounting for the hope that is in you; yet do it with gentleness and reverence....*
> — 1 Peter 3:15-16

Learning to live in a society that is at best skeptical and at worst hostile to your way of life is difficult. The author of 1 Peter is writing to a church whose members live as resident aliens in a foreign country. They are different from their neighbors and therefore easily the victim of suspicion and fear. Apparently hope was one of their distinguishing characteristics. Can you be too hopeful in a manner that upsets your more fearful neighbors? "Do not fear what they fear," Peter advises, "and do not be intimidated, but in your hearts sanctify Christ as Lord." Given the amount of attention that 1 Peter devoted to how you should respond to unjust treatment, it would seem that the Christians may have been the object of their neighbor's hostility frequently. How should Christians respond to hostility, slander, and unjust treatment? "Keep your conscience clear, so that, when you are maligned, those who abuse you for your good conduct in Christ may be put to shame."

While Christians are encouraged not to retaliate, they are not asked to play victim. Rather their response is to be modeled after Christ. "For Christ also suffered for sins once for all, the righteous for the unrighteous, in order to bring you to God." Christ did not play the role of victim but rather sought by his response to benefit others, even those who were mistreating him. The challenge for our church is twofold. First, is there any evidence that our behavior is so strikingly distinct from the surrounding community that anyone would have reason to become upset with us? If surveys are correct, there does not seem to be much difference between Christians and non-Christians in their social behavior. Second, how are we to react when we are treated unjustly? Is our response to such mistreatment any different from other people in society? If the answer to both of these questions is that there is no difference, then the question becomes what does it mean to declare Jesus Christ as Lord?

John 14:15-21

If you love me, you will keep my commandments.
— John 14:15

It is as simple and as difficult as that. Jesus was preparing his disciples for his departure. He promised them that they would not be left alone with this task but that he would send another advocate to be with them forever. There is a spirit of truth that transcends all of our philosophical arguments and bids us love one another as Jesus had commanded (13:34-35). This very direct statement stands over all the divisions within the Christian community and calls us to task. The truth of our failure to obey this direct commandment of our Lord stands as a continuing indictment of the church. The proliferation of divisions within the church continues to shame the body of Christ. In John 13:35 Jesus said, "By this everyone will know that you are my disciples, if you have love for one another."

The evidence for why many in this world question the validity of our faith is all too apparent. Jesus promised to send the spirit of truth to be an advocate for the living out of the faith. "This is the spirit of truth, whom the world cannot receive, because it neither sees him nor knows him." The difficult question for the church is whether we too have become too worldly to receive the spirit of truth. Perhaps a beginning point for every church is to ask themselves daily, "What have we done today that has demonstrated our love for other Christians within our church, among our churches, among our denominations, and for the world?" Perhaps if we focused on that question, we would see Christ more clearly among us. "They who have my commandments and keep them are those who love me; and those who love me will be loved by my Father, and I will love them and reveal myself to them."

Easter 7

Acts 1:6-14

> *He replied, "It is not for you to know the times or periods that the Father has set by his own authority. But you will receive power when the Holy Spirit has come upon you; and you will be my witnesses in Jerusalem in all Judea and Samaria, and to the ends of the earth."*
> — Acts 1:7-8

This is the Luke/Acts version of the great commission (Matthew 28:19-20). It came in response to a question about the timing of God. "Lord, is this the time when you will restore the kingdom to Israel?" As Jesus had said before, and as many seem unable to understand, "It is not for you to know the times or periods that the Father has set by his own authority...." It is difficult for humans to resist the temptation to want to eat of the tree of the knowledge of good and evil (Genesis 2:17). In essence, even if we would acknowledge that we are not God, we at least want to be included in the secret of how God will complete the creation. As it was in the Garden of Eden, the question here is also one of obedience. Jesus gave his disciples their marching orders. They were to be his "witnesses in Jerusalem, in all Judea and Samaria, and to the ends of the earth."

The task of the church is not to serve themselves but to serve the world. In preparation for that task, they were to return to Jerusalem and await the coming of the Holy Spirit. So that there would be no question that this responsibility rested on the entire church, we are told that included in those who were in Jerusalem awaiting the Holy Spirit were "certain women, including Mary the mother of Jesus, as well as his brothers." Acts began to tell the story of the unfolding of the mission of the church accompanied by the Holy Spirit. It was made clear from the beginning of the life of the church that we are not to spend our time gazing into the heavens seeking signs of Jesus' return but are to be about the work of Christ as guided by the Holy Spirit here on earth.

Psalm 68:1-10, 32-35

> *God gives the desolate a home to live in; he leads out the prisoners to prosperity, but the rebellious live in a parched land.* — Psalm 68:6

The context from which you listen to a psalm can completely alter your response to it. If you hear this psalm from a position of comfort in the world, there seems to be a certain vindictiveness to its celebration. "As smoke is driven away, so drive them away; as wax melts before the fire, let the wicked perish before God. But let the righteous be joyful; let them exult before God; let them be jubilant with joy." If you hear this psalm from a condition of poverty and powerlessness, having felt the sting of injustice many times, there is an anticipation of a reversal in fortune that has scarcely been dreamed of. "God gives the desolate a home to live in; he leads out the prisoners to prosperity, but the rebellious live in a parched land." This image of God who caused a reversal of fortunes in the world was consistent with Israel's memory of how they began as a people when they were slaves in Egypt. At that time, God met every enemy and protected his people. "O God, when you went out before your people, when you marched through the wilderness, the earth quaked, the heavens poured down rain at the presence of God, the God of Sinai, at the presence of God, the God of Israel ... your flock found a dwelling in it; in your goodness, O God, you provided for the needy."

For Christians, this psalm recalls the Magnificat in which Mary welcomed the coming birth of Jesus. "He has shown strength with his arm; he has scattered the proud in the thoughts of their hearts. He has brought down the powerful from their thrones, and lifted up the lowly; he has filled the hungry with good things and sent the rich away empty." Perhaps both passages remind us that God is not pleased with the way the world deals with the needy and that we endanger our soul when we become too comfortable with the way things are.

1 Peter 4:12-14; 5:6-11

> *Discipline yourselves, keep alert. Like a roaring lion your adversary the devil prowls around, looking for someone to devour.* — 1 Peter 5:8

While 1 Peter had made many references to suffering and facing hostility, in this passage it would seem as if he was concerned less with physical suffering than he was with spiritual suffering. First Peter had used the image of the congregation being like a flock of sheep under the care of a shepherd (1 Peter 2:25). In 1 Peter 5:2 he has exhorted the elders to tend the flock of God. Further, he warns that this must be done with a sense of humility — "Then he warned that the devil was like a roaring lion that prowled around looking for someone to devour" (1 Peter 5:5). One of the roles of shepherds was to keep the flock together because a single sheep that wandered from the flock was easy prey for the predators. While the leaders in a Christian community need to lead with humility, the entire congregation needs to understand that they need each other if they are going to resist the temptations that seek to seduce them into wandering from the faith. In an expansion of that image, First Peter also reminded the faithful of their connection with Christians all around the world. "Resist him, steadfast in your faith, for you know that your brothers and sisters in all the world are undergoing the same kinds of suffering."

This was an appeal to the solidarity of the community of faith for the resisting of the distorting influences of the culture around them. "Beloved, I urge you as aliens and exiles to abstain from the desires of the flesh that wage war against the soul" (1 Peter 2:11). In our culture, which celebrates individualism in a way that is destructive to the building of community, it is important to be reminded of the necessity of communal support if one is going to be able to alter practices that are present in the surrounding community. Many of the disciplines of Christianity run counter to the selfishness of our culture. When the surrounding community supports the practice of protecting yourself first, even at the expense of your wounded neighbor, it takes the support of a community to resist such fear. Imagine the strength we could develop if we felt connected to the worldwide community of Christ that was seeking to support each other in loving our neighbor and forgiving those who mistreat us.

John 17:1-11

> *I am asking on their behalf; I am not asking on behalf of the world, but on behalf of those whom you gave me, because they are yours.* — John 17:9

Jesus knew that he would soon be leaving his disciples. In preparation for his departure, Jesus prayed for his disciples. He prayed for those whom God had given him. The implication was that there were others whom God had not given to the name of Jesus. The ones given to Jesus were called Christians. Jesus' prayer for Christians was that they "may be one even as we are one." The prayer of Jesus was that Christians might have the same intimate relationship with each other that God had with Jesus. While in the historical sense, there is a differentiation between Jesus and God, at a deeper level, there is an identification. "In the beginning was the Word, and the Word was with God, and the Word was God" (John 1:1). If God answered Jesus' prayer, then, even though in a historical sense there were differences between one Christian and another in the church, at a deeper level, we are one. Therefore when we argue with one another, we are arguing with ourselves. If we separate ourselves from or reject another Christian, we are wounding ourselves. We are not permitted the luxury of demonizing those with whom we disagree in the church. If they claim Christ, then they are part of us. It makes a difference in how we debate the issues in the church if we recognize that we are debating with ourselves.

The Day Of Pentecost

Numbers 11:24-30

> *But Moses said to him, "Are you jealous for my sake? Would that all the Lord's people were prophets, and that the Lord would put his spirit on them!"*
> — Numbers 11:29

It is interesting how quickly we become possessive of the very Spirit that is graciously given to us. In this particular story, God decided to spread some of the Spirit that rested on Moses so that it empowered some seventy elders to assist Moses in the work. But as the gospel of John would later confirm (John 3:8), the Spirit, like the wind, blew where it chose. Some of the Spirit fell on two men who had remained in the camp, and they also began to prophesy. Several factors are important to remember. First, the Spirit was a gift from God. Second, the men's use of the Spirit neither harmed anyone nor was used for selfish purposes. Third, the Spirit was not a respecter of status and position in a community. With that in mind, we also can notice the stubborn presence of envy that has plagued the community of faith from its beginning.

On Pentecost Sunday, when we celebrate the infusion of the Christians' community with the Holy Spirit, it is an important reminder that we do not possess the Spirit. When it is present, it empowers us to act on God's behalf in ways that transcend our limitations, but it is always a gift and not a possession. Moses' response to this expression of envy was, "Would that all the Lord's people were prophets, and that the Lord would put his spirit on them!" Consider the effect of all of our churches rejoicing in the spiritual manifestation of power in any of our churches. Would that not be a more powerful witness than the petty jealousies that are so often manifest in our response to another church's successes?

Psalm 104:24-34, 35b

Bless the Lord, O my soul. Praise the Lord!
— Psalm 104:35b

On Pentecost we reflect on various aspects of the Spirit. In the famous interchange between Jesus and Nicodemus in John 3:1-10, we hear of the essential nature of the Spirit for a fully embodied life. "Very truly I tell you, no one can enter the kingdom of God without being born of water and of the Spirit" (John 3:5). Then we are quickly reminded that this empowering Spirit is absolutely free from our manipulations. "The wind blows where it chooses, and you hear the sound of it, but you do not know where it comes from or where it goes. So it is with everyone who is born of the Spirit" (John 3:8). In Psalm 104, the psalmist celebrated the creation of God and reminds us that all aspects of our life are dependent on God. "When you hide your face, they are dismayed; when you take away their breath, they die and return to their dust." In both Hebrew and Greek, the word for breath and spirit are the same. "When you send forth your spirit, they are created; and you renew the face of the ground."

God's creative and sustaining power is a mystery beyond our comprehension and control. At the same time, in an echo of the celebration of wisdom in Proverbs 8, there is recognition that God's creation, while beyond our full comprehension, nevertheless is reflective of a wisdom that brings order out of chaos. "In wisdom you have made them all; the earth is full of your creatures." As an example, the psalmist noted that Leviathan, the sea monster that was often seen as a symbol of chaos, was a creature that God created to sport and play in the sea. To explore the secrets of this universe is to engage in appreciating the wonders of God. On Pentecost we are invited to reflect on the creative, wonderful, and sustaining power of the Spirit that reflects both the absolute freedom of God and also the empowering love of God. While Pentecost is often celebrated as the birthday of the church, the church is but a microcosm of the power that also created and sustains the universe. When we truly comprehend the power behind all of creation, we are led to a natural response of praise. "I will sing to the Lord as long as I live; I will sing praise to my God while I have being." Pentecost would be an appropriate season to reflect on our treatment of the environment as an act of worship or, far too often, an act of blasphemy.

1 Corinthians 12:3b-13

> ... no one can say "Jesus is Lord" except by the Holy Spirit. — 1 Corinthians 12:3b

What does it mean to say, "Jesus is Lord"? It is more than allowing the words to come pouring out of one's mouth. It is a commitment that transcends all others. It means when you have to determine whether to skip worship to catch up on office work or to get a little extra sleep, the decision is clear. It means when reasoning whether you can afford to give 10% of your income to God or hedge your gifts to determine first what is needed for life's necessities, the decision is clear. It means when you are frustrated with your marriage, angry with your parents, tempted to cheat to get ahead, the decision is clear. It means when important social friends you have worked hard to acquire make disparaging remarks about the poor and you are tempted to agree in order to continue the relationships, the decision is clear.

Can we live such a life? We can only if Jesus is experienced as our Lord deep within our hearts, because to do so we have to confront powerful fears that dwell within each of us. Can churches say, "Jesus is Lord"? If all of our churches demonstrated obedience to a common Lord, would it not enable them to resist envy and competition and to acknowledge the strength of our variety? Imagine the witness that would be made if all the churches in one city could clearly agree that "we were made to drink of one Spirit." It would be an interesting spiritual discipline for all the members of a church to agree that, for one month, each member would take a few moments three times a day to reflect on what it means for us to say "Jesus is Lord." By the power of the Holy Spirit, it might change our experience of the faith of in our community.

John 20:19-23

> *When he had said this, he breathed on them and said to them, "Receive the Holy Spirit. If you forgive the sins of any, they are forgiven them; if you retain the sins of any, they are retained."* — John 20:22-23

When the disciples were locked away in fear, Jesus came and was present to them offering them peace. Their fear was a fear of the violence that those in power could afflict on them. Jesus showed them his wounds, the signs of what the world had done to him. He revealed to them that when the world had done its worst, the world had not conquered him. He again offered them peace. He was the proof of God's triumph over evil. The disciples did not need to be afraid, but to receive the peace of God was also to receive the mandate of God to spread that peace to others who are fearful in this world. "As the Father has sent me, so I send you." So Jesus breathed on them just as God had breathed on Adam in the first creation (Genesis 2:7). The breath that gave Jesus life, Jesus gave to his disciples. Jesus empowered them to offer peace to others who are fearful.

The visible sign of peace was the power to forgive. It is the incredible power and responsibility of the church to be God's agent of forgiveness. Consider the implications. What if marriages broke up because the church had failed to convey forgiveness? What if wars happened because the sins of people were retained? What if the history of racism, greed, and violence awaited the church's resolution? Do we believe that the central message of the church to the world is a message of forgiveness? To offer forgiveness is not to ignore the sin of another but to heal it. Jesus' power to heal this troubled world, which he has given to the church, is to be God's agent of forgiveness. When people experience forgiveness, they know the peace of God.

The Holy Trinity

Genesis 1:1—2:4a

> *See, I have given you every plant yielding seed ... you shall have them for food.*   — Genesis 1:29

This hymn of creation begins by speaking of God's relationship to the chaos of life. It uses several prominent symbols of chaos — formlessness, watery void, darkness, even sea monsters. God demonstrated mastery over all that threatens us. By merely speaking a word, God could bring order and purpose out of chaos. Even seasons and times are products of God's creative word. In God's plan of creation, the living creatures are provided with food. Since this story wished to emphasize the harmony of creation and the absence of violence, the food provided was that of fruit and vegetables. Later, in the story of Noah, as a reflection of the real nature of our world, God allowed for birds, animals, and fish to also be food for humans (Genesis 9:3). The human creature, which at that point displayed the dual character of male and female, was given the task of dominion. The creature's role was not to dominate but to give order to the rest of creation. Such dominion did not simply mean the exercise of power over other aspects of creation but a respect and care for the various parts of creation. In turn, creation cared for humans by providing them with food. Food was a gift from God, and a part of human dominion was to see that it was distributed among the human populace in a manner that allowed God's intention to be fulfilled. From the beginning, hungry people were not in accordance with God's intention.

Psalm 8

> *O Lord, our Sovereign, how majestic is your name in all the earth!* — Psalm 8:9

The praise of God finds its expression in creation in a manner that cannot be silenced. The very majesty of creation evokes praise. The incredible conditions that had to come together to enable life to exist on this planet makes belief that it was all by chance more incredible than belief in God. The very complexity of the human body, from the way it converts food into energy to the muscles in the foot that enables us to stand, makes design far more plausible than chance. Yet, the risky wisdom of allowing the human animal to have the capacity to exercise "dominion over the works of thy hands" fills us with both wonder and fear. The responsibility given to humans for the care of the universe is at times overwhelming. We are all too aware that the necessary creative drive within humans can easily be distorted by arrogance, fear, and greed. Dominion is a carefully balanced power and responsibility. When we forget that it was God who had entrusted us with such a responsibility, dominion can easily become a desire for domination. Only regular praise enables us to retain the perspective that keeps us truly human. "O Lord, our Lord, how majestic is thy name."

2 Corinthians 13:11-13

> *The grace of the Lord Jesus Christ, the love of God, and the communion of the Holy Spirit be with all of you.* — 2 Corinthians 13:13

Paul concluded what we now call the second letter to the church at Corinth with this threefold blessing. While the doctrine of the Trinity is not explicit in scripture, it is at least implicit in the early church. The strength of the church is experienced in grace, love, and communion. When we invoke the three persons of the Trinity, we lay claim to these three qualities in our life together in the church. As the church repeatedly discovers, we are not held together by our moral strength but by the grace of Christ. In that grace, we discover the love of God that is not defeated by the principalities and powers of our world. As that love of God infuses our lives, the communion of the Holy Spirit connects us. Paul's appeal to the Corinthians that they "agree with one another, (and) live in peace" suggested that the Corinthians had as much trouble doing that as our current churches do. The image of the Trinity provides us a picture of how we are to live in peace. Each part of the Trinity is distinct; yet they exist together in perfect harmony. We do not think of the Trinity as competing with each other or needing to defer to one another in order to maintain peace. Rather each part is thought of as fulfilling its full identity in a way that enhances the other parts. They greet each other with a "holy kiss" as it should also be in the community of the church.

Matthew 28:16-20

And remember, I am with you always, to the end of the age. — Matthew 28:20

This passage is often referred to as the great commission. It has inspired the church to take on the task of mission throughout the world. But imagine what it must have sounded like to those first disciples. Remember that the disciples had lost both their leader and had their ranks thinned by the betrayal of Judas. From a human perspective, it is amazing that they stayed together at all. Now, try to imagine this small band of frightened disciples hearing that their task was to transform the whole world. "Go therefore and make disciples of all nations ... and [teach] them to obey everything that I have commanded you." In our contemporary experience, we know how easy it is for a church to be overwhelmed by the challenge before them and be convinced that they do not have the resources or ability to succeed.

It might be helpful for such a church to reflect on the challenge before the original disciples. Jesus framed the task before the disciples with two statements. First, all authority in heaven and on earth belonged to Jesus. Therefore, the disciples actually had far more resources than they realized. Second, Jesus promised that he would be present with them. In our contemporary situation, if Jesus has the authority, then the issue is not whether we have the ability but whether we are clear about his commission for us. If Jesus is Emmanuel, God with us, then we need not fear the challenges we confront in the world. When any church seeks to determine what its specific mission is, the discussion should center on what God wants the church to do and not whether they have the ability or resources to accomplish their mission. God, who brought order out of chaos by merely speaking a word, can give order to our chaos when we listen to the word God speaks to us.

Proper 4
Pentecost 2
Ordinary Time 9

Genesis 6:9-22; 7:24; 8:14-19

Now the earth was corrupt in God's sight, and the earth was filled with violence. — Genesis 6:11

The story of Noah and the ark might be considered the first "rapture story," such as was made popular in the "Left Behind" series. If you have ever wondered why a good God does not simply snatch the good people away to safety and then cleanse the earth of evil, this story can help you explore how Genesis reflected on the same question. The temptation to believe that you can overcome evil by destroying it with superior force would be faced by Jesus in his wilderness temptation (Matthew 4:8-10). Further, it is the temptation that every strong nation faces. For Noah the issue, as it was also described in the Garden of Eden, was one of trust and obedience to God. Like Abraham in Genesis 12:1-3, Noah was asked to turn his back on the familiar and prepare for a journey of unknown dimensions based on his trust in God. In preparation, one saw the care of God for his creation. God acted to preserve a representative sample of all forms of life. God did punish, but God also protected. What is not described in this portion of the scripture, but what we discover in the larger story, is that this attempt to purify by separation failed because the temptation to evil is not an external force outside of ourselves but a temptation inherit in our human nature. If some are saved out of this corrupt world, unless their human nature is sacrificed, the same problem will reoccur wherever they find themselves.

Psalm 46

"Be still, and know that I am God!..." — Psalm 46:10

Psalm 46 is a psalm of praise of the sovereignty of God. In the midst of chaos, God stands as a refuge. The psalm is divided into three parts. The first part described the chaos of nature where mountains shake and waters roar (vv. 1-3). When the entire world seemed to be falling apart around the people, God was present as both strength and refuge. The second part described God's response to the chaos created by the instruments of war. God made wars cease, broke bows, shattered spears, and burned chariots (v. 9). Between these two descriptions of chaos was an image of the river of God flowing through the city of God. This recalled the river in Eden where God was first seen overcoming chaos and bringing about life (vv. 4-5). This river would again make its appearance in Revelation 22. As was true in the first encounter with chaos in Genesis, God needed merely to speak to reshape chaos (v. 6). It was this God, who so effortlessly overcame the chaos of nations raging and kingdoms tottering, who was Lord of hosts and the God of Jacob (v. 7). This God was both the God of the forces of the universe and also the God of a people. Our response, regardless of the chaos we experience, is to "Be still and know that I am God" (v. 10). This God, who is exalted by both the natural world and the nations in the world, is present to us and offers to us refuge (v. 11).

Romans 1:16-17; 3:22b-28 (29-31)

For in it the righteousness of God is revealed through faith for faith.... — Romans 1:17

Romans 1:16-17 is a key summary of Paul's understanding of the faith. The gospel, he declared, was not a secret path by which one escaped from this evil world and defeated death as the gnostics believed. Rather, the gospel was God's power to set right a world that had gone wrong. It was a challenge to Caesar who also offered a gospel of salvation. It directly addressed the tension between Jew and Gentile that was so much a part of the Roman experience. In 49 CE, the Jews had been expelled from Rome leaving the leadership of the Christian community in Rome to the Gentiles. A few years later, the edict was removed and Jewish Christians returned to Rome. They found a church whose leaders were not inclined to cede leadership to the returning Jews. In the midst of this tension, Paul spoke of the righteousness (or right relationships) that God had revealed in the death and resurrection of Christ. Like Habakkuk, whom Paul quoted, Paul painted a picture of a corrupt world whose relationships were all distorted. Such a world challenged the belief that God was in charge. Paul declared that the gospel of Jesus' death and resurrection revealed how God was working in the world to restore all righteousness or right relationships. "The one who is righteous will live by faith."

The lectionary skips the frequently quoted passage that included Paul's comments on homosexuality and the infrequently quoted passage where Paul warned against making self-righteous judgments on such conditions. The lectionary picks up on Paul's conclusion that "there is no distinction, since all have sinned and fall short of the glory of God." For Paul, our current debate about homosexuality would simply illustrate the inability of such distinctions to save us. What happened in Jesus' death and resurrection was the critical moment in history that revealed the power of God to overcome all of the divisions of creation. "He did this to show his righteousness because in his divine forbearance he had passed over the sins previously committed."

Matthew 7:21-29

> *Not everyone who says to me, "Lord, Lord" will enter the kingdom of heaven, but only the one who does the will of my Father in heaven.* — Matthew 7:21

There is an interesting tension in the Christian understanding between faith and works. We can say with Ephesians 2:8-9 that we are saved by faith and not by works, but then we hear Jesus say that we cannot be saved by what we say but by what we do. To further complicate the matter, not all religious actions are effective. "... Many will say to me, 'Lord, Lord, did we not ... cast out many demons ... [and] do many deeds of power' ... [and] I will declare to them, 'I never knew you.' " It was not that casting out demons or doing deeds of power in Jesus' name was wrong, but the attitude or intent was also crucial. "If I hand over my body so that I may boast, but do not have love, I gain nothing" (1 Corinthians 13:3b). So it is not enough to declare our faith or even to do good deeds in Jesus' name. To build our house on a rock is to allow our faith in Jesus Christ to transform our lives in such a way that our works are done not to secure our salvation but to praise God who already loves us. James 2:26 may be right that "faith without works is dead," but works done to curry favor with God or neighbor is self-serving and eventually fall apart like a house built on sand. We are saved by faith and therefore set free to love our neighbor in a manner that praises God and demonstrates our love for God. We no longer live out of guilt or fear but are free to let our lives be a living thanksgiving.

Proper 5
Pentecost 3
Ordinary Time 10

Genesis 12:1-9

> *... and in you all the families of the earth shall be blessed.*
> — Genesis 12:3

This is one of the key passages in the Old Testament. It is the beginning of the family of faith that will become known as the Jews. Prior to this story, the Bible stories were about humanity in general. Now they begin to speak of history and a particular family in a particular place and time. God entered history by speaking to a specific person and making a promise to that person. No explanation is given as to why God chose this family and not another. It happened when Abram was 75 years old. What would normally be seen as the end of life became a radical new beginning. It began with the God of the universe asking one person, Abram, to trust God enough to leave behind all the normal signs of security and to venture forth into an unknown future based on a promise from an invisible God.

All the challenges in our own faith journey are pictured here. Faith is a relationship between finite humans and an infinite, invisible God. Faith requires trust in the promise offered by this God. It asks us to leave behind the normal ways we seek to secure our lives. Abram left behind the familiarity of place, connections, and status and responded to a call to a better way of life that was never fully described. Faith asks us to venture toward a future beyond ourselves and affects not only our unborn family but also the whole world. While our story of faith is particular, God's intent is universal. The reason God entered time to speak to Abram was to begin a process by which "all the families of the earth shall be blessed." God's purpose from the beginning was to reconcile the whole world to himself (2 Corinthians 5:19).

Psalm 33:1-12

> *Let all the earth fear the Lord; let all the inhabitants of the world stand in awe of him.* — Psalm 33:8

As one is meditating on the Lord's Prayer, one could use Psalm 33 to deepen our understanding of the petition, "Hallowed be thy name." This psalm is a song of praise that can help us understand the implications of God's name being hallowed. The righteous, or those who stand in right relationship with God, are called to hallow God's name with melody, song, and loud shouts (vv. 1-3). Praise is an appropriate character trait of those in right relationship with God. "Praise befits the upright." The word of the Lord demonstrated the Lord's love of righteousness and justice (vv. 4-5). One can see that in how God brought about the created universe. "For he spoke, and it came to be; he commanded, and it stood firm." It is by the word of God that the chaos is brought into right relationship or righteousness. God's love of justice is also seen in how the plan of nations may falter, but the council of the Lord is perpetual. "The Lord brings the counsel of the nations to nothing ... the counsel of the Lord stands forever and the thoughts of his heart to all generations." It is the nature of God never to forget, and we offer praise to God when we celebrate the memory of God's actions. To hallow God's name is to celebrate God's faithfulness in the past and future through the music of song and instruments that announce to the world around us that God is our joy.

Romans 4:13-25

> *... (for he is father of all of us, as it is written, "I have made you the father of many nations") ...* — Romans 4:16-17

It is customary for us to believe that Abraham is the original father of the Jewish people. Paul, however, suggested that Abraham was the father of the whole community of faith — both Jew and

Gentile. "... The promise may rest on grace and be guaranteed to all his descendents, not only to the adherents of the law (the Jews) but also to those who share the faith of Abraham...." To follow the logic of Paul, Abraham received the promise of God and it was "recognized to him as righteousness" before he was a Jew — that is before he was circumcised. This also happened several generations before the people received God's commandments at Mount Sinai. This all illustrated for Paul the effectiveness of grace that God released on the world and which was available to both Jew and Gentile. The critical turning point for Paul was trusting in God "who gives life to the dead and calls into existence the things that do not exist." It is important for contemporary Christians to recall that, for Paul, the Jews continued in the promise of God even as the Gentiles who had learned to trust in the God "who raised Jesus our Lord from the dead" were then included in. There is a modern irony to the fact that many Christians, who have been saved by the grace of God, want to deny that same grace to the Jewish people and create a new name, Jesus, that they must adhere to in order to be saved. This is a distortion of what Paul believed.

Matthew 9:9-13, 18-26

> *... Those who are well have no need of a physician, but those who are sick. Go and learn what this means, "I desire mercy, not sacrifice." For I have come to call not the righteous but sinners.* — Matthew 9:12-13

In this scripture, Jesus encountered a woman that had been hemorrhaging for twelve years. The laws of Judaism made it clear that such a condition rendered her unclean (Leviticus 15:25-33). For her to reach out and touch Jesus would render him unclean. The tassels that she wanted to touch on his robe were a reminder of the commandments that all Jews were to obey (Numbers 15:37-41). The story confronts us with the classic choice between our human need and following the practices of our faith. Her need was so great that she risked rebuke and violation of the law in order to touch the mercy of God. The lectionary passage combines this story with the question from the Pharisees as to why Jesus ate with tax collectors and sinners. Jesus insisted that his ministry, and therefore our ministry, needed to demonstrate to the outer world a compassionate mercy. The challenge for the church is to consider what we should be doing that demonstrates a welcome for those who may have been hemorrhaging in body and soul and need to reach out and touch the fringe of the church's cloak.

Notice in the story that Jesus did not require her to accommodate herself to the practices of the faith before he would respond to her need. Nor did Jesus rebuke her for interrupting his journey to help someone who was part of the community of faith. Jesus' response challenges the church to consider whether they have allowed their beliefs or busyness in otherwise legitimate ministry to become a barrier to offering mercy to those on the fringes of their community. If Jesus came "to call not the righteous but sinners," then, perhaps, we can hear in this story, and the challenge it presents to the church, an opportunity to recognize ourselves as sinners in need of the healing love of Christ.

Proper 6
Pentecost 4
Ordinary Time 11

Genesis 18:1-15 (21:1-7)

Is anything too wonderful for the Lord?...
— Genesis 18:14

This mysterious story of Abraham meeting God at the oaks of Mamre has become an important text for Christians. In Hebrews 13:2, Christians were told, "Do not neglect to show hospitality to strangers, for by doing that some have entertained angels without knowing it." The offering of hospitality was a central ethic in both the Old and New Testaments. In Luke 24:13-33, it was through the offering of hospitality to a stranger that they encountered the risen Christ. Abraham went to elaborate means to offer hospitality to the three strangers that had come to him. There is no indication that he was aware that there was any transcendental quality to the strangers that had come to him. Yet, it was because of his act of offering hospitality that he discovered that God was addressing him. As people would repeatedly discover throughout the scripture, just because God addressed you did not mean that everything made sense. When God, in the form of one of the strangers (or perhaps all three), told Abraham that Sarah would become pregnant, Sarah overheard them and thought that the promised child was an impossibility. As often happens to people when they hear the promises of God in light of the practical realities of life, Sarah laughed. In a society that is increasingly fearful of strangers, we risk missing the experience of the divine and discovering the power of resurrection in our lives.

Psalm 116:1-2, 12-19

> *I will lift up the cup of salvation and call on the name of the Lord.* — Psalm 116:13

Psalm 116 is a psalm of deliverance from death or what appeared to be a hopeless situation. It is the awestruck wonder of one having been delivered against all expectation. You can hear a cancer patient who had been diagnosed with terminal cancer suddenly finding herself in complete remission. She expresses her love for the Lord because her desperate pleas have been answered (vv. 1-2). She was in a hopeless state, and she cried out to the Lord as her only source of hope (vv. 3-4). She can only stand in awe at God's gracious act (vv. 5-6). From a state of total anxiety, she has rediscovered the peace of trusting God (v. 7). She has been delivered not only from death but also fear and distrust (v. 8) and has received again the gift of life (v. 9). She has learned in this deep distress to place her hope in God rather than human wisdom (vv. 10-11). But now she faces the question of how to respond to the unexpected gift of life (v. 12). Her decision is to lift up her saving experience as praise to God and to witness to God's people (vv. 13-14). She acknowledges how God values the lives of the faithful (v. 15) and how her experience has set her free of the fear of death (v. 16). It has released her to devote her living as a thanksgiving to God (vv. 16-17). To live a life away from fear and toward thanksgiving is a testimony before people as to the grace of God (vv. 17-18).

Romans 5:1-8

> *But God proves his love for us in that while we still were sinners Christ died for us.* — Romans 5:8

The glory of God, the clear evidence of God's active, caring presence among us, reveals the grace of God. Our saying the right prayer or demonstrating the perfect life does not cause God's active presence. Unlike some pagan religions, God is not a spiteful being that must be appeased or an indifferent being that must be wooed. Rather, even before we do anything to please God, God takes the initiative to reach across the divide and draws us to him. "While we were still sinners, Christ died for us." This fact alters our perspective on all of life's experiences. When we suffer, we do not conclude that God is punishing us. Rather, like the Israelites in the wilderness, we know that God can use our suffering to build our character. Knowing that gives all our experiences purpose. We need not despair; therefore, we have hope. Because God has already proved his love to us, we can trust that the hope we have in life will not disappoint us. We do not assume that God is manipulating our lives through a series of calculated rewards and punishments — a sort of behavior modification project. We do believe that God is not absent from our sufferings, however. God is not a distant God. Our faith is that God has closed the gap and by grace is present to us in all circumstances.

Matthew 9:35—10:8 (9-23)

... You received without payment, give without payment.
— Matthew 10:8

What was it that the disciples had received without payment? At its most basic level, reflect on what you have received from God without payment. There are the normal gifts of life, health, friends, family, country, and class of birth, as well as our natural talents and intelligence. If we have any of these, it is clear that there are equally deserving people who did not receive these in life. Add to these gifts the gifts of prayer, scripture, freedom to worship, and a church community. As you look out into the world, you can see many people who hunger for what God has given us without payment. But transcending all of these benefits, the disciples also received the gift of God's undeserved love as experienced in Jesus' calling them to be disciples. Note who the disciples were — Peter the impetuous, James and John the status seekers,

Matthew the tax collector, Thomas the skeptic, Simon the Zealot, and Judas the betrayer among others. Notice also that Jesus invited them to respond to this gracious love of God without first asking them to either change their ideas or their behavior.

For many of them, though not all, such change would come later, but first he asked them to be his disciples. Then he asked them to go out and spread the news of God's gracious love that could result in miraculous transformations. He asked them to do so without preconditions. As he led them in that ministry, he introduced them to strangers. He first invited them to share with the strangers among them, but later he would encourage them by his own ministry to reach out to the Samaritans, the Gentiles, and all the excluded of God's world. The only reason you and I are part of this community of love is because Jesus led his disciples to reach out to the stranger beyond them that eventually included Gentiles like us.

Proper 7
Pentecost 5
Ordinary Time 12

Genesis 21:8-21

> *... And as she sat opposite him, she lifted up her voice and wept.*
> — Genesis 21:16

The story of Hagar and her son is perplexing. An aspect of Israel's relationship with their neighbor was reflected in Sarah's jealousy toward Ishmael. She was afraid that he would share in Isaac's inheritance. Did she suspect that Abraham might have favored Ishmael, his firstborn son? To protect Isaac, Sarah asked Abraham to cast him out. Strangely, God told Abraham to cooperate with Sarah's selfish behavior because of the importance of this family line. "... For it is through Isaac that offspring shall be named for you." It was as if God would tolerate some ethically questionable behavior because there was something of greater importance at stake here. At the same time, it was made clear that God was active in the future of people other than Israel. "As for the son of the slave woman, I will make a nation of him also, because he is your offspring." Abraham was seen as not only the father of the Jews but the family of humanity.

As God had promised, "in (Abraham) all the families of the earth shall be blessed" (Genesis 12:3b). God seemed to pay particular attention to the lives of slaves when they cried out to him. "... She lifted up her voice and wept. And God heard the voice of the boy...." While it is only hinted at here, it is clear that God paid attention to the sufferings of other nations and made promises to them as well. "... God was with the boy, and he grew up...." The complexity of our relationship with other people of distinct faith is hinted at here. From the beginning, God's story is much more complex than just God's relationship with us. We are part of a vast puzzle that God is putting together throughout the entire universe.

Psalm 86:1-10, 16-17

Incline your ear, O Lord, and answer me, for I am poor and needy.   — Psalm 86:1

As a response to the lectionary passage of Genesis 21:8-21 that tells the story of God's hearing Hagar's cry on behalf of her son, Ishmael, this passage emphasizes an important aspect of the character of God. While God elected a specific people to be God's people, God continued to be the God of all people. If we hear this part of the psalm with the story of Hagar and Ishmael in mind, we recognize that God's hearing the cry of the slaves in Egypt, while specifically told of the Hebrew people, is characteristic of God with respect to all people. While Hagar and Ishmael were not to share in the heritage of Abraham and Sarah, God was not unmindful of their fate. When Hagar lifted up her voice and cried out, she represented all of the cries of pain that come from humans that suffer in this world. Beginning with Abel's blood that cried out (Genesis 4:10), we learn that we worship a God who refuses to be indifferent to human suffering. The first act of faith is not a statement of belief but a cry of pain.

To lament the state of the world is to affirm that injustice is abnormal. To cry out in complaint is to affirm that if someone hears our cry, it will make a difference. "In the day of my trouble I call on you, for you will answer me." Most of the descriptions that we have of pagan gods suggest that one's worship and sacrifice was meant to appease them so that they would not bring suffering upon the people. The God of the Hebrews was shown as someone who was offended by such suffering. Even when Jesus prayed Psalm 22 from the cross, "My God, My God, why have you forsaken me ..." it was a challenge to God to respond. In challenging God to respond, one is affirming that not to respond violates the very character of God. This is true even if we have not been faithful. "For you, O Lord, are good and forgiving, abounding in steadfast love to all who call on you." This psalm could encourage us to teach our people the value of lifting their complaint to God. In doing so, they can reconnect with the source of all their healing.

Romans 6:1b-11

Should we continue in sin in order that grace may abound? — Romans 6:1b

In Romans 5:20, Paul asserted that where sin increased, grace multiplied. Since the grace of God is a sign of the incredible love of God, the cynic could well conclude that by sinning we are providing the opportunity for the grace of God to shine all the more brightly. Paul quickly challenged this ridiculous conclusion with the rhetorical question, "Should we continue in sin in order that grace may abound?" As wonderful as grace is, sin is an affront to God and only overcome at a cost. The reason Christ died for us was to set us free for a new life. "So that, just as Christ was raised from the dead by the glory of the Father, we too might walk in the newness of life." Paul used the analogy of slavery and spoke of us being "enslaved to sin." If you were a slave and someone came and set you free, it would be a wonderful moment, but you would not want to return to slavery so that you could experience that moment of liberation again. The "newness of life" is a life that is shaped by a new focus. If sin is reflected in the self-centered focus of living in response to our personal desires and fears, then the "newness of life" is "living to God." With Christ, we have overcome death and are set free for a whole new life. "So you also must consider yourselves dead to sin and alive to God in Christ Jesus." Since Paul was speaking to the community of the church, his invitation was for the church to refuse to make its decisions according to what would make the church prosper and to shift to making decisions according to what would be pleasing to God. It is a worthy consideration for the contemporary church as well.

Matthew 10:24-39

> *... for nothing is covered up that will not be uncovered, and nothing secret that will not become known.*
> — Matthew 10:26

One of the most powerful destroyers of community is secrets. A community can be destroyed because of secrets. Marriages are ripped apart because of secrets. People commit suicide because of secrets. The psalmist warned over and over that the most destructive weapon an enemy had was a deceitful tongue. When a secret is exposed, it is rarely as powerful as a secret that is hidden. Lies that are exposed to the light can be challenged and corrected. Lies that are spoken in secret eat away at the bonds of trust that are essential to community. That is why the scriptures are so harsh on the sin of gossip. Gossip is the sharing of supposedly secret, inside knowledge. Most often it is damaging to one person or another, but because it is shared in the dark, its truth cannot be challenged. Why do we love to gossip? Often it is an attempt to build our own ego by demonstrating our inside knowledge. It also is an attempt to bond us to another by virtue of our sharing a secret about a third party. But what if we knew that on a certain day everything we had uttered in secret would be exposed to the light of day? It would be embarrassing for us because we would have to cope with errors that we have made. But imagine the freedom of not having to cover up for ourselves. Jesus promised us a life free from secrets. It can seem a fearful life unless we recognize the healing power of forgiveness. In some ways, we already have that exposed life before God from whom no secrets are hidden. Yet, we try to delude ourselves into thinking that we can hide from God. God awaits our confession of what God already knows because then we can receive forgiveness. In taking that step, we discover what can also happen with our neighbor. We begin to taste the kingdom.

Proper 8
Pentecost 6
Ordinary Time 13

Genesis 22:1-14

Then Abraham reached out his hand and took the knife to kill his son. — Genesis 22:10

This story is one of the most horrifying and troublesome stories in the Bible. It confronts us not only with the literal horror of a father willing to slay his own son but also with the fearful image of the cruelty possible in religious fanaticism. Here we have a man determined to be obedient to God. Just prior to this story, this same Abraham was willing to let his other son, Ishmael, be driven out into the wilderness to die. God had to intervene in that story, also, to save the life of the child. It is helpful to remember the meaning of the two names. Ishmael means "God hears" and Isaac means "laughter." When we forget that "God hears" the suffering of the oppressed, religion becomes a faith of the powerful. When we are willing to sacrifice "laughter" in our faith, we are easily seduced by the fanatical in religion. One of the decisions of faith has always been whether we will serve God or the powers of our age. In making the choice for God, too often the attempt has been seen as also requiring the sacrifice of laughter. This story suggested that laughter (Isaac) was a special gift of God and critical to the development of the family of faith. Without laughter, we misunderstand the true sacrifice God asks of us. Laughter allows us to step back from our own pretentiousness and hear what God hears. We can become overly serious in our determination to be "perfect" in our faith and sacrifice the very future that God invites us to pursue.

Psalm 13

How long, O Lord? Will you forget me forever?...
— Psalm 13:1

This classic lament psalm guides us in how we should bring our complaints to God. To hear its personal power, we need only to bring to it any of numerous situations of distress. Imagine that you had lost your job, could not pay the rent, and were forced to depend on soup kitchens. Can you not hear yourself cry out, "How long, O Lord? Will you forget me forever? How long will you hide your face from me?" Without money or a place, would you not feel stripped of your dignity? How long before you would feel the disapproving stares of those bothered by your presence? How long must I bear pain in my soul, and have sorrow in my heart all day long? How long shall my enemy be exalted over me? Picture the burden of just staying alive and the living death of never seeing any prospect for change. Hear yourself cry out to the only source of real help available, "Consider and answer me, O Lord my God! Give light to my eyes, or I will sleep the sleep of death." In that setting, everyone else becomes your adversary — wanting your bed, wanting you off the street, wanting you out of their mind, wanting you to be continually grateful, and refusing to believe that you have thoughts of your own. "And my enemy will say, 'I have prevailed'; my foes will rejoice because I am shaken."

Yet there is a source of dignity and strength that you cling to because it keeps clinging to you and telling you that you are a person of worth. It keeps telling you that you are loved. "But I trusted in your steadfast love; my heart shall rejoice in your salvation." It is because God keeps surprising you with signs of love that you know that the world is wrong when they dismiss you. It is as if God is putting a tune in your mind that the noise of the world cannot drown out. "I will sing to the Lord, because he has dealt bountifully with me." Now that you have heard the prayer in a context of extreme need, listen to it again but insert your own situation of suffering or distress. Hear again that whatever the situation is that challenges you, God is stronger, and God's love is full of transforming surprises. Life makes sense in praise, letting the song out that God has planted in you.

Romans 6:12-23

> *... so now present your members as slaves to righteousness for sanctification.* — Romans 6:19

There is a temptation in some forms of Protestant thought to become so focused on the moment of experiencing salvation that we forget that it is the beginning and not the end of a lifelong process. To turn from sin and accept Christ as one's Savior is a radical re-orientation of one's life. As we begin to live this new grace-filled life, we begin to mature in the faith. Sanctification is the process by which we develop a maturity in the faith. When members of a church begin to present themselves "to God as instruments of righteousness," they enter into the ethical realm of the faith. We engage in ethical actions not in order to be saved but as evidence of our desire to grow in the faith. "But now that you have been freed from sin and are enslaved to God, the advantage you get is sanctification." Some churches want to avoid becoming involved in taking ethical stands because many of the issues we face as a society are complex and often controversial. The result is that they focus almost exclusively on the personal moment of salvation. The unfortunate result is that they remain "babes in the faith." To engage in ethical reflection and action is to risk being wrong, but that is why we are saved by grace. We do not sin so that grace may abound, but we risk sinning because we are saved by grace. "For the wages of sin is death, but the free gift of God is eternal life in Christ Jesus our Lord."

Matthew 10:40-42

Whoever welcomes you welcomes me, and whoever welcomes me welcomes the one who sent me.
— Matthew 10:40

What a frightening and awesome statement. Jesus not only identified completely with God but also completely with the community of his disciples. Perhaps even more frightening, how people receive and perceive Christ's disciples, is how they are going to perceive Jesus and choose to respond to God. God had identified with Jesus' disciples. Jesus was entrusting the message to his disciples. It is incredible that God, through Jesus, would make the divine self so vulnerable to our response. But, if we choose to respond to what God sees in us, there are possibilities for others as well. If we are faithful to God's call to be a prophet, then those who receive our word receive a prophet's reward. A prophet's reward is none other than an identification with God's word. Such identification at times brings suffering but ultimately means life. Recall the story of Elisha and the Shumanite woman (2 Kings 4:8-37). Those who receive a righteous person will receive a righteous person's reward. Recall Joseph's story in Matthew 1:18-25. If we are responsive to God's word and to right relationships with others, we share in Christ's complete identification with God and people. Because God has so thoroughly identified with Jesus' disciples, those who receive such disciples with even the minimum of hospitality will discover they are receiving God (Genesis 18:1-16). The task of a congregation, in response to Jesus' identification with God and us, is to respond to God's word and be in right relationship with others because in us others see Christ and, through Christ, God.

Proper 9
Pentecost 7
Ordinary Time 14

Genesis 24:34-38, 42-49, 58-67

> *... let the young woman who comes out to draw, to whom I shall say, "Please give me a little water from your jar to drink...."* — Genesis 24:43

There is an almost fairy-tale quality to this mysterious story of the choosing of a woman to be Isaac's wife. It began with Abraham's concern to not let this special family line simply be absorbed into the stream of humanity. He wanted Isaac to have a wife from his own people. In a demonstration that God was at work behind the scenes to guide the decisions of the faithful, the servant set up a test by a well where the community came to draw their water. He discovered that the very woman who met his test was also the daughter of Abraham's relative. Yet, even though it was made clear that God was operating behind the scenes, it was also made clear that humans were free to make their own choices. Not only did Rebecca's family make their decision as to whether to respond to the servant's choice of Rebecca, but she was given the freedom to choose as well.

Beginning with Sarah and continuing on through the family line, the women of these early patriarchs had a strong role to play, and God respected the freedom of their choices. Not only did Rebecca make the choice to leave her family, but she also took the initiative when she saw Isaac from a distance. The unique combination of God's actions and human freedom to make choices was displayed here. The journey of faith was a complex one played out in the lives of strong-willed people and an infinitely patient God. We continue to experience that interplay with our freedom and the sovereignty of God.

Psalm 45:10-17

> *I will cause your name to be celebrated in all generations; therefore the peoples will praise you forever and ever.* — Psalm 45:17

Psalm 45 is a love song for the king. In Christian symbolism, Jesus is our Lord and king, and the church is the bride of Christ. Reflecting on the psalm in these terms allows it to transcend its immediate historical context. The psalm becomes God's love song for Christ and Christ's bride, the church, that is called on to emulate her Lord's grace, truth, and love of righteousness. Beginning in verse 10, the church is invited to leave behind the values of the world from which she has come and submit to her Lord. "... Forget your people and your father's house, and the king will desire your beauty. Since he is your lord, bow to him." If the church does that, the world will see the church as a source of blessing (v. 12). Like a bride decked in royalty, the church is led to her king (vv. 13-14). "With joy and gladness they are led along as they enter the palace of the king" (v. 15). In an era when the church seems consumed with how to attract new members, it is important to hear God's promise of how the church will increase. If the church is faithful to Christ, God will cause it to bear children who will serve the world. "In the place of ancestors you, O king, shall have sons; you will make them princes in all the earth." When Christians choose to be servants of Christ and therefore servants of the world, all generations will celebrate this bride of Christ and praise her forever (v. 17). To hear the power of this psalm for the church, substitute the church for the bride and Christ for the king. "Hear, O [church], consider and incline your ear; forget your people and your father's house, and (Christ) will desire your beauty. Since he is your Lord, bow to him."

Song Of Solomon 2:8-13

... Arise my love, my fair one, and come away; for now the winter is past, the rain is over and gone.
— Song Of Solomon 2:10-11

The church has historically seen in the Song of Solomon a metaphor for the church as the lover of Christ. This selection draws upon the joy and sense of renewal that comes with the arrival of spring after a long winter season. It is important as one reflects on this passage as a metaphor to not avoid the full carnality of the passage. One should first hear this as the reflections of a young, lovesick woman who has been fantasizing about the pleasures that her lover has brought her (Song Of Solomon 2:2-7) and now sees him coming toward her house calling to her. "Look, there he stands behind our wall, gazing in at the windows, looking through the lattice." Like the thrill of the first sign of spring after a long winter, so she responds to his arrival after an absence. "The flowers appear on the earth; the time of singing has come...." She hears him call to her, "Arise, my love, my fair one, and come away." Only when you feel the full power of that moment of star-crossed lovers, are you ready to turn to this passage as a metaphor of the relationship of the church with Christ.

There are times when the church is sustained by the memory of her relationship with Christ, but there are also times when the church hears Christ calling to her like a lover who has come for a visit. "Look, there he stands behind our wall, gazing in at the windows, looking through the lattice." There is that moment in a church's life when they hear Christ calling to her like a lover who wants to renew the power of their love for each other. "Arise, my love, my fair one, and come away; for now the winter is past, the rain is over and gone." There is a rhythm in the life of any church. Not all of our time can be what is often called mountaintop experiences. There are times of ordinary living out of our faithfulness. But we must also be ready when we hear our lover call. "The flowers appear on the earth; the time of singing has come...."

Romans 7:15-25a

> *For I delight in the law of God in my inmost self, but I see in my members another law at war with the law of my mind, making me captive to the law of sin that dwells in my members.* — Romans 7:22-23

It is important to remember that Paul focused on the corporate nature of the faith. Sometimes by speaking about faith only from the perspective of the individual, we miss some of what Paul was saying. For example, by simply altering the pronouns of the passage above, we see how what Paul was saying, using himself as an example, applies to the church community. "For [the church] delights in the law of God in [her] inmost self, but [she] sees in [her] members another law at war with the law of [her] mind and making [her] captive to the law of sin which dwells in [her members]." Reading it that way, does it not remind you of some of the tension between the faith we proclaim as a church and the reality we experience far too often? We want desperately to believe that the way of life that Jesus proclaimed in the gospels expresses who we are as a church. We get angry when people point out the contradictions between what we proclaim and the behavior of our members. Sometimes we are even willing to violate Jesus' commandment of forgiving another member in the name of defending the standards of the church for ourselves. It is difficult for us to be as honest about our church as Paul was about himself.

The result is that we seem to be at war with ourselves. Individuals and whole groups seem to be at war with the gospel that we accept with our minds. Our inability to acknowledge this makes us captive to the law of sin that dwells within us as members of the church. When an individual refuses to acknowledge his or her sin but rather rationalizes and excuses his or her behavior, he or she cannot be healed. Perhaps a major factor in the inability of the churches to be at peace with each other is seen in this same truth. "Wretched [church] that we are! Who will rescue [us] from this body of death? Thanks be to God through Jesus Christ our Lord!

So then, with [our] mind [we are] a slave to the law of God, but with [our] flesh [we] are a slave to the law of sin."

Matthew 11:16-19, 25-30

> *Come to me, all you that are weary and are carrying heavy burdens, and I will give you rest.*
> — Matthew 11:28

Jesus held out this magnificent promise to us of rest from our burdens. There is probably little that could be better news to our generation, and yet, many Christians do not experience such rest even among Christians. Jesus spoke of God revealing the truth to infants while hiding it from the wise and intelligent. The latter were intent upon mastering and controlling their situation while infants lived in trust. Is part of our burden the result of our insistence that we be in control? How does Jesus offer us rest for our souls? First, Jesus offers us a path to integrity. It was his consistent prayer life and being guided by scripture that enabled him to be in touch with God who guided his life. A significant part of our stress is because of a confusion of our souls in the face of the multiple demands of life. Second, the humbleness in heart of Jesus was his awareness that he did not need to control events but only be faithful in response to them. One can quickly grow weary trying to control the uncontrollable. When you let God be God, then you can learn to trust that the Creator is still creating out of the often-chaotic events of life. There is rest in that trustful Spirit that is similar to the trust of an infant in the arms of a parent. When Jesus said that his yoke was easy and his burden was light, he was declaring that he knew the one true source of the fulfillment of life and his faith in God could shape his response.

Proper 10
Pentecost 8
Ordinary Time 15

Genesis 25:19-34

Isaac loved Esau, because he was fond of his game; but Rebekah loved Jacob. — Genesis 25:28

Rebekah had gone directly to God concerning the struggle that was taking place in her womb, and she was told of the twins that would be born to her. If Rebekah serves as the mother of our faith, then the twins reflect the dual emphasis that struggles within our faith. Esau is the action-oriented, physical one. He is the man of the world that focuses on what can be done. Jacob is the mind-oriented thinker. He is the person of reflection who plans ahead. In a way, this could be seen as the prefiguring of the later Mary and Martha story (Luke 10:38-42). Within the community of faith, there are the action-oriented members who are always asking, "What are we going to do?"

There is also an element that is more focused on reflection. For them, the path of faith centers on the mind. Each element needs the other to guard against their own inherent dangers. The action-oriented are tempted to believe that what is done in the moment is what is important. Their whole energy is focused on the project. They are always in danger of selling their soul for a mess of pottage. Those who focus on the mind are tempted to use their minds to manipulate the other and become lost in their schemes. A person who only reflects on faith can easily become lost in thought, and there is no fruit from their faith that others can feed upon. Faith without deeds is dead according to James. But action without reflection can become superficial. When the twins continued to struggle against each other, as they have a tendency to do within the church, they were failing to realize how much they needed each other. We are saved by faith, but faith without deeds is dead. Neither can despise their birthright nor neglect the gifts of the other.

Psalm 119:105-112

> *Your word is a lamp to my feet and a light to my path.*
> — Psalm 119:105

This section represents the fourteenth letter of the Hebrew alphabet (*Nun*) in the acrostic reflection by the psalmist on the gift of God's law to the people of faith. It is important to remember that by the law the entire Torah or first five books of scripture is intended. The law is not just a set of rules, as we might refer to it in our Western tradition, but a whole way of life that God has revealed in the stories of the life of the early people of God. It certainly includes rules and commandments, but it is fleshed out in the life of a people. Because Christians see Christ as the fulfillment of the law, one can also see this psalm as a poetic reflection on the life of Christ. "[God's] word [or Christ] is a lamp to my feet and a light to my path." Because Jesus' life embodied the life of Israel in a single person, we can see in him how God is at work in this world. As Christians, "[We] have sworn an oath and confirmed it to observe [Christ's] righteous ordinances." Like the psalmist, when our life is afflicted, we too act in faith and cry out to God, "Give me life, O Lord, according to your word." We come to worship asking God to "accept my offerings of praise, O Lord, and teach me your ordinances." While we accept responsibility for our own behaviors, we "do not forget [the law of Christ]." We know that the way to avoid the evil distortions of our life is to "not stray from [Christ's] precepts." Because faith must shape the way we live our life, we can say with the psalmist, "I incline my heart to perform your statutes forever, to the end."

Romans 8:1-11

> *For those who live according to the flesh set their minds on the things of the flesh, but those who live according to the Spirit set their minds on the things of the Spirit.*
>
> — Romans 8:5

"To set [your] minds on the things of the flesh" is to view life from the perspective of our immediate needs, desires, and fears. In a sense, it is to follow our animal nature in that we are guided by a basic instinct to survive and to pleasure ourselves. We act from the assumption that we are the center of the universe, and everything revolves around us. In contrast, to set our minds on the things of the Spirit is to allow our lives to be directed by a transcendent perspective. When Jesus was in the Garden of Gethsemane, his prayer to let the cup pass from him was an expression of the natural human desire to survive. To then pray "yet not what I want but what you want" (Matthew 26:39) was to give himself over to the spiritual perspective of the divine. Life based on things of the flesh centers on death and is "hostile to God." The reason that the law, "weakened by the flesh," cannot save us is that we are always rationalizing and interpreting the law through our own personal needs and fears. Recall how we struggle to reinterpret the commandment "You shall not kill" (or murder) to permit war, capital punishment, and so forth. God sent "his Son in the likeness of sinful flesh" to deal with sin. Jesus lived his life centered on God rather than on self, Spirit rather than flesh. "But if Christ is in you, though the body is dead because of sin, the Spirit is life because of righteousness." By the power of the Spirit in us, we are able to live life from a divine perspective.

Matthew 13:1-9, 18-23

> *When anyone hears the word of the kingdom and does not understand it, the evil one comes and snatches away what is sown in the heart; this is what was sown on the path.* — Matthew 13:19

Matthew offered Jesus' interpretation of this very familiar parable. For Matthew's community, and for ours, it must have helped them understand a very disturbing but familiar experience in the Christian community. One does not have to belong to the church for many years until one can see this parable being demonstrated in the life of the community. Glance through an old church directory and notice how many once active members have faded away. The reasons that they are no longer active are numerous, but this parable begins with the most familiar reasons. Who has not witnessed someone enter the Christian community with great enthusiasm and immediately volunteer for many of the opportunities within the community? They are so busy living out their faith that they do not take time to probe the depths of their faith. Like seeds that sprout up quickly on rocky ground, they lack the roots to withstand the challenges that occur and soon burn out. Others, like those seeds that grow amidst the thorns, allow the pressures and pleasures that surround their lives to choke out their faith. Fortunately, amidst those discouraging realities, there are also those who are like the seeds that fell on good soil and bring forth a rich harvest.

It is humbling but instructive to realize that our task is to sow the seeds, but that which takes root and produces much fruit is beyond our control. The church, and the clergy that guide it, are to provide the best soil possible in which the seeds of faith can grow. Evangelism is not recruiting new members but planting seeds by helping people explore and affirm the good news that God is offering them if they have eyes to see and ears to hear. Isaiah's prophecy suggested that we are to continue to sow the seeds in all soils because God can even use resistance to further God's purpose.

Proper 11
Pentecost 9
Ordinary Time 16

Genesis 28:10-19a

> *... Surely the Lord is in this place — and I did not know it!*
> — Genesis 28:16

It is a sobering reminder to recognize that Jacob, who would be the father of the twelve tribes of Israel that made up the people of God, was not exactly a person of high moral virtue. Prior to this incident, he had, with the help of his mother, cheated his brother out of his birthright and deceived and dishonored his father. As our passage begins, Jacob was running from the consequences of his scheming life. Because he had cheated his brother, Esau, out of his father's blessing, his brother was so angry that he wanted to kill Jacob. It was during Jacob's flight that God met him. Jacob was not looking for God, but God found him. When the consequences of his schemes had caught up to him, and he was in fear for his life, God met him. It is a less noble version of God hearing the cry of the people who suffer. It was in a dream, when Jacob's normal defenses were down, that God penetrated his self-centered life.

It is a very human trait that while we are experiencing some success at manipulating and controlling the events of our lives, we often shut God out. Even very successful clergy are often subject to this delusion that they know how to "manage" the church. It often is only when we are frightened and vulnerable that we allow God to penetrate our awareness. For the most part, we live our lives without an awareness that God is in this place. When Jacob became aware of God's presence in his life, he called the place of his encounter Bethel or house of God. He spoke of it as the gate of heaven. It is not unusual for people to designate certain places, often places on a mountain, as places that seem particularly close to God. The Christian church has had the audacity to suggest that the church is a mobile Bethel or gate of heaven. We declare that where two or three are gathered together in Christ's name, Christ is present to them. We are continually subject to the temptation, however, to become so mired down in our attempts to manipulate and control the shape of the church, so that it conforms to our ideas, that we fail to stop to consider the awesome fact that "God is in this place."

Psalm 139:1-12, 23-24

> *You search out my path and my lying down, and are acquainted with all my ways. Even before a word is on my tongue, O Lord, you know it completely.*
> — Psalm 139:3-4

It is often helpful to hear a psalm in the context of another biblical story. The lectionary offers us the opportunity to hear this psalm in the context of the story of Jacob. When Jacob had his dream at Luz, which he would rename Bethel, he recognized that "surely the Lord is in this place" (Genesis 28:16). Considering what had previously taken place in Jacob's life, he could easily have believed that he was about to feel the wrath of God. He had been running, and now he was lying down. "O Lord, you have searched me and known me. You know when I sit down and when I rise up; you discern my thoughts from far away. You search out my path and my lying down, and are acquainted with all my ways." There are moments in our lives when there is no place to run and hide. It does not do any good to try to talk our way out of the situation. "Even before the word is on my tongue, O Lord, you know it completely."

Jacob realized there was no escape from the God who had found him. "Where can I go from your spirit? Or where can I flee from your presence? If I ascend to heaven, you are there; if I make my bed in Sheol, you are there." From a human perspective, such a moment, when we are stripped naked and totally vulnerable, is a fearful moment. Yet, from a spiritual perspective, there is also a freedom to such a moment. Since there is no place to go, one will finally experience the truth. The startling truth that Jacob experienced was that God was not a vengeful God but rather a God of promise. "Know that I am with you and will keep you wherever you go, and will bring you back to this land; for I will not leave you until I have done what I have promised you" (Genesis 28:15). When we discover that God is a God of promise and that God promises to be with us, then our life also is a life of promise and has a future that is significant. We can pray with the psalmist, "Search me, O God, and know my heart; test me and know my thoughts. See if there is any wicked way in me, and lead me in the way everlasting."

Romans 8:12-25

> *We know that the whole creation has been groaning in labor pains until now....* — Romans 8:22

In this remarkable passage, we are given a whole new perspective on suffering and sin. First, it is a mistake to avoid all suffering. With Christ as our model, there is a redemptive possibility in suffering. By the Spirit we are invited to be "heirs with Christ — if, in fact, we suffer with him so that we may also be glorified with him." Second, there is an intimate link between the sin of humanity and the damage done to our ecology. Nature is trapped in a "bondage to decay" that is reflected in the sinfulness of humanity. The background of this statement is Genesis chapters 2-3 in which humanity was set in a gardenlike world as stewards but the ground was cursed by the couple's disobedience (Genesis 3:17). For example, the exploitive greed of humanity has led to the pollution of our atmosphere.

But this intricate relationship between sin and suffering (both human and of nature) is not a hopeless path to destruction. The whole spiral of sin and evil is not a threat to God's triumph but rather a necessary part of God's unfolding purpose. Instead of looking at the painful state of the world and feeling despair, we are offered hope. "We know that the whole creation has been groaning in labor pains until now, and not only the creation, but we ourselves, who have the first fruits of the Spirit, groan inwardly while we wait for adoption, the redemption of our bodies." To see both the suffering of nature and of humanity as "labor pains" is to find meaning and purpose to our struggle to be faithful. The difficult challenge of living a faithful life is given new meaning if God is using our efforts for a larger purpose. Like a woman who endures labor pains because of her anticipation of a new baby, so we can see our struggle "as a necessary passage to a glory that will be revealed." And "if we hope for what we do not see, we await for it with patience."

Matthew 13:24-30, 36-43

> *He answered, "The one who sows the good seed is the Son of Man; the field is the world, and the good seed are the children of the kingdom...."*
> — Matthew 13:37

If we had been designing the nature of the church that we would have established on the earth to effect the salvation of the world, we would probably have made it a perfect organization. Our church would have been a model of moral perfection that would have demonstrated for the world how God wants us to live in this world. We certainly would not have allowed it to have within it the petty bickering and often tragic, immoral behavior that too often convinces many that the church is a lost cause.

From the beginning of church history, there have been movements to reform and purify the church. There are churches in our time that seek to be a righteous organization by excluding all those who they feel are sinners. They are quick to explain that they are simply wanting people to be accountable for their behavior. "Let them repent first, and then we will accept them." The parable suggests that such an approach will do damage to those who are truly good. One only has to see the hopelessly fractured body of Christ in our time to verify the truth of the parable. None of the reformers wanted to split the body of Christ, but that has been the result. Jesus' approach was to "associate with sinners" and to let his goodness speak for itself. We see in his behavior and ministry the danger of our wanting to quickly exclude sinners from our community. If, as Paul reminded us, we have all sinned and fallen short of the glory of God (Romans 3:23), it might even result in our being the ones that would be excluded. Jesus suggested that the timing and decision of judgment be left to God. To want to be among the good seed is natural. Yet, Jesus warns of the damage to our souls in being too quick to exercise judgment.

Proper 12
Pentecost 10
Ordinary Time 17

Genesis 29:15-28

> *... What is this you have done to me? Did I not serve with you for Rachel?...* — Genesis 29:25

While some of the elements of this story challenge credibility, a major theme is that the deceiver is deceived. The reason that Jacob was in Haran was that he had deceived his father and stolen the birthright of his brother, Esau. Then the equally deceptive Uncle Laban challenged Jacob, the deceiver. Jacob, who would eventually be called Israel, would be the father of twelve sons who in turn would father the twelve tribes that formed the nation of Israel. Our community of faith had its origin in deception. God would work out the covenant among a people who demonstrated the same untrustworthy qualities as the rest of humanity. From the beginning, God's people had no reason to boast of their special qualities of character. They could only stand in wonder at the grace of God who had chosen them. While the whole story of Jacob is filled with incidents of deception, Jacob also proved to be faithful to the commitments that he made. He loved Rachel but was also faithful to Leah. While God was not mentioned in this part of the story, it would become evident that Jacob was grasped by this mysterious God and would eventually discover his path in life by grasping God in return. Deception and treachery may be part of human reality, but God can be trusted in all that we experience.

Psalm 105:1-11, 45b

> *O give thanks to the Lord, call on his name, make known his deeds among the peoples.* — Psalm 105:1

This verse could well serve as a mission statement for any congregation. A gathered people of God must continually give thanks to the Lord. It is in expressing our gratitude that we bring to mind how present God is in our lives. Even in our low moments and our acts of rebellion, God is gently weaving a possibility of transformation. No one can read the story of Joseph's brothers selling him into slavery and conclude that that was an act of faithfulness. Yet, it was in selling Joseph into slavery that God prepared the way for Israel to be saved from famine. We need to nurture our attitude of gratitude as a means of strengthening our faith. Also, since God has been actively present in our history, we need to call upon God's name in our present life. By continually naming God in our lives, we activate the power of God in our lives. "Whatever you ask in my name ..." (John 14:13), but thanking God for what God has done and calling on God's name is not enough. We need to make known God's deeds to the peoples. It is in this way that we become a light to the nations. We have a responsibility to make public what we have discovered about how God acts in the world. In this way we bring hope to a despairing world.

Romans 8:26-39

> *We know that all things work together for good for those who love God, who are called according to his purpose.* — Romans 8:28

The Revised Standard Version translated this verse as, "We know that *in everything* God works for good...." This translation is carried in the footnote of the NRSV. The RSV translation helped clarify that the Bible was not saying that everything worked for good, as many had interpreted it from the even earlier King James

Version. The danger of this earlier translation is that it fosters a passive acceptance that everything has a purpose, and we just have to trust that someday we will understand. In the ultimate sense, that may be true, but in the most immediate sense not everything reflects God's intention. Those who "love God [and] who are called according to his purpose," still need to resist sin, but they are not defeated by it. God can work a redemptive possibility in even the most negative of circumstances. That is certainly a central truth of the cross. It was not a good thing that happened to Jesus, but rather the cross was a reflection of the sinful rebelliousness of humanity. God was not defeated by this sinful act, however, but God transformed it into an instrument of redemption for the world.

Even in this horrible act of rebellion, God was working for good for his Son who loved him and who was seeking to live according to God's purpose. "If God is for us, who is against us?" We have now seen, in the faith of Jesus Christ, "that neither death nor life ... nor anything else in God's whole creation, will be able to separate us from the love of God in Christ Jesus our Lord." Because we live in a world that still awaits the completion of God's purpose, we will continue to experience hardships, distress, persecution, famine, nakedness, peril, and the sword, but by the Spirit of God intervening for us, we need not be defeated by these negative experiences. "No, in all these things we are more than conquerors through him who loved us."

Matthew 13:31-33, 44-52

"Have you understood all this?" They answered, "Yes."
— Matthew 13:51

Perhaps a challenge for the church is to answer Jesus' question with respect to these parables. This is a collection of parables that seek to reveal the kingdom of God or how God governs. If people within the church are going to live in relationship to each other and the world according to God's way, these parables help us understand what our life and relationships should be like.

The first parable is that of the mustard seed that begins small but grows large and provides shelter for the birds of the air. The birds of the air are a biblical symbol of the nations. It is for the sake of the world that God called the people together. When we are feeling our work, however faithful, is insignificant, this parable is a parable of promise. The faith that changed the world began with a Galilean Jew who could not even gain the loyalty of his own people. The parable of the yeast suggests that we proclaim a faith that infiltrates and changes all around it. The yeast is an almost invisible element that affects the whole loaf. The church does not need to get great publicity to be effective. The next parable is about a treasure hidden in a field and then a fine pearl that is so precious it is worth all that one has. Finally, the kingdom is compared to a net that gathers up the good and bad and leaves the separation until later.

If the church as the body of Christ is to reveal how God governs, the parables are suggestive. God's rule is built on small things (mustard seeds) that build a structure that protects the nations. Like yeast, it infiltrates from within rather than conquers from outside. God rules in our life by enticing our spirit by the value of serving God (fine pearl) and is worth all that we have. God governs by a grace, like a fishing net that gathers everyone in and leaves the separation of good and bad to God at a later time. It is a different way to govern our lives than that which the world offers.

Proper 13
Pentecost 11
Ordinary Time 18

Genesis 32:22-31

> *Then the man said, "You shall no longer be called Jacob, but Israel, for you have striven with God and with humans, and have prevailed."* — Genesis 32:28

In some ways Israel was a people with an almost haunted look on their face. As they moved through life, they were both the same as and different from other people. For reasons only God understands, this was a people who had glimpsed the face of God and limped through life with that memory in their soul. The people of God, formed out of the twelve sons of Jacob, were called Israel. The biblical origin of the name Israel was given here in this story of Jacob wrestling with God. The story reflects several characteristics of the self-understanding of the people of God. Because, as Christians, we see ourselves as included into God's choice of a people, sometimes referred to as a new Israel, the story applies to us as well. First, in Jacob we see the church characterized as a people marked not by their moral superiority but by the fact that God touches our lives. Second, Israel is a people who wrestles with God and humanity, with the divine and the human dimensions of life. What makes us distinctive from humanity in general is our audacious refusal to let go of either our humanity or the way we have been touched by the divine. We wrestle with what it means to be God-struck; with what the divine presence brings to our understanding of life.

Our glimpse of eternity changes how we view the most ordinary of events. Jacob would continue to experience many events, good and bad, in life as he watched his twelve sons and a daughter grow. But, each would be experienced in light of having wrestled with God. God could no longer be denied. Finally, we are wounded by our interaction with the divine. Those touched by God limp through life. They do not stride through history in arrogance but limp with a wounded awareness that there is more to life than meets the eye. Everything has a vertical as well as a horizontal dimension.

Psalm 17:1-7, 15

> *As for me, I shall behold your face in righteousness; when I awake I shall be satisfied, beholding your likeness.* — Psalm 17:15

When you consider that the book of psalms was Jesus' prayer book, it is interesting to hear this psalm as a prayer that Jesus might have prayed in the Garden of Gethsemane. Picture Jesus having left the meal with his disciples and having gone to the Mount of Olives and the Garden of Gethsemane. He had told most of his disciples to wait in one place in the garden and took Peter and the two sons of Zebedee with him. He went a little further and threw himself on the ground. He began to pray. While Matthew 26:36-46 tells us that he prayed to let the cup pass from him, he clearly prayed more than the words recorded in Matthew.

Psalm 17 may provide an example of the type of prayer that he might have engaged in. This was a prayer of a faithful one who, surrounded by the enemy, was crying out to God. "Hear a just cause, O Lord; attend to my cry; give ear to my prayer from lips free of deceit." The prayer was a plea for vindication for a life lived in faith that was now threatened by a world that did not consider his life to be of value. He laid his case before God. "If you try my heart, if you visit me by night, if you test me, you will find no wickedness in me; my mouth does not transgress." Later Jesus would demonstrate that he had chosen not to exercise violence against his enemy (Matthew 26:52-53). "As for what others do, by the word of your lips I have avoided the ways of the violent."

Jesus confronted the question that has always haunted believers throughout the ages. If people are not to respond to their enemies with violence, how should they respond? Jesus' prayer placed the issue before God. "I call upon you, for you will answer me, O God; incline your ear to me, hear my words. Wondrously show your steadfast love, O savior of those who seek refuge from their adversaries at your right hand." Jesus' hope in the garden, our hope in our confrontation with evil, was (is) that God would arise and confront those who measured life by physical victory or defeat. Jesus demonstrated in his passion that there are times in life when we do not receive an answer ahead of time but must trust God as we "walk through the darkest valley ..." (Psalm 23:4). So we hear the psalm that might have guided him in offering that trust: "As for me, I shall behold your face in righteousness; when I awake I shall be satisfied, beholding your likeness." As we imagine Jesus praying this prayer in his time of distress, we hear how, in our time of distress, this might be our prayer.

Romans 9:1-5

They are Israelites, and to them belong the adoption, the glory, the covenants....   — Romans 9:4

Having just concluded the ringing declaration that nothing "will be able to separate us from the love of God in Christ Jesus our Lord," Paul then turned to the most difficult challenge to such a belief. If Jesus was the Messiah who God had sent to God's people, the Jews, why had the majority of the Jews rejected Jesus? Did not such rejection either mean that Jesus was not the Messiah or Christ or that the plans of God couid be defeated by the rebellious choice of humanity? Paul would develop his answer in chapters 9-11. But in these verses, Paul made clear that the change that had occurred in his life on the Damascus road had not meant that he had ceased to be a Jew. His identity was so complete that if it would have made a difference, he would gladly have sacrificed himself for the sake of his people. "For I could wish that I myself were accursed and cut off from Christ for the sake of my own people, my kindred according to the flesh."

The hope of humanity was seen in what God had done through Israel. Paul catalogued the gifts of God to humanity through the Jews — adoption, glory, covenants, the giving of the law, worship, and the promise. It is good for Christians to be reminded of their indebtedness to Judaism. Christianity is not a rejection of the beliefs and experience of Judaism, as Marcion taught, but a further development and understanding of the truth of God first revealed in Judaism. We are the heirs of faith that began with the promise to Abram that through his progeny all the families of the earth would be blessed (Genesis 12:3). We are the recipients of that blessing. For the church to divorce itself from Judaism is to reject our own family.

Matthew 14:13-21

> ... *the disciples came to him and said ... send the crowds away so that they may go into the villages and buy food for themselves.* — Matthew 14:15

Since we are the contemporary disciples of Jesus Christ, we note the role of the disciples in this event with special interest. Note that it was the disciples who first noticed the hunger of the crowds. Their natural compassion caused them to want to respond before the hunger of the crowd became a serious concern. They brought their concern to Jesus. It was natural for them, and us, to bring the concerns noted in the world to Jesus. It is Christ who is head of the church and should guide our response. But the disciples did not just bring a concern. They also offered a very practical and pragmatic solution to the problem. They suggested that Jesus send the people away into the villages so that they might buy food for themselves to eat. This was not a heartless act but a practical solution. There is no indication that the people lacked the ability to purchase their own food. We do not know why Jesus did not accept the disciples' solution. There was no suggestion of a rebuke from Jesus. He simply suggested another solution to the problem. He told the disciples that they should provide for the crowd. The disciples immediately gave voice to their concern. They had only five loaves and two fish. It was barely enough for them, let alone for the entire crowd.

The church is a naturally compassionate community, but it often measures its response in terms of what it sees as the limitations of its resources. The disciples did not hold back but gave what they had to Jesus who blessed it and gave it back to the disciples. It was the disciples who had the stewardship responsibility to use their resources on behalf of the needy. Trusting in Jesus, they responded by giving away what could have been used to meet their own needs. When they did that, it multiplied, and they had twelve baskets left over. The disciples, by acting in faith, discovered that they not only had enough but they had an abundance for themselves. "I came that they may have life and have it abundantly" (John 10:10). The unsettling message for the church is to discern when pragmatic thinking needs to be replaced with a response of faith that trusts in the abundant grace of Christ.

Proper 14
Pentecost 12
Ordinary Time 19

Genesis 37:1-4, 12-28

> *... and sold him to the Ishmaelites for twenty pieces of silver....*
> — Genesis 37:28

The name of Judas stands in infamy because of his betrayal of Jesus. The story of Joseph being sold into slavery became a prototype of that later betrayal of Jesus. The first was done by Judah for twenty pieces of silver and the second by Judas for thirty pieces of silver. By examining the first story, we begin to glimpse how God works through even our ignoble actions to accomplish the divine purpose. The Judah story lays the foundation for our understanding of the second story. In the same way that there remains a mystery about why Judas acted as he did, so it is not entirely clear why Judah acted as he did. Did he act out of greed or from a nobler motive? Whatever Judah's motive was, the result, contrary to the intentions of the brothers, became God's means of salvation for God's people. It was because Joseph went into slavery that he eventually became the second in command in Egypt and the one who not only saved Egypt from famine but also Jacob's family. Without Judah convincing his brothers to sell Joseph into slavery, there would have been no means by which Israel and his family could have survived the famine in their land. Not only was Israel saved from a destructive famine because of the betrayal, but Egypt was also saved.

We see the mysterious hand of God that can take what is meant for evil and transform it into God's intention for good (Genesis 50:20). This becomes a pattern that we will see in its most complete form in the passion of Christ. It was Judas' betrayal that led to the evil of the cross. It was in the cross that the faithful saw God take what was intended for evil and transform it into an instrument of salvation, not only for the faithful but also for the world. It is in the pattern of the cross that we see that we need not despair when evil seems so powerful because God is able to redeem even that which is meant for evil.

Psalm 105:1-6, 16-22, 45b

> *He had sent a man ahead of them, Joseph, who was sold as a slave.* — Psalm 105:17

In Genesis 37, the story of Joseph's being sold as a slave is told from a human perspective. It is a story of jealousy and greed resulting in the brothers acting violently toward their youngest brother. This is the opposite of loving your neighbor as yourself, and it is happening in the family of faith. We see this story being echoed in denominations fighting among themselves, churches being split by issues of greed and vicious gossip, and Christian neighbors acting in cruelty toward each other. It is our worst nightmare of churches failing to behave according to the basic gospel message.

In Psalm 105, however, the story was viewed from the perspective of eternity. God was working through the ignoble behavior of Joseph's brothers to put Joseph in a position whereby he might save the lives of those very brothers who had betrayed him. This was not something that was apparent to any human on earth, including Joseph. "The word of the Lord tested him." Only God could see how these events would serve God's purpose. It was not that God arranged to have Joseph sold into slavery so that the impact of famine could be averted. Rather, God transformed Joseph's sojourn into slavery as a means of averting the impact of the famine. Only God could see how these events could be transformed and redeemed to serve God's purpose. If Joseph had allowed the immediate events to defeat him, then God would have had to use other means. How often do people allow the ignoble behavior in the church to convince them to leave God's people rather than allow God to test their faith and redeem the situation?

Romans 10:5-15

For, "Everyone who calls on the name of the Lord shall be saved." — Romans 10:13

It is important to remember that Paul was quoting Joel 2:32. If one strips the quote of its context, one can easily misconstrue what Paul intended by using it. For some in the Christian community, this quote has become almost a ticket by which people can claim their salvation from God. For Paul the original quote from Joel of calling on the Lord was filled with content by the person of Jesus Christ. You cannot call on God and be saved unless you know whom you are calling upon. "But how are they to call on one in whom they have not believed?" Jesus' life, death, and resurrection gave content to the character of God who was a God who called us into a community of love and forgiveness.

Earlier in Romans, Paul used the example of Abraham to make clear that God's love and grace extended to both Jew and Gentile. "For this reason it depends on faith, in order that the promise may rest on grace and be guaranteed to all his descendants, not only to the adherents of the law [Jews] but also to those who share the faith of Abraham," which Paul demonstrated included all nations (Romans 4:16 ff). In pursuing this line of thought Paul declared, "For there is no distinction between Jew and Greek; the same Lord is Lord of all and is generous to all who call on him."

To say one accepts Jesus as Lord and to refuse to be part of the community of Christ or the church, as many in our culture are attempting to do, is a contradiction in terms. In the same manner, to say that one accepts Jesus as Lord and Savior but to refuse to strive to be as loving and forgiving as God gives us the grace to be is to deny content to the statement that Jesus is Lord. To call on the name of the Lord is to invoke God's character as seen in Jesus Christ as the way of living by which we find salvation.

Matthew 14:22-33

... You of little faith, why did you doubt?
— Matthew 14:31

There is a book titled, *If You Want to Walk on Water, You've Got to Get Out of the Boat*. One has to admire Peter for having the courage to get out of the boat. None of the other disciples took that step. Despite the fearsome storm that was raging around the boat, Peter did get out of the boat and actually walked on water, at least for a little while. It was an extraordinary act of faith. Not long after that wonderful act of faith, Peter looked around and saw the waves and the storm around him, and he began to sink. When Jesus asked Peter later, "Why did you doubt?" Jesus was implying that if Peter had kept his faith and kept his focus on Jesus, he could have continued to walk on the water. When we read the story, however, we know how easy it is, even for the most faithful, to suddenly be aware of the heights of the waves and the fierceness of the storm around us.

It is not easy to keep our focus on Jesus. Caught up in the miraculous vision of Christ walking on water, Peter stepped out onto the water himself. That was the miracle that should inspire us. It was not just Jesus but Peter, a very human person, who actually walked on water. We are capable of miraculous acts of faith. Yet, even in our most faithful moments, we are not immune from the fearful forces that impinge upon us. It is not a choice between faith and doubt for most of us. Rather, it is a life lived with a mixture of both. It is important to remember that Jesus does not abandon us to our own resources. When fear begins to overcome us, Christ is there offering us an extra hand. We are invited to get out of the boat, and we are not alone when we take those first steps.

Proper 15
Pentecost 13
Ordinary Time 20

Genesis 45:1-15

> *And now do not be distressed, or angry with yourselves, because you sold me here; for God sent me before you to preserve life.* — Genesis 45:5

How does one learn to live with the dark shadows of one's own history or the history of one's country? Some people live in denial, creating glorified versions of their history that deny the evil of the past. Others feel the guilt of the past as a burden and try to absolve themselves by denouncing it loudly and righteously. Most of us in the United States have benefited from the accident of our birth in a time and place that benefits from a violent beginning that involved the near genocide of the Native Americans and the enslavement of Africans for inexpensive labor. The story of Joseph's response to his brothers provides a valuable faith story with which to reflect on our own condition. Out of jealousy and greed, the brothers had sold Joseph into slavery. Many years later, after he had become an enormous success in Egypt, his brothers came to Egypt in desperate need. Joseph did not deny the evil of their actions but reinterpreted the events from God's transforming perspective. "Do not be distressed, or angry with yourselves, because you sold me here; for God sent me before you to preserve life."

How could they not be distressed? They had not only acted in an evil way, but now they stood vulnerable before their brother who had the power to exact a punishment for what they had done. Yet, Joseph's words were based on his realization of how God had used such evil deeds for good. Whether it is the dark chapters in our own personal history or that of our country or church, we are invited to see how God can transform such events into saving possibilities for the future. This does not gloss over what was wrong in the past but gives us a freedom to thank God for a good future. Once Joseph had identified God's transforming hand in these events, it set him free from the need for vengeance and allowed him to use his gratitude for how God had blessed him to release others from their past as well. If we have eyes to see God's transforming hand even in the dark shadows of our history, does that release us to act more graciously toward others who have not been so fortunate?

Psalm 133

> *How very good and pleasant it is when kindred live together in unity!* — Psalm 133:1

The inability of people of faith to avoid division among themselves continues to weaken our witness of God's goodness in the world. In this psalm, there was a celebration of the blessing of community. In the second story of creation, there is a recognition that it is not good for humans to be alone (Genesis 2:18). Jesus summarized the law in the great commandment that declares all of reality is expressed in love of God and love of neighbor. We demonstrate the power of sin when we fail to live together in unity. The imagery that the psalmist used to illustrate the blessing of community was drawn from the physical realities of their lives.

In the Middle East, with its dry climate, it was a sign of hospitality to anoint a guest's head with olive oil that could refresh the skin dried by the weather. Human community (v. 1) is refreshing like the generous oil put on Aaron's head (v. 2). Aaron, Moses' brother, became the head of the priesthood in Israel and Moses' interpreter for God's word. God's will was for a generous hospitality among God's people. The dew of Hermon was the life-giving water that enabled the plants to bloom. Life together was like that precious water that enabled life to flower (v. 3). It flowered in Zion, the place where God had chosen to make his presence visible. God's presence becomes visible and productive where people dwell together enriching and refreshing each other under God's guidance. All attempts to demonstrate our goodness that result in division of community are a failure to discover the blessing of God that produces the fullness of life (v. 3b). We cannot love God and hate our neighbor (1 John 4:20). It is in building the community of the church that we demonstrate to the world "a more excellent way" (1 Corinthians 12:31).

Romans 11:1-2a, 29-32

> ... *the gifts and the calling of God are irrevocable.*
> — Romans 11:29

The integrity of God and the future of the church are on the line in this argument. If, as many in Christianity have taught, God rejected the Jews because they had rejected Jesus as the Christ, then we know that God's promises cannot be counted on. When God first made his promise of a covenant relationship with Abram in Genesis 15:1-20, it was not a conditional covenant dependent on people's behavior. In the scene in which God sealed his promise to Abram, it was only the "smoking fire pot and a flaming torch," symbols of the presence of God, that passed through the split animals. God guaranteed the fulfillment of the covenant. This unconditional covenant was reaffirmed through David and throughout the scriptures.

If God reneged on his promise by rejecting the Jews because of their behavior, then how can the church trust that God will not do the same with the church? Clearly, the church has not proven to be a paragon of faithfulness in its own history. Paul answered with a ringing declaration, "I ask, then, has God rejected his people? By no means ... God has not rejected his people whom he foreknew." So what is the answer? Paul's conclusion was that God had integrated the Jewish rejection of Jesus as the Christ into his overall plan for the salvation of the world. "Just as you [Gentiles] were once disobedient to God but have now received mercy because of their [the Jews] disobedience, so they have now been disobedient in order that, by the mercy shown to you, they too may now receive mercy." However the church chose to relate to Judaism, Paul made it clear that Christians were responding to the continuing covenant people of God.

Matthew 15:(10-20) 21-28

> *... Listen and understand: it is not what goes into the mouth that defiles a person, but it is what comes out of the mouth that defiles.* — Matthew 15:10-11

Jesus was contrasting the religious tradition and practices that were intended to shape a person's character with the character itself as evidenced by what a person says. His emphasis was on the purpose behind the tradition — to build God-like character — rather than the tradition itself. Many of the common people, because of the nature of their life and their regular contact with foreigners, could not possibly keep all of the cleanliness laws. In Psalm 80:8 and Isaiah 5:7, the people of Israel were referred to as God's planting. The religious leaders were to be the guides or stewards of God's plantings, but they had become blinded to their responsibility for the people by their commitment to protecting the tradition. In a humorous reference to their leadership ability, Jesus suggested that if one blind person led another, they both would fall into the pit. The Pharisees recognized his challenge to the framework of religion and, therefore, took offense. Lest the church become self-righteous in thinking that Jesus was only referring to Israel and not also the church, Matthew recorded that Peter (the rock on which the church was built) was also misunderstood. Jesus emphasized the difference between what passes through people and what became an expression of their character. Evil thoughts such as murder, adultery, fornication, theft, false witness, and slander came out of one's heart or character. Except for slander, this list followed the order of that part of the Ten Commandments that spoke of our obligations to other people. God's law was intended to cultivate God's plantings so that they might produce good fruit. When tradition becomes insensitive to the realities of people's lives, then the structure of religion becomes oppressive rather than liberating. The story of the Canaanite woman that follows illustrated that even the disciples could be tempted to use the law to excuse their lack of compassion for another human being. The story stands as a caution for the entire church.

Proper 16
Pentecost 14
Ordinary Time 21

Exodus 1:8—2:10

> *... Look, the Israelite people are more numerous and more powerful than we. Come, let us deal shrewdly with them, or they will increase and, in the event of war, join our enemies and fight against us and escape from the land.* — Exodus 1:9-10

There has always been a fear of the immigrants, especially when they stick together and remain identifiable. The pattern of the treatment of the Hebrew immigrants in this story becomes a familiar pattern. Pharaoh could easily identify them as "the Israelite people" reflecting the fact that they had refused to be assimilated. Because they did not fit into the dominant culture, Pharaoh began to question their loyalty. "... In the event of war, [they will] join our enemies." They began to discriminate against them (deal shrewdly with them) and in guilt assumed that the Israelites would be disloyal to them. They began to develop laws that made use of their services but made their lives more difficult: "Therefore they set taskmasters over them to oppress them with forced labor." Then they developed a rationale for treating their lives more cheaply than the life of an Egyptian. "When you act as midwives to the Hebrew women ... if it is a boy, kill him...." They were shocked to discover that members of the Egyptian society became advocates for the Hebrews out of a sense of common decency. "But the midwives feared God; they did not do as the king of Egypt commanded them...."

The Bible delights in revealing how God uses the least powerful in society to transform unjust situations. In this case there is a common thread of the work of women from all levels of society resisting the evil that was operating. First, it was the midwives who refused to practice infanticide. Second, a mother refused to give up her child and placed him in a basket on the Nile. Third, "by chance," the baby was found by the one person close enough to Pharaoh to defy his policy of infanticide. To complete the irony, Moses' sister convinced Pharaoh's daughter that she could find a woman (actually the baby's mother) to care for him on her behalf. And it was this child, preserved by this chain of women, that would eventually lead God's people to the very freedom that Pharaoh had sought to prevent.

Psalm 124

If it had not been the Lord who was on our side ... then they would have swallowed us up alive....
— Psalm 124:1, 3

Psalm 124 is a prayer of thanksgiving for Israel's deliverance. While one could easily imagine this psalm as a song of celebration following the crossing of the Red Sea, the specific context was not provided. This enables the psalm to apply to many situations. It should first be prayed in the context of the miraculous history of Israel's survival from any of numerous attempts to destroy them as a people both in the scriptures and up to the present day. The psalm can then become a model of prayer for any of numerous seemingly miraculous escapes from dire situations. It is a psalm of wonder at the unexpected escape from what seemed to be certain disaster (vv. 1-3). It does not suggest that God had been visibly present in the battle but, in retrospect, that is the only possible explanation for the remarkable turn of events.

Whether it is a nation, church, or individual, it is a fearful thing to experience the raging, irrational anger of an opponent. All reason is swept aside, and life seems to have returned to that primordial chaos (vv. 3-5). Such a formless void is overcome by God who speaks the divine word to bring order out of chaos (Genesis 1:2-3). The only response to such an unexpected salvation is to praise God who has not let you be ripped apart by such anger (v. 6) nor trapped by its overwhelming power (v. 7). Despite all of our attempts to be in control of our lives, the unexpected grace by which we are saved from seemingly impossible situations continues to remind us that our true source of help is not in ourselves but in "the name of the Lord who made heaven and earth" (v. 8). The illusion of self-sufficiency is shattered by the creative word of grace that helps us see beyond the darkness that threatens us.

Romans 12:1-8

> *Do not be conformed to this world, but be transformed by the renewing of your minds, so that you may discern what is the will of God — what is good and acceptable and perfect.* — Romans 12:2

Many commentators suggest that, with Romans 12, Paul turned to the subject of ethics. While this is true, it would be a mistake to not keep in mind the connection with the prior theological argument in which Paul explored the mystery of God by which both Jew and Gentile would be reconciled as the one people of God. Because the emperor Claudius had expelled the Jews from Rome in 49 CE, the leadership of the church had fallen upon the Gentile Christians who had remained. A few years later, the Jewish Christians returned to find Gentiles in charge. It is in this context that Paul said, "For by the grace given to me I say to everyone among you not to think of yourself more highly than you ought to think, but to think with sober judgment, each according to the measure of faith that God has assigned." It was easy for Jews to claim that since Jesus was a Jew and the faith had come from Judaism, Gentiles were of a lesser quality. It was equally easy for Gentiles to claim that since the majority of Jews had rejected Jesus as the Christ, the Gentiles were now the favored of God. Paul had just shown how the mercy of God in the face of the disobedience of both groups had opened the possibility of a reconciled world. Instead of jockeying for position within the community, they were called upon to follow Christ and "present your bodies as a living sacrifice, holy and acceptable to God, which is your spiritual worship."

The lesson for both Judaism and the church in these verses is that instead of competing with one another we are of the same body, but we have different functions. Consider the challenge to the world that would be made by these currently two distinct faiths recognizing that "we have gifts that differ according to the grace given to us...." This same truth might guide our different denominations and local competing churches in relating to each other. Is it possible that in the mystery of God's plan, there is a proper function for conservative and liberal, liturgical and free churches in the one purpose of God? "Do not be conformed to this world, but be transformed by the renewing of your minds, so that you may discern what is the will of God — what is good and acceptable and perfect."

Matthew 16:13-20

> ... Who do people say that the Son of Man is?
> — Matthew 16:13

Unlike Mark, who put it more directly — "Who do people say that I am?" — Matthew had Jesus say, "Who do people say that the Son of Man is?" In both Aramaic and Hebrew, such a phrase could simply mean "human" as in Psalm 8:4. In the book of Daniel, which Jesus made direct reference to (Matthew 24:30), the phrase referred to the community of the faithful (Daniel 7:13-18). While his disciples clearly understood Jesus to be referring directly to himself as seen by their response, Matthew may have been indicating all three understandings to be accurate but in reverse order. Jesus was referring to himself, but as will be clear in 16:18, Jesus saw himself intimately connected with the community of the faithful as seen in the twelve disciples. They, in turn, were to be the true Israel, a light to the whole world, as reflected in the original promise to Abraham (Genesis 12:1-4).

As the true Israel, they were to reflect to the world what God intended to be ultimately true for all humanity. Thus to respond accurately to the question: "Who do [people] say that the Son of Man is?" was to understand who the church was meant to be through faith and what the church was to reflect as God's purpose for all of humanity. Then Jesus asked them, "But who do you say that I am?" which raised the question of what the role of the church (the body of Christ) was and its vision for humanity. "Simon Peter answered, 'You are the Messiah, the Son of the living God.' " When Jesus responded, "Blessed are you, Simon son of Jonah...." he was confirming not only his own identity but the identity of the body of Christ or the church. It was this recognition of the very presence of God in their midst, and not Peter's steadiness of faith or consistent moral courage, that was the basis of Peter's blessedness. God was not someone apart from life but was revealed in the very center of life. The challenge for Christians is to recognize that same truth in the midst of the church.

Proper 17
Pentecost 15
Ordinary Time 22

Exodus 3:1-15

> *... I must turn aside and look at this great sight, and see why the bush is not burned up.* — Exodus 3:3

There are significant clues for our own spiritual life in this story of Moses' experience. First, Moses was not looking for a spiritual revelation. He was simply doing his job caring for his father-in-law's sheep. Second, when he first saw the bush, it could have been dismissed as a natural experience, but Moses noticed something different. He deliberately chose to turn aside and examine it. It was only as he chose to take time out in the midst of work to be open to the special within the normal that God spoke to him. God's revelation did not impose itself on Moses in a manner that robbed him of his freedom to choose. Notice how many possibilities there were that would have prevented Moses from receiving God's revelation. Even when God spoke out of the bush, God still awaited Moses' response. Moses took the next step by responding, "Here I am." Then God responded by saying, "Come no closer! Remove the sandals from your feet, for the place on which you are standing is holy ground."

It was then, after Moses acknowledged the sacred quality of the moment by taking off his shoes, that God began to reveal who it was that was speaking to him. Up to this point, the burning bush had only been experienced as an abnormal phenomenon. It was when Moses removed his shoes that God identified Godself from the history of God's actions in the past. "I am the God of your father...." The God who reveals Godself to us is consistent with the God we have known in scripture. Moses was appropriately afraid and hid his face. But God continued by revealing that God had heard the people's cry and now desired to respond by sending

Moses. That which triggered this amazing experience was not Moses' piety but the pain of a people who were trapped in slavery. Our personal spiritual experiences are closely tied to both our willingness to notice the unusual within the normal and God's compassion for the sufferings of the world.

Psalm 105:1-6, 23-26, 45c

> *Seek the Lord and his strength; seek his presence continually.* — Psalm 105:4

The reader is referred to Propers 12, 14, and 20 (Ordinary Time 17, 19, and 25) for further commentary. (The lectionary obviously likes this psalm.) This psalm is a celebration of the glory of God as it was manifested in the history of the people of Israel. The psalm can serve as a reminder to the church of the critical importance of worship. The character of God for Israel and the church is made known by a continual recalling of the deeds that God had performed among God's people. We do that through worship. "Sing to him, sing praises to him; tell of all his wonderful works." It is when the worshiping community rehearses how God has been faithful to God's people in the past that it gains courage for its future. "Seek the Lord and his strength; seek his presence continually." A church should be instructed by such psalms as these to rehearse the deeds of God's faithfulness as they are recounted in the scripture and in the church's history as well. God is not always visible in our current struggles, but frequently in retrospect, we can see glimpses of the invisible hand guiding us. It is precisely in the difficult passages of our lives that we become most aware of the mysterious, often unexpected, ways that God has cared for us. "Then Israel came to Egypt; Jacob lived as an alien in the land of Ham. And the Lord made his people very fruitful, and made them stronger than their foes." There is gospel in the minutes of our church's history that need to be celebrated.

Romans 12:9-21

Let love be genuine; hate what is evil, hold fast to what is good; love one another with mutual affection; outdo one another in showing honor. — Romans 12:9-10

This entire passage is a template for how Christians are to live in community and thereby offer an alternative to the way that the world lives. The mandate for Christians as they live together in community and as they relate to the larger world around them is summed up in Paul's statement, "Do not be overcome by evil, but overcome evil with good." While Paul insisted that evil could not defeat God, he was very aware that as humans we are constantly struggling with the temptations to allow evil to defeat us in our life. There is full recognition that people will experience persecution, but Paul suggested we could overcome such experiences by blessing the very ones that persecute us. In a Christian community, there will be differences in experiences of pain and joy, differences in class and wisdom, and also experiences of injustice. The full range of experiences is present in the church as they are in the world. It is our response to such experiences that will make all the difference. Because we are to live as Christ lived, Paul suggested an alternative response to what the world would normally expect. "Live in harmony with one another; do not be haughty, but associate with the lowly; do not claim to be wiser than you are. Do not repay anyone evil for evil, but take thought for what is noble in the sight of all." Given the current state of the church, which often causes our worldly companions to mock us, it might be a significant beginning for the church to focus on Paul's advice as central in our relationships with each other. It is by practicing such behavior that we gain the courage and strength to offer such an alternative way of living to the world around us.

Matthew 16:21-28

For what will it profit them if they gain the whole world but forfeit their life?   — Matthew 16:26

This gospel lesson provides a stark challenge to a trend in our society. As we have grown more affluent in our society, the trend has been against sacrifice. There is a temptation toward hedonism, a desire for the good life, and certainly a tendency to choose the comfortable over the uncomfortable. Along with that is a tendency, even within churches, to want to build a fortress to protect ourselves against all forms of fears.

When Peter heard that Jesus was heading to Jerusalem and that he would "undergo great suffering at the hands of the elders and chief priests and scribes ..." Peter spoke for us. He said, "God forbid it, Lord! This must never happen to you." When was the last time that a church chose to risk suffering because this was where the faith journey seemed to be leading them? When Jesus responded with one of his fiercest responses recorded in scripture, "Get behind me, Satan! You are a stumbling block to me; for you are setting your mind not on divine things but on human things," Jesus was laying a significant challenge at the doorstep of every church. The irony is that despite our fears, we know the underlying truth of which Jesus was speaking.

Even in our secular society, we know that there are few experiences that are so satisfying and fulfilling as finding a cause for which you can make great sacrifice. Whether it is a sports team, defending your country, or identifying with a great project in your corporation, we gain great satisfaction in being able to devote ourselves to something bigger than ourselves. The problem, of course, is that many of our goals, once achieved, fail to deliver their promise to us. Human life needs a cause to dedicate itself to that will not let us down. When Christ offered his followers the chance to "deny themselves and take up their cross and follow me," he was offering them life. To sacrifice is to set apart something we value and to dedicate it to a greater cause. In Christ, we see one who was willing to sacrifice himself for us and invited us to do the same for him that we might experience the full love of God.

Proper 18
Pentecost 16
Ordinary Time 23

Exodus 12:1-14

> ... *when I see the blood, I will pass over you, and no plague shall destroy you when I strike the land of Egypt.*
> — Exodus 12:13

This is the biblical explanation of the origin of the Passover feast that has been a center of the Jewish faith ever since. The Israelites had been slaves in Egypt and had cried out to God who initiated a process to liberate them. This was the final plague of a series of plagues that God invoked in Egypt to loosen Egypt's control over the slaves. Note the careful ritual that was established to recall this event. The Jewish calendar was arranged to mark this anniversary of freedom as the beginning of a new year. The meal celebrating this event was a family celebration. While the people were eating the lamb, it was clearly a sacrifice to God. The lamb was to be one year old and without blemish. It was to be completely eaten that night. They were to eat it hurriedly and dressed ready to travel at a moment's notice. The blood of the lamb, which bore God's gift of life, was to be painted on the doorposts and lintels of the house. When the final plague began, God would move through Egypt bringing death to the firstborn animals and humans except on those homes in which God saw the mark of the blood. God would pass over those houses. As Jews continue to celebrate this event, they are reminded that they are the people whom God loved and rescued from slavery. This festival reveals a critical aspect of the nature of God. God is willing to get involved to correct injustice. Our freedom is a gift from God and an expression of God's love for us. "You shall celebrate it as a festival to the Lord."

Psalm 149

> *Let the high praises of God be in their throats and two-edged swords in their hands.* — Psalm 149:6

We tend to treat worship so casually in our society. Even for believers, it is a nice thing to do but hardly a critical thing, let alone a dangerous thing to do. The central event in Israel's liberation from slavery is re-enacted in worship. The Jewish liturgy stands as a challenge to all forms of slavery. It is a remembrance of the liberating power of God. Our time of worship becomes an act of celebrating victory over the forces of chaos and darkness. We have made it through another week without being overcome by the enemy. The psalmist suggested that continual praise of God was like a two-edged sword that executed vengeance on nations and punishment on people. Edward Gibbons, in *The Rise and the Fall of the Roman Empire*, suggested that when Christians praised God, it gave them a loyalty greater than the state and that was the beginning of the fall of the empire. So one cut of our sword of worship is that it reminds us that even nations are accountable to the God of justice and that our ultimate loyalty is to this God. The other cut of the sword of worship is that we also are accountable to God for justice and mercy to others in need. The "glory for all faithful ones" is to recognize again that it is God, not kings, nobles, CEOs, judges, or senators who shape the world. In praising God, we regain perspective on reality and are once more liberated to reenter the world to love our neighbor. It is an appropriate occasion for a party.

Romans 13:8-14

> *Owe no one anything, except to love one another; for the one who loves another has fulfilled the law.* — Romans 13:8

How are we to love one another when sometimes we do not even like each other very much? That is often the challenge within a church, let alone in the larger society. We would prefer to keep our religion at a more formal level. Laws such as not committing adultery, not stealing, and not coveting can codify correct behavior. And indeed, these are good commandments because they teach us appropriate boundaries. Yet, we can keep all of these commandments and still remain strangers to each other. You can refrain from stealing from another person without ever having to interact with that person. You can break one of these commandments and still need to be cared for by others. The intimacy we are starved for requires us not only to be correct in our relationships but also to love one another as Jesus loved us. Jesus' love revealed a passion for our well-being even when it meant a sacrifice for him. Jesus' love offered an acceptance of us with all our irritating and offensive characteristics. It offered a forgiveness that restored us again and again to wholeness. The challenge for the church in its internal relationships is enormous. We need to continue to strive to overcome our desire to focus on our own comfort and pleasure, and we need to seek the best for those other members who make us uncomfortable. "Instead, put on the Lord Jesus Christ, and make no provision for the flesh, to gratify its desires."

Matthew 18:15-20

> *For where two or three are gathered in my name, I am there among them.* — Matthew 18:20

A dialogue between two church members:
"Have you seen Jesus lately?"
"I'm not one of those religious fanatics who is always seeing visions. What are you talking about?"
"I want to see Jesus. He must be around here somewhere. He promised."
"Are you crazy? Jesus lived almost 2,000 years ago."
"But he promised to be here if two or three of us gathered in his name. You and I make two, don't we?"

"He didn't mean physically. He just meant his Spirit would be among us."

"Okay, have you seen Jesus' Spirit among us?"

"You can't see a spirit. You just feel its presence."

"What would it mean to feel Jesus' presence among us right now?"

"Well it would mean that we would feel his continuing to urge us to love one another as Jesus loved us."

"So how did Jesus love us?"

"Jesus was always thinking of the other person and trying to act in a way that released the best in the other person."

"But what if some people in this church are mean to me? What if they don't deserve my love?"

"If we only received Jesus' love when we deserved it, where would we be?"

"But if you were always seeking the best in others, aren't there people in this world who would take advantage of you?"

"That is our cross to bear."

"Have you seen Jesus, lately?"

Proper 19
Pentecost 17
Ordinary Time 24

Exodus 14:19-31

> *The Egyptians said, "Let us flee from the Israelites, for the Lord is fighting for them against Egypt."*
> — Exodus 14:25

This was the climactic moment in the story of God's liberation of the Israelites. The story is impossible, and that is the point. Like the resurrection of Jesus, the event defied the laws of nature. People will write volumes trying to explain the Exodus. Yet the story would, like the resurrection, become the critical energy that formed the faith of Israel. The theological point is clear. God can defeat the greatest military power in the world. The God who created the world remains Lord over nature as well. No matter how strong the power of evil is in the world, it can only flee in panic when it recognizes with whom it is contending. Here is the real truth in the battle between good and evil. Trust and obedience in God, which is what faith is, can overcome the laws of nature, the military force of nations, and any other force that exists. From the story of Adam to the present time, the issue has always been whether one can trust and obey God. Later, in the life of Jesus, that would become the critical issue in the Garden of Gethsemane. The story of Israel was a continual struggle for obedience against all the logic that suggested there must be a better way. The energy that drives the quest is found in this critical story of the Exodus that described when Israel once put everything in the hand of God, and God proved to be faithful. Is that not the challenge for the church as well?

Psalm 114

Judah became God's sanctuary, Israel his dominion.
— Psalm 114:2

Psalm 114 is the fourth psalm of praise in a row. The first one, Psalm 111, praised God for establishing and being faithful to the covenant that God had established with God's people. The second, Psalm 112, praised God for the way that God had guided Israel in responding to their material blessings by being conscious of the issues of justice and generosity to the poor. "They have distributed freely, they have given to the poor; their righteousness endures forever ..." (Psalm 112:9). The third, Psalm 113, celebrated the sovereignty of God over all nations and the way in which God acted on behalf of the poor and the needy in the world. In Psalm 114, the focus was on God's lordship over the forces of nature. All of these psalms can be read with the memory of how God had dealt with them when they were slaves in Egypt. God remembered God's covenant with them as a people, demanded the same justice and mercy from Egypt that he expected from Israel, and acted on behalf of those who cried out to God from their pain of slavery.

It is helpful to recall the significance of the names of Jacob and Israel and Judah. Jacob signified an aggressive striver after that which would benefit him in life. Israel signified one whose striving had been transformed into striving with God. Recall that Jacob wrestled with God at Jabbok and refused to let go of God until he was blessed. He was then named Israel because he had wrestled with God and humanity and prevailed (Genesis 32:22-30). Still later in the story, it was his son, Judah, who, perhaps out of greed, it is not clear, was used by God to preserve Joseph's life so that he could go into Egypt and prepare the way to save all of Israel from famine (Genesis 37:26-28). It is this very ambiguous reflection of humanity, only distinguished by God's choice, that becomes "God's sanctuary."

As further evidence of God's sovereignty, the psalmist celebrated how even the forces of nature are God's instruments to effect God's purpose. When we remember that God is sovereign over both human nature in all of its ambiguity and the natural forces of creation, we can only tremble and offer our praise.

Romans 14:1-12

> *Welcome those who are weak in faith, but not for the purpose of quarreling over opinions.*
> — Romans 14:1

A major theme of chapter 14 is the witness of paying attention to the faith of our neighbor. The essential ingredient for true Christian community is acceptance of Jesus as our Lord. Within that context, our relationship with other Christians is summed up by the statement, "Owe no one anything, except to love one another" (Romans 13:8). Paul addressed the Christian that sincerely believes he has a more correct understanding than another Christian and urged that person to make room for the person of weaker faith, not for the purpose of correcting the other person but for the purpose of bringing that person into the presence of the Lord. If you think another person is weaker than you are in his or her understanding of the faith, then you are not to engage that person in dispute to prove your faith but to welcome that person so that he or she may be nurtured in the Lord.

In the current heated debates within the Christian community, that would mean each of us would have to turn to those who hold contrary positions, which we think are a weaker understanding of the faith, and welcome them. To follow that admonition is to place more trust in the Lord than in the rightness of our opinion. "It is before their own lord that they stand or fall. And they will be upheld, for the Lord is able to make them stand." The Reformed faith places the confession of sins in a prominent place in worship precisely to remind us that there is always a distance between what we consider right and what God sees as right. In our pursuit of purity, we seem to need to defeat the arguments of those who differ with us. Paul placed the pursuit of faithfulness in a whole different context. To be pure in faith is not centered in ideas or even in personal morality alone but in community relationships. That which causes my fellow church member to stumble reveals a defective faith in me. No matter how correct my ideas, if my advocacy of them weakens the bonds of community, I am not "walking in love."

Matthew 18:21-35

> *Jesus said to him, "Not seven times, but, I tell you, seventy-seven times."* — Matthew 18:22

Peter probably thought he was being bold to suggest that a Christian might forgive another Christian as many as seven times. Indeed, that might be an improvement over what sometimes happens in our own churches. Some manuscripts have Jesus saying that we should forgive seventy times seven times. Regardless, it is clear that Jesus was suggesting that our forgiveness of another member in the church should be endless. It is natural for us to move to a psychological defense that it might not even be good for the person to be forgiven so frequently. People might become so accustomed to our forgiveness that they would feel no need to change their behavior. We easily slip into an explanation of the importance of "tough love." Yet, just as we gain some satisfaction for such a defense, we read Jesus' parable that drew the connection between how God treats us and how we treat others. In the parable, Jesus was not speaking of toleration but forgiveness. Each slave in the parable clearly owed the debt. The tension of the parable is in the inability of the first slave to see a connection between his being forgiven of his enormous debt and his being willing to forgive the second slave of a much smaller debt. Is it possible that it is only through our forgiving others that we can allow the forgiveness of God to heal the cancer within us? For many of us there is a deep-seated hurt planted in our soul that tells us we are inadequate. Only when we pay the price of forgiving others, do we realize the price that God paid for us, and then we realize our true value. When

Jesus taught us to pray, "Forgive us our debts as we forgive our debtors," was he not drawing that same connection? The church becomes the laboratory in which we learn how to live with each other in a manner that reflects God's purpose for the world.

Proper 20
Pentecost 18
Ordinary Time 25

Exodus 16:2-15

> ... *I am going to rain bread from heaven for you, and each day the people shall go out and gather enough for that day....* — Exodus 16:4

For Christians, this is a foundational story that illuminates several aspects of Christian teaching. Bread and its source are a critical element in our journey of faith. People will worship the source of bread whether it is an ancient fertility goddess or the wealthy corporation that employs them. Jesus' first temptation was to turn the stones into bread. The person who can supply bread to the hungry will be their god. It is important in our journey of faith to continually learn that one does not live by bread alone (Matthew 4:4 and Deuteronomy 8:3). Also, this story is the background for Jesus' petition, "Give us this day our daily bread" (Matthew 6:11). Jesus did not teach us to pray for bigger barns (Luke 12:13-21) to secure our future but to trust God each day. Will we trust God to provide for us each day, or will we expend our energy in useless anxiety about tomorrow? (Matthew 6:34). "In that way I will test them, whether they will follow my instructions or not." Greed and mistrust of the faithful generosity of God continues to plague the Christian community. We also have trouble recognizing what we have has been given to us. "Moses said to them, 'It is the bread that the Lord has given you to eat.'" But perhaps the most important connection with this story is that of communion or the Eucharist. At the table, we hear Jesus say of the bread, "This is my body which is broken for you." Once again, it is God who provides us with the bread of life. We are sustained by the love of God.

Psalm 105:1-6, 37-45

*They asked, and he brought quails, and gave them food
from heaven in abundance.* — Psalm 105:40

This is the fourth use of this psalm in recent weeks. See also Propers 12, 14, and 17 (Ordinary Time 17, 19, and 22). All call our attention to verses 1-6 and verse 45 that emphasized the importance of the praise of God in worship. This reading also emphasized God's various ways of providing for the people with both the necessities and recompense for past suffering. The psalmist recalled the moment of Israel's departure from Egypt when the Egyptian people were so anxious to be rid of them that they gave them silver, gold, and clothing for their journey (Exodus 12:35-36). This may have been the first demand by former slaves for reparation for the work they had been forced to do. The psalmist then celebrated God's protecting and providing for the Israelites in the wilderness journey. God could not be defeated by the army of the Egyptians or by the deprivation in the desert in fulfilling God's promise to their ancestor Abraham so long ago. God further provided for this people by giving "them the lands of the nations, and they took possession of the wealth of the peoples...." All of this is a celebration of the mystery of God's generosity on behalf of this people.

One may wonder why this people was blessed at the expense of other peoples but no explanation is given. The psalm might provide a helpful context for reflecting on the unexplained favor that has been showered on America. Certainly we have been blessed with far more benefits than most people in the world, and it has often come at the expense of other nations and people. While the psalmist does not attempt to explain this anomaly in history, it was clear that Israel had a clear responsibility in light of this reality. This has been done so "that they might keep his statutes and observe his laws." How might this be applied to our own responsibilities in light of our blessings?

Philippians 1:21-30

I know that I will remain and continue with all of you for your progress and joy in faith....
— Philippians 1:25

Paul struggled with his reason for living. Death was not a fearful thing for him but rather an appealing completion of his faith journey. "For to me, living is Christ and dying is gain." The reason for living was not a selfish clinging to life but rather an acknowledgment that God could use him to contribute to the journey of faith of others. His joy of life was found in the way that God enabled him to be a means by which others could mature in the faith. "... To remain in the flesh is more necessary for you." There are times when any clergy person can grow weary with all of the struggles of ministry. There are times when any Christian can grow weary with trying to live a life of integrity within the context of the temptation of life. Sometimes when we are confronted with the possibility of death and survive, we discover that we do not fear death. We also believe that all the struggles in our life and ministry have value if we can believe that God is using our efforts for a greater purpose. It is immensely satisfying and refreshing when we glimpse how our efforts have made life better for someone else. Even when we feel inadequate in the demonstration of our faith, we are encouraged when we are allowed to understand how God can use our efforts to build up someone else. It is at those moments that we experience "the privilege of not only believing in Christ, but of suffering for him as well...."

Matthew 20:1-16

... Or are you envious because I am generous?
— Matthew 20:15

On the surface, we can identify much more with those who grumbled in the parable than with the landowner who represented

God. If we had toiled all day and then received the same wages as those who had worked only an hour, we would grumble, too. It would seem unfair to us. To understand the parable, we must first understand the labor pool. Each day the men lined up waiting to be hired. Their ability to feed their family depended on being picked. The owner was not questioned when he offered the usual daily wage of one denarius. This was not an unjust situation. When he kept returning to get more workers, they assumed that he would be fair. When he questioned those standing idle late in the day, it was clear that the reason they were not working was not laziness but because they had not been hired. Through no fault of their own, their family would not eat that night. The turning point of the parable was the owner's compassion on the last to be hired. He wanted their families to eat, as well. Those who worked longer saw this generous act and expected that since they worked longer they would get more pay. But the owner only paid what he had agreed to pay. The suggestion of the parable is that God is interested in "giving us this day our daily bread" and would extend God, himself, to provide such to the less fortunate, also. God was not interested in keeping the world divided along the lines of who had worked hardest. God was interested in our sufficiency and not our gathering wealth.

Proper 21
Pentecost 19
Ordinary Time 26

Exodus 17:1-7

> ... *Moses said to them, "Why do you quarrel with me? Why do you test the Lord?"* — Exodus 17:2

This becomes a pivotal text in the story of our journey of faith. Both the Israelites, and later the Christians, would return to this story to understand the mystery of their relationship with God. Something happened that caused God to decide not to permit Moses to accompany the people into the promised land (Deuteronomy 32:48-52). Later, Paul would return to this story and say that the rock that provided living water for the people was Christ (1 Corinthians 10:4). The language that is used here to describe the people's complaint is in the form of a lawsuit. "Why do you test the Lord?" Israel's whole journey, which becomes a metaphor for our journey of faith, became a series of tests both from God (Exodus 15:25-26) and the people (Exodus 17:2). God wanted to know if the people would trust and obey God. The people wanted to know "Is the Lord among us or not?" The same set of questions would be part of the Christian journey of faith. Jesus' ministry was filled with signs of God's healing presence, but once Jesus was gone, the community of faith still quarreled with their leadership as to whether Christ was the living water that could slake their thirst. Many a Christian leader has been ready to cry out as Moses did, "What shall I do with these people? They are ready to stone me." Repeatedly we are asked to go ahead of the people and provide a sign of God's loving presence. Christ, the living rock, is a mystery that calls for our trust and obedience.

Psalm 78:1-4, 12-16

> *I will open my mouth in a parable; I will utter dark sayings from of old, things that we have heard and known, that our ancestors have told us.*
>
> — Psalm 78:2-3

This is a rather strange selection from a very long psalm. The psalm itself is a wisdom psalm that drew upon the history of God's actions among the people of Israel to reveal the character of God. Using a variety of incidents from Israel's history, it demonstrated how the failure of Israel was the failure to remember the variety of ways that God had been present to them and provided for them. It was the lack of memory that caused the Ephramites, another name for northern Israel, to lose the battle and be defeated as a nation. This particular selection was probably chosen because it recalled the time in the wilderness that God provided water from the rock to slake their thirst, which is the incident referred to in the Exodus reading for this Sunday. But the thrust of the entire psalm was that what destroyed Israel and could yet destroy Judah was a national form of dementia. The parable that the psalmist wished to declare was the parable seen in the history of Israel's defeat. But it was also a parable that revealed that when God's people suffered dementia, God continued to remember and act on their behalf. The damaging effect of forgetfulness also can be seen in the contemporary Christian church. How often are we so consumed by whatever current crisis occupies our attention that we forget how God has been there for us in the past? It would be well for churches to occasionally tell their own parable derived from their personal church's history and pass it on to their children.

Philippians 2:1-13

... Work out your own salvation with fear and trembling.
— Philippians 2:12

We should remember that Paul, whose central message was that salvation was a gift, gave this admonition. He was not suggesting that we achieved or earned our salvation but rather that as a community of faith we should live out the implications of our salvation. Since salvation is a gift, we do not respond to it with arrogance. "Do nothing from selfish ambition or conceit...." In the church, we have the context to explore the implication of looking not to our own interest but to the interest of others. That does not mean that the church is a safe place to explore the implications of our salvation. Rather, it is God's place to explore the mind of Christ, who became obedient to the point of death. What would it be like for a church to have the mind of Christ? Do we first think of the power to perform miracles or do we think of the refusal to use one's power to dominate others? Can we imagine not using any of the abilities that we have in order to gain advantage for ourselves? How would our church be different if the goal of its members was not to use any of their power for selfish ambition or conceit but, in humility, to regard other members as better than themselves? Would that not be a very concrete way of "working our faith out with fear and trembling"? We would be practicing what it would mean to believe that God is at work in us not through our exploiting others but in our continuing to will and work according to God's pleasure. The "God community" is the community that lifts up Christ despite itself, and God offers us a saving experience within it.

Matthew 21:23-32

> *... By what authority are you doing these things, and who gave you this authority?* — Matthew 21:23

In many ways, clergy have become quite reluctant to be specific about how Christians should be living their lives. If a clergyperson were to speak to a member or group in his or her church and say, "God wants you to set aside time to pray and read scripture twice a day, worship every Sunday without fail, give ten percent of your income back to God's work through the church, actively forgive all who have offended you, and deliberately reach out to the least among us at least once a week," what would you expect the response to be? Most clergy, under pressure to attract new members and keep everyone happy, fear that if they attempt to do that, they would make people angry. They would hear a challenge to their authority. Who gave you the right to question my way of life? Who do you think you are telling us how to live our lives? The origin of such a challenge is usually the same. We do not want to change. Consider the difference between one who publicly becomes a Christian but continues to resist changing one's life in response to God and a person who realizes life is going nowhere and turns to God in grateful obedience. This is the implication of the question Jesus posed about the two sons going or not going to work in the vineyard. It is not enough to declare one's faith. Sometimes we get just enough of the Christian faith to inoculate us against catching the full faith. If clergy are not permitted to raise such questions regarding the fruit of one's faith, one needs to find another way in which Christ can address the congregation.

Proper 22
Pentecost 20
Ordinary Time 27

Exodus 20:1-4, 7-9, 12-20

> *You shall have no other gods before me. You shall not make for yourself an idol, whether in the form of anything that is in heaven above, or that is on the earth beneath, or that is in the water under the earth.*
> — Exodus 20:3-4

What we now call the Ten Commandments came thundering down from on high. The story is clear that this was not a set of suggestions that emerged out of people's wisdom or life's experiences. This was a set of commandments that were spoken from out of eternity into our finite world. They were meant to provide the boundaries that gave shape to a community's life. There was lots of room for choosing what to do within these boundaries, but these were the parameters within which one should live. They came as a voice of authority from beyond the human experience.

Such a voice is resisted by our modern, independent mind. They raise the question, if not this authority then what authority do we obey in our lives? Who or what can speak in a way that brooks no debate in us but only obedience? "You shall have no other gods before me." What are the other gods that seek to claim our loyalty? Have we simply renamed what the Bible refers to as gods and called them forces or influences that weaken our sense of obedience and compete for our loyalty? In Exodus, the people were frightened by the thundering voice of God and urged Moses to be God's interpreter so that the people did not have to listen to God's voice.

It raises a question as to what the screens of interpretation are that we insist stand between God and us. Do we insist that what God asks of us be screened through what we call "reasonableness" or "psychological truth"? Is there any word of God, any commandment from God that we would allow to penetrate directly into our soul and claim complete obedience? Have we not created a whole pantheon of little gods to compete for our obedience? Does our need of leisure time activities compete with God for the sabbath? Do we allow our emotional needs to lure us to commit adultery? Does self-preservation permit killing, fear justify false witness, and economic pressures override the honoring of parents? Moses said, "Do not be afraid; for God has come only to test you and to put the fear of him upon you so that you do not sin." Perhaps a major question for our time is whether there is any fear of God in us that would cause us to simply obey.

Psalm 19

> *The heavens are telling the glory of God; and the firmament proclaims his handiwork. Day to day pours forth speech, and night to night declares knowledge. There is no speech, nor are there words; their voice is not heard.* — Psalm 19:1-3

There is a sense in which the intricate design of creation proclaims the loving hand of the Creator. This psalm could have provided the foundation for Paul's statement in Romans 1:19-20, "For what can be known about God is plain to them, because God has shown it to them. For since the creation of the world his eternal power and divine nature, invisible though they are, have been understood and seen through the things he has made." Yet, for many it is a speech that is not heard. People can live in the midst of this miraculous universe designed to balance the fragile elements that sustain all life and presume that nothing more than an accident created it. The existence of this marvelous envelope in which we live does not in itself command a response from its creatures. The beauty of the heavens does not speak the word "You shall not steal" or "You shall not bear false witness against your neighbor."

The law of the Lord is God's gift that informs us, in a way that nature cannot, of how we can respond to this mysterious power that orders the universe. It is the law of the Lord spoken through revelation that "revives the soul" and connects the creature with the Creator. By God's commands we know that our life has meaning and purpose beyond mere survival. To be commanded "to not make for yourself an idol" suggests that God is beyond any aspect of creation and cannot be captured in the works of our hands. To be commanded "not to covet" tells us life is more than the possessions we gather. To hear the command of the God of the universe tells us our lives have meaning and are connected to the one who created us.

Philippians 3:4b-14

> *If anyone else has reason to be confident in the flesh, I have more.* — Philippians 3:4b

To the modern Western ear, Paul's words sound like boasting in the extreme. He described his pedigree as a Jew and asserted that he had an enviable record. We can hear the rich, young man say to Jesus, "Teacher, I have kept all these since my youth" (Mark 10:20). Paul said, "As to the law, blameless." If one can accomplish salvation through one's zeal and accomplishments, Paul had done so. Jesus said to the rich, young man who claimed that he had kept the commandments, "You lack one thing; go, sell what you own, and give the money to the poor, and you will have treasure in heaven; then come, follow me" (Mark 10:21). Paul, in parallel fashion, said, "Yet whatever gains I had, these I have come to regard as loss because of Christ." It is not that this faithful behavior was wrong. What was wrong was to depend on one's own behavior as a means of securing the grace of God. After Paul had experienced the transformation on the Damascus Road, he continued "to press on," but now it was in response to what Christ had already done. "... Because Christ Jesus made me his own." Paul believed that his life served a higher purpose that transcended his personal needs.

Now it was not a record of achievements but a commitment to join Christ in the redemption of life. "... Forgetting what lies behind and straining forward to what lies ahead, I press on toward the goal...." Ministry that is liberated from the need to achieve is an exciting, if demanding, discovery of what God is doing with us.

Matthew 21:33-46

> *... Have you never read in the scriptures: "The stone that the builders rejected has become the cornerstone; this was the Lord's doing, and it is amazing in our eyes"?* — Matthew 21:42

In an agrarian society, the wealthy owned large tracts of land that they rented to peasants to cultivate. The description of the vineyard in this parable was based on Isaiah 5:1-7, which was a strong protest against the injustice of securing large landholdings at the expense of others (Isaiah 5:8). Jesus stepped into the tension between the wealthy and the poor. The wealthy and the religious leaders disdained contact with the working peasants who they considered subhuman and would have been horrified at their violent response (Matthew 21:41). The more vulnerable in the society would have raised a different set of questions upon hearing Jesus' parable. How had the landowner gotten that piece of property? Had he foreclosed on a loan that had been given at exorbitant interest rates? How high was the rent on the peasants who did all the work? Some peasants would have seen the ejection of the servants as the beginning of a revolution for justice against an oppressive landlord like the Exodus event of their tradition. In the sending of the son, the owner was bringing the aura of the "natural order" of the elite over the peasant to bear on the situation. But, like the firstborn in Egypt (Exodus 12:29-32), the son's presence was no barrier to the ongoing revolt of the tenants.

How should we respond to such a situation? We are tempted to agree with the chief priests and the elders when they responded that "[the owner] will put those wretches to a miserable death, and let out the vineyard to other tenants who will give him the fruits in their seasons." We are shocked to hear Jesus respond by quoting Psalm 118:22-33, "The very stone which the builders rejected has become the head of the corner; this was the Lord's doing...." The psalm is one of thanksgiving to God for deliverance from oppression. Jesus was challenging those who supported the landowner. He suggested that those whom they so quickly rejected would be the cornerstone of God's reformed future.

While it disturbs us that Jesus did not clearly reject the violence of the parable, it lifts up Jesus' concern for systemic violence that oppresses the poor quietly. The Pharisees and chief priests quickly understood that Jesus was denouncing their alliance with the world as it was (Matthew 21:45). The challenge for the church, which often consists of people who are caught in between the rich and the poor, is whether we place security over justice in our response to the inequities of our society.

Proper 23
Pentecost 21
Ordinary Time 28

Exodus 32:1-14

> *... These are your gods, O Israel, who brought you up out of the land of Egypt.* — Exodus 32:8

When the going got tough, the tough wanted visible gods they could manipulate. It is not unusual for a community of faith to express their anxiety about their security by redirecting their resources toward a more visible program or strategy for success. Golden calves come in a variety of forms in the contemporary church. "Come, make gods for us, who shall go before us." Aaron tried to blend their demand for a successful plan with the worship of God. "Tomorrow shall be a festival to the Lord." God's reaction was described with a touch of humor. Pay attention to the choice of pronouns. God says, "*Your* people whom *you* brought up...." Moses responds to God, "Why does your wrath burn hot against *your* people whom *you* brought up...." Sometimes clergy want to speak of the church as "my people," but at other times, we would be quite pleased to remind God that it was God who formed them as a church. In either case, the role of spiritual leadership is displayed in this story. We are pressed by people's anxieties to make faith address the instrumental values of the people. Such pressure often centers on economical issues of survival. It is difficult for people to have confidence in leaders who absent themselves as Moses did by staying on top of the mountain.

A major role for spiritual leadership that is often overlooked, however, is seen in Moses' pleading with God on behalf of the people. It is precisely when people have been unfaithful that they most need clergy to plead with God on their behalf. The role of the priest is to be the person caught in the middle between God and the people. Moses did not walk away in despair just because the people had committed a grievous sin, and neither should that be the response of the clergy.

Psalm 106:1-6, 19-23

> *Remember me, O Lord, when you show favor to your people; help me when you deliver them ... Both we and our ancestors have sinned; we have committed iniquity, have done wickedly.* — Psalm 106:4, 6

This psalm was a celebration of the character of God as revealed repeatedly in the life of Israel. God repeatedly demonstrated an unshakeable love in the face of an obstinate and rebellious people. The psalmist reviewed a series of incidents in which the people of Israel rebelled against the purpose of God. In each of the incidents, we see that God would not tolerate evil. Yet, even God's punishment of the people for their sins was always designed to save. However, in the midst of celebrating the infinite love of God, there also was displayed the critical role of the priest in the midst of this relationship. The psalmist recounted that when the people of Israel built the golden calf, God was furious and would have destroyed them "had not Moses, his chosen one, stood in the breach before him to turn away his wrath from destroying them." It provides an important reminder for pastors that their responsibility does not end when their people sin.

When Luke was seeking to explain what had happened on the cross, he apparently drew on this psalm to develop words for one of the thieves that was crucified with Jesus (Luke 23:39-43). In response to the other criminal's mockery of Jesus, one thief paraphrased these words from the psalm. "Remember me, O Lord, when you show favor to your people; help me when you deliver them ... Both we and our ancestors have sinned; we have committed iniquity, have done wickedly" (vv. 4, 6). From Luke's perspective, the thief understood what we continually forget — that God's redeeming love is available to all who turn to it. Neither Israel's rebellion nor ours exhausts the transforming possibility of God's love.

Philippians 4:1-9

> *Rejoice in the Lord always ... Let your gentleness be known to everyone....*
> — Philippians 4:4, 5

This passage would clearly challenge the frequently accepted conclusion that Paul believed that only men should be leaders in the church. In Philippians, Paul was speaking of two women, Euodia and Syntyche, who have been partners with him in the ministry. He spoke of them as two strong leaders whose disagreement had ripped the church apart, and he was urging them, along with the rest of the church, to follow a path to conflict resolution that he was laying out. Paul entreated the women to recognize that they have a common Lord who transcended their arguments (v. 2). He then urged the congregation to provide support for both women and acknowledged the valuable contributions of each in the work of the gospel (v. 3). Without any attempt to resolve the specific issue in terms of one being right and one being wrong, he then urged the whole congregation to engage in praise — "Rejoice in the Lord." Finally, he urged them to display forbearance for each other and to put whatever the issue was in the hands of God. "Do not worry about anything, but in everything by prayer and supplication with thanksgiving let your requests be made known to God."

Imagine this as a strategy for churches in conflict: first, to acknowledge we are bound by a common Lord who is greater than any disagreement; second, to urge the body to acknowledge the authentic contributions of all parties; third, to emphasize the praise of God in the face of conflict; and, finally, to release our anxiety by putting the issues in the hands of God. By facing the issues that cause tension among us in this manner, we could hear Paul's urging, "Finally, beloved, whatever is true, whatever is honorable, whatever is just, whatever is pure, whatever is pleasing, whatever is commendable, if there is any excellence and if there is anything worthy of praise, think about these things." In this way we could experience the peace of God.

Matthew 22:1-14

Then he said to his slaves, "The wedding is ready, but those invited were not worthy." — Matthew 22:8

Look at the events of the story. Royal weddings were an opportunity to reconfirm the loyalty of the king's followers. Their refusal to come was a sign of open rebellion against the king's authority. The fact that he sent a second invitation showed the king's patience. Yet, they not only refused because of their own personal concerns but also mistreated his messengers. They had concluded that the king was so weak that they taunted him in their refusal. The king declared war against the rebels and then sought new subjects to demonstrate loyalty to the kingdom. His slaves gathered people indiscriminately, both good and bad. Then the royal party began, but, again, it became apparent that not everyone respected the king. While even the least peasant would have some kind of wedding garment, there was one guest who came without dressing in such a garment. He did not come to honor the king and the wedding party but to indulge himself in the food and drink.

From Genesis' image in the Garden of Eden to Jesus' image of a banquet prepared, we are encouraged to see life as something to be enjoyed and celebrated. Jesus saw some in open rebellion against God's invitation and others too preoccupied to take God seriously. In the parable, we see why God favors the poor over against the well to do. The poor recognized their neediness and rejoiced in the invitation. If worship is a window onto the banquet of life, how frequently do our preoccupations interfere with our acceptance of the invitation? God's invitation is indiscriminately generous, but we are expected to show honor by the manner of our response.

Proper 24
Pentecost 22
Ordinary Time 29

Exodus 33:12-23

> *... And while my glory passes by I will put you in the cleft of the rock ... and you shall see my back; but my face shall not be seen.* — Exodus 33:22-23

Here we see an example of the very honest exchange that is expected between God and God's people. Moses challenged God, "Now, if I have found favor in your sight, show me your ways...." He also demanded of God that God be present with them in their journey. "If your presence will not go, do not carry us up from here." It was not morality, intelligence, strength, or wealth that distinguished God's people from other nations. It was God's presence among them. "In this way, we shall be distinct." Later, Jesus made the same promise of being present with the Christian community in Matthew 28:20. Moses was not content with God in the abstract but asked for concrete signs of God's presence. "Show me your glory, I pray." God was responsive to Moses' very demanding prayer. "I will make my goodness pass before you, and will proclaim before you the name, 'The Lord....' "

But, there are limitations on God's self-disclosure. "You shall see my back; but my face shall not be seen." While this is a very physical scene, its theological importance is profound. To see the backside of God was to see where God has been. It is as we reflect back on our journey that we can see signs of God's presence. To see God's face is to see where God will go. If Moses saw God's face, it would mean he saw God coming toward him. We know God by reflecting on how God has been faithful to us, but we cannot know God's future. God is free. "... I will be gracious to whom I will be gracious...." As our future unfolds, we trust in God's presence and his faithfulness is confirmed by our memory.

Psalm 99

The Lord is king; let the peoples tremble!
— Psalm 99:1

Can you picture coming out to begin a worship service in a contemporary Christian church in America and announcing, "The Lord is king; let the peoples tremble! He is enthroned upon his cherubim; let the earth quake!"? Is it not likely that the people would sit there wondering what the first hymn was or reflecting on the nice decorations in the sanctuary? Few people in our churches tremble at the thought that God might really be in charge and have some definite expectations of us. This was a psalm for a people of God who had grown comfortable and perhaps even indifferent in their relationship with God. The psalm was a challenge to people who treated God as an emergency resource or even as a personal friend. It challenged people to praise God because God is holy — totally different from and apart from us and, yet, is ruling over us. It lifted up a God who was a mystery; who cannot be grasped and understood. "Let them praise your great and awesome name. Holy is he!" The psalmist recognized that God was not a total mystery.

There are aspects of God's character that have been revealed to us. "Mighty King, lover of justice, you have established equity; you have executed justice and righteousness in Jacob." We are charged with worshiping (giving first priority to) God, which means that God's desire for justice and equity must be our desire as well. As further revelation of the character of God, the psalmist reminded them of Moses, Aaron, and Samuel as people who cried out to God and God responded to them (v. 6) and told them how they should live (v. 7). This same God who answered them was both a forgiving God and, also, a God who punished their wrongdoing (v. 8). Now we know why we should tremble. God is more than a magic amulet that assists us in living. God is someone totally different from us who expects us to reflect God's love for justice and equity (v. 9). Precisely because God has responded to us, we know that God expects something from our lives. "The Lord is king; let the peoples tremble!"

1 Thessalonians 1:1-10

> *For we know, brothers and sisters beloved by God, that he has chosen you.*   — 1 Thessalonians 1:4

What if it is true that you have been chosen by God? We know the stories of Israel having been the chosen people, and we read the story of the disciples being chosen by Jesus. It did not mean for either that their lives were free from mistakes and more than a share of suffering. It did mean that there was a power working in their lives that was from beyond them. A message came to them and through them that was not of their own making. Paul spoke of that message as "not in word only but also in power and in the Holy Spirit...." This power working through us does not overpower us but does enable us to be good news. It sounds forth from us in ways that are convicting in the lives of others. Paul said of the Thessalonians that their deeds of faith rippled out from their congregation in a way that was so convincing that it proclaimed itself. The theme of the church's internal ministry is the equipping of the saints, those called out of the world into the church, so that they might go back out into the world and proclaim the gospel. It is often the fruit of the Spirit that is the most effective witness. To be chosen by God is less a reason for arrogance than amazement. We are the same people and yet utterly different.

Matthew 22:15-22

> *... Teacher, we know that you are sincere, and teach the way of God in accordance with truth, and show deference to no one....*   — Matthew 22:16

Sometimes we hide our malice behind the cover of compliments and a smile. The Pharisees sent both their disciples and the Herodians, representatives of both the faith community and the political community, to entrap Jesus. Their words suggested respect, but their question was meant to entrap. There was a negative spirit that betrayed them in their questions. Their questions were not for information or learning the truth but to ensnare Jesus. "Is it lawful to pay taxes to the emperor, or not?" If Jesus answered that they should pay taxes, he would lose the support of the people who chaffed under Roman rule. They looked for a Messiah that would liberate them from the Romans, not support the Romans. If, on the other hand, Jesus said that they should not pay taxes, then the Romans could arrest him. He asked for a coin, and they gave him a denarius that had the image of Caesar and words that claimed divinity for Caesar.

When Jesus gave his now-familiar response, he was speaking on two levels. On one level, the very image on the coin that claimed divinity for Caesar would suggest that Jesus was saying, "Give therefore to the emperor [a false god] the things that are the emperor's, and to [the true] God the things that are God's." But on another level, there is a legitimate separation of what should be directly given over to visibly honor God and what should be used for earthly responsibilities. Yet, the overall impact of what Jesus was saying is to suggest that each time we spend our money, we need to weigh whether we are doing it in such a way as to honor God or to support false idols in our lives.

Proper 25
Pentecost 23
Ordinary Time 30

Deuteronomy 34:1-12

> *... I have let you see it with your eyes, but you shall not cross over there.* — Deuteronomy 34:4

One of the great unresolved mysteries of our faith story was why Moses was not permitted to cross over into the promised land. Surely, whatever error he committed at the rock would not seem to compare with some of the failures of other servants of God such as Abraham or David. Even as we ponder this mystery, we are faced with a profound theological truth. We cannot accomplish everything we would like to in our lives. Even if we live to be 120 and are in excellent health, as Moses was reported to have been, there are still things that we cannot complete. There is always a "promised land" out there ahead of us that we will not enter. "Yet all these, though they were commended for their faith, did not receive what was promised, since God had provided something better so that they would not, apart from us, be made perfect" (Hebrews 11:39-40).

Even during our life, there are good things to do that we are really interested in doing but which we do not have time to accomplish. For some people that is reason for despair, but for people of faith, it is an admonition for good stewardship. Just because Moses could not enter the promised land himself did not mean his life was a failure. As a steward of the Spirit of God, Moses laid his hand on Joshua so that Joshua could carry on. Earlier Moses had shared God's Spirit with seventy elders that they might do what Moses did not have time to do. Moses shared his gifts so that God could use the greater community to further God's witness. While Moses was a key figure in the story of our faith, the completion of God's purpose was not dependent on him alone. There always comes a time when we must transfer the responsibility to those who come after us. Hopefully, we will have had the grace to share the Spirit that will enable them to continue on.

Psalm 90:1-6, 13-17

> *Lord, you have been our dwelling place in all generations. Before the mountains were brought forth, or ever you had formed the earth and the world, from everlasting to everlasting you are God.* — Psalm 90:1-2

Psalm 90 is a helpful reminder of the everlasting nature of God as the center of existence. When we lose perspective and begin to assume that our lives and the events that impinge upon and at times threaten our existence are critical for the fate of the universe, it is helpful to be reminded that God has been here before and will be here after we are gone. The psalmist reflects on the fact that God existed before even the mountains, the most solid thing the eye could behold (v. 2). The mountains that had witnessed kingdoms come and kingdoms go were a cautionary reminder that all hope does not rest on our decisions and us. Human arrogance evaporates in the light of the eternal nature of God who makes our measure of time insignificant. "You turn us back to dust, and say, 'Turn back, you mortals.' For a thousand years in your sight are like yesterday when it is past, or like a watch in the night." Our greatest achievements are like a briefly flourishing plant that quickly fades from sight (vv. 5-6). Such sobering thoughts are not to denigrate our importance but to bring our achievements into proper perspective.

In that context, it is even more amazing that the eternal mystery that created the universe and will, in time, bring it to completion takes note of us. "Satisfy us in the morning with your steadfast love, so that we may rejoice and be glad all our days." Our hope and joy rests in God's mercy and grace by which God grants us the good that we could not achieve ourselves (v. 15). The incredible truth is that such grace and mercy are available to us because, out of the infinite possibilities in creation, God chooses to care for us.

When we recognize the good that God does in us and the power of God to manifest God's purpose in ourselves (v. 16), our life takes on new meaning (v. 17). It would be easy to consider the briefness of our lives and the ephemeral quality of whatever we accomplish and be in despair. When we recognize the eternity of God and God's taking note of our lives, we begin to understand that what we do can have eternal significance.

1 Thessalonians 2:1-8

> *... we speak, not to please mortals, but to please God who tests our hearts.* — 1 Thessalonians 2:4

It almost seems to be built into ministry to be tempted to shape our words and actions so as to please people rather than God. Our visible signs of success seem so tied to having people like us that the use of flattery and manipulation are constant temptations. There is a form of greed attached to this temptation. The immediate rewards of pleasing people are great. When our measure of success is the response of people, and things go wrong, it is hard not to blame people for failing us. In contrast, when our objective is to please God, we are still focused on the needs of people because they are loved by God, but our perspective is different. Now when difficulties arise, we see it as God testing our hearts and thus we ask, "Where is God in this?" Paul testified to the fruits of having been willing to suffer on behalf of the gospel. For Paul the suffering he had endured was seen not as a sign of failure but as a test provided by God. The challenges of his ministry became God's way of saying, "Whom do you trust?" From such a perspective, we are set free of the flattery/blame continuum and, therefore, are able to look upon the people with continued affection. Paul resisted the temptation of claiming special privileges as an apostle of Christ. Instead he tried to be "gentle among you, like a nurse tenderly caring for her own children."

Matthew 22:34-46

On these two commandments hang all the law and the prophets. — Matthew 22:40

Given all the arguments over doctrine and ethics that have torn at the very fabric of the body of Christ, consider how radical this passage of scripture is. Jesus was saying that these are the essential commandments and everything else is simply commentary on the love of God and the love of neighbor. The essence of the faith is experienced in relationships. Sometimes we seem to insist on making things complex. The Christian community easily falls into the ancient trap of arguing about the little stuff so that we do not have to face the important things. If the essence of faith is expressed in this dual commandment of loving God and neighbor, then the test of much of our complex arguments will be whether they result in more love for God or neighbor. How many conflicts in church life could be resolved by each side striving to be more loving toward the other? It is not a simple thing to be more loving. It requires being faithful to the other person even when it hurts. Sometimes it requires sacrificing what is important to us on behalf of our neighbor. It asks us to put our neighbors' best interest ahead of ours. It does not require sacrificing the truth, but it does ask us to express the truth in a way that uplifts rather than demeans our neighbor. To love God means to trust that God will be for us if we are for our neighbor.

Proper 26
Pentecost 24
Ordinary Time 31

Joshua 3:7-17

> *When the soles of the feet of the priests who bear the ark of the Lord, the Lord of all the earth, rest in the waters of the Jordan....* — Joshua 3:13

The crossing of the Jordan River was a key transition in the life of Israel. Now Joshua, rather than Moses, was their leader. They would begin to be a settled people rather than a wandering people. To make this transition, they had to demonstrate a faith in the impossible. This was not the generation that had crossed the Red Sea. This was a new generation who had only heard stories of that crossing. The Jordan looked formidable as it overflowed its banks. The people had to walk through it as on dry land. They had to reexperience the power of God in their lives. They could not live off the faith of their parents. If they were to be able to stand strong against their enemies that would threaten their living in the promised land, they had to experience that "the living God" was among them.

Notice how this story becomes a template for our own experiences. For example, some very courageous leaders have led us out of the Egypt of legal discrimination. We have been wandering in the wilderness of racism for a number of years. There have been people who have tried to spy out the land of a society free from racism, but after a time they report back that it is a land of giants too difficult to conquer. We have been wandering in this wilderness for so long that we begin to doubt that anything will ever change. There is this huge Jordan River, with its flood-swollen waters, that stands between the promised land and us. There is the tree of job discrimination, the rock of intermarriage, and the flotsam of religious styles that keep hurtling down this Jordan River and preventing us from crossing over: These are our Canaanites, Kittites, and Perizites. How could the living God drive out these enemies who are so much a part of who we are? Where do we get the faith to get our feet wet in the Jordan? How do we learn to trust in the "living God" who is among us and risk crossing the Jordan and tasting the fruit that is waiting for us?

Psalm 107:1-7, 33-37

> *Let the redeemed of the Lord say so, those he redeemed from trouble and gathered in from the lands, from the east and from the west, from the north and from the south.* — Psalm 107:2-3

The lectionary placed these verses as a commentary on the story of Joshua's leading the people into the promised land. While the entire psalm commented on God's redeeming activity in a variety of circumstances — wandering in the wilderness (vv. 4-9), imprisoned (vv. 10-16), physical sickness and affliction (vv. 17-22), and crisis in the pursuit of business (vv. 23-32) — this selection focused on God's rescuing those wandering in a wilderness and being brought into the safety of a new home. Later, Jesus would begin his ministry with a sermon that suggested that he embodied similar redeeming activities (Luke 18). It is important to note the hint toward God's universal redeeming activity. While both Judaism and Christianity focus a great deal of attention on the internal issues of the community, the faith began with the revelation that God's intention of relating to a particular people was for the purpose of benefiting the entire world (Genesis 12:3).

In this psalm, God's redeeming activity came to people from all points of the compass. In this particular selection, it was not suggested that those suffering in the desert had sinned against God. Their need, and not their spiritual health or lack of it, entitled them to call on God, and God responded. The closing part of this selection emphasizes the universal theme of Psalm 1 and

God's complete control of nature in effecting God's purpose. Christians saw Jesus embodying these characteristics of God in redeeming the less fortunate and also demonstrating a creative control of the forces of nature (Matthew 8:23-27). The central focus of the entire psalm was that people should give thanks continually to this God who redeemed people from their troubles in all circumstances. "O give thanks to the Lord, for he is good; for his steadfast love endures forever."

1 Thessalonians 2:9-13

> *We also constantly give thanks to God for this, that when you received the word of God that you heard from us, you accepted it not as a human word but as what it really is, God's word, which is also at work in you believers.* — 1 Thessalonians 2:13

To our modern ears, it would appear that Paul was making an incredible claim. In many liturgical churches, when the liturgist finishes reading the scripture lesson, he or she will look at the congregation and say, "The word of the Lord." Paul took it a step further and suggested that when they heard his sermon, they were listening to God's word. How many congregants in our contemporary churches begin to listen to a sermon with the assumption that what they are listening to is the word of God? Isn't it far more likely that they assume that they are listening to an interpretation of scripture that they will evaluate as individuals? Many classic theologians, such as John Calvin, believed that when a faithful preacher rose, and a faithful congregant listened, God's word was being enacted in their presence. Between the words flowing from the pastor's mouth and the ear of a faithful listener, God was at work speaking to each person. Both the preacher and the listener bore a responsibility to approach this event with awe.

It is significant that Paul connected the effect of his words with the conduct of his life. "You are witnesses, and God also, how pure, upright, and blameless our conduct was toward you believers." As is abundantly clear in our situation, when our words are not consistent with our life, the possibility of people hearing the word of God is seriously damaged. One can imagine, however, the impact of a congregation approaching the proclamation of the word with the expectation that God was about to speak to each of them. One can also imagine the impact on preachers if they recognized that God would use their efforts in this way. It might cause us all to tremble as we entered the sanctuary and prepared for worship.

Matthew 23:1-12

> *The greatest among you will be your servant. All who exalt themselves will be humbled, and all who humble themselves will be exalted.* — Matthew 23:11-12

There is a disturbing contemporary ring to this passage as churches and church leaders strive to ascend the ladder of popularity, success, and power. Jesus saw the accommodations that religious leaders were tempted to make to the class stratification of society as a contradiction to the egalitarian relationships called for in the law of Moses. The ruling elite, of which the Pharisees were a part, disparaged manual work of all types and insisted that the lower class perform it for them. Status in agrarian societies was displayed in very clear modes of dress. Religious symbols like phylacteries (Deuteronomy 6:8-9) and long, long tassels (Numbers 15:38-39) became a luxury that working people could not afford but were clear symbols of the elite class. Places of honor at feasts, the best seats in the synagogues, proper salutations in the market place, and being called rabbi by others were all ways that lower-class people gave deference to their betters

In contrast, Jesus called on his disciples to reject such inequality and to live in equality with each other. One should challenge such inequality in society by responding to the needs of others as if you were a servant because you recognize that God intends to upset the structure of society that places some people in exalted classes above others. The increasing development of a service class in our own society and the widening gap between the wealthy and the poor provide uncomfortable challenges to our contemporary church. The expansion of the megachurch movement will also create clear challenges to clergy in the areas of status and influence. The consumer mentality of our society presses churches to emulate rather than challenge the values of our society. It is not an easy gospel to proclaim. This gospel calls on clergy and members to seek their satisfaction in serving others and to resist the temptation to exalt oneself or one's church at the expense of others. Try to picture the impact of all our individual churches seeing themselves as part of the one body of Christ and seeking as servants of that body to build up the other parts of the body.

Proper 27
Pentecost 25
Ordinary Time 32

Joshua 24:1-3a, 14-25

> *... Far be it from us that we should forsake the Lord to serve other gods....* — Joshua 24:16

There are frequent moments of decision in our journey of faith. There are times when we have to decide where our loyalties lie. As Israel was about to move from a nomadic to a settled, agrarian way of life, Joshua confronted them with their choice. Well aware of the temptation of split loyalties, he asked them to choose the god they would serve. He reminded them that their earlier ancestors "lived beyond the Euphrates and served other gods," and that they had had other gods in Egypt. The basis of the people's choice was their memory of how God had stepped into history and "protected us along all the way that we went...." The mystery of election, why God chose to be involved in their lives, is beyond human comprehension. Who can explain why God has evoked faith in some lives and not in others? Yet, because an essential aspect of our God-given life is freedom, God refused to force us to be loyal. We must choose God who has chosen us. It is not a simple choice. There are consequences to our choice. God "is a jealous God." Choosing to trust in God means that we have to give up our loyalties to other gods in our lives. As Jesus would later say, "You cannot serve God and wealth" (Matthew 6:24b). There are critical turning points in our journey of faith in which we must renew our trust in God over against the many competing loyalties. It helps, when we are facing an uncertain future, to recall how faithful God has been to us in the past.

Psalm 78:1-7

> *Give ear, O my people, to my teaching; incline your ears to the words of my mouth. I will open my mouth in a parable....*   — Psalm 78:1-2

This psalm opens in the form of a wisdom teacher trying to counter the inevitable problem of future generations not remembering the lessons learned by their ancestors. Israel's faith had always been empowered by the recalling of their history. The Torah recounted the stories of how God had been faithful to them through all their highs and lows as a people. Scholars will sometimes question the historical accuracy of some of these stories and debate whether there is any objective verification to them. In doing so, they forget the nature of these stories. They were not meant to be a video recording of an event but a theological reflection on the meaning of life. When the psalmist suggested that he would "open my mouth in a parable," he was setting the stage for reflecting on how the character of God had been revealed in the life of Israel. The truth was even more important than the facts. In our own culture, for example, one might question the historical accuracy of whether Washington chopped down a cherry tree and refused to lie about it, but the enduring truth is that this country was founded on a reverence for truth even when it was unpleasant. The same was true for Israel.

The rest of the psalm that is not included in this selection recounts the dark side of Israel's life and the gracious way that God responded to it. The Hebrew scriptures have always refused to whitewash their failings. Rather, they lifted them up that they might reflect on and learn from them. The history of Israel was not meant to celebrate the heroic feats of a people but to celebrate the amazing character of God that had been revealed through God's relationship with this people. The life of Israel was the "parable" by which they learned of God. The wisdom teacher of this psalm emphasized the necessity of continually recounting the truths they had learned to future generations. It was only through the words by which one recounted their history that future generations could keep the memory of God's faithfulness fresh in their own lives. It would be a challenging but valuable experience for a church to recall their particular history and treat it as a parable for what it could teach them about the character of God. One of the sad realities of our culture is its loss of memory. We need to hear the wisdom of the parable again, "I will open my mouth in a parable; I will utter dark sayings from of old, things that we have heard and known, that our ancestors have told us."

1 Thessalonians 4:13-18

> *But we do not want you to be uninformed, brothers and sisters, about those who have died, so that you may not grieve as others do who have no hope.*
> — 1 Thessalonians 4:13

These are common verses that are read at funerals. Mostly they are read as an affirmation of the resurrection and are intended to provide some comfort in the midst of the grief that is felt at the death of a loved one. It is probably rarely mentioned that they challenge a myth that many people cling to at the time of the death of a loved one. The myth is that death is not real but only an appearance. The myth suggests that we do not really die but simply pass on to a new life, often believed to be a spiritual life unencumbered by our bodies. Behind such a myth is the belief in an immortal soul that never dies. What did Paul mean when he suggested that we should "not grieve as others do who have no hope"?

The Greeks, as well as many others, believed in an immortal soul. What the Christians suggested was that the soul is not immortal. When Paul returned to the central image of the cross for his understanding, he was recognizing that Jesus did indeed die. His soul did not escape from his body, but death had laid claim to his body and his soul. It was God, not an immortal soul, that defeated death. God raised Jesus, body and soul, and broke the power of death. It is the power of God that will effect the final triumph of God over death. "For the Lord himself, with a cry of command, with the archangel's call and with the sound of God's trumpet, will descend from heaven and the dead in Christ will rise first." It is God, not some indestructible soul, that is not defeated by death. The mystery of life is the mystery of God who breathes the breath of life into us. As it has been from the beginning, our hope is in God who created and sustains us and will defeat the power of death.

Matthew 25:1-13

> *Then the kingdom of heaven will be like this. Ten bridesmaids took their lamps and went to meet the bridegroom.*
> — Matthew 25:1

This parable has been traditionally interpreted to reinforce the Boy Scout motto: "Be Prepared." The opening line suggested that the kingdom of heaven was compared to all ten maidens and not just those who were prepared with an extra flask of oil. We all want to go to the marriage feast. As we begin to take charge of our life, we intend it to be a happy life. But some of us are not as prepared for the unexpected as others are. The wise maidens were prepared for the unexpected delay of the bridegroom, but they did not seem very sensitive to their neighbors' needs. Can you imagine that Jesus would commend as a loving response the answer of the five prepared maidens to the unprepared: "No! There will not be enough for you and for us; you had better go to the dealers and buy some for yourselves." Is that not the stereotypical response of the "haves" to the "have nots" of this world? Does it not fly in the face of Jesus' example of sacrificial love for the sinners of our world? It is easy to say to those in need, "Go and find your own resources."

But the kingdom of heaven in the parable included both the prepared and the unprepared. Even the bridegroom of this parable seemed harsh. If we identify with the wise maidens, we conclude with the rest of the world that those who are in need have only themselves to blame. The image hardly corresponds to the image we have of Jesus. This parable does come after a series of warnings to be watchful because we do not know when the master will come. It is instructive, however, that this parable was included in the same chapter with the parable of the judgment of the nations that is interpreted as saying, "Truly I tell you, just as you did not do it to one of the least of these, you did not do it to me." Is there a danger that we could enter the wedding feast only to find our Master is locked outside with the foolish that had been unprepared?

Proper 28
Pentecost 26
Ordinary Time 33

Judges 4:1-7

> *At that time Deborah, a prophetess ... was judging Israel.* — Judges 4:4

We seek to understand what might be called the natural order of things and relationships. We observe our universe and try to discern how God intended life to be. We conclude that it is natural that plants produce food for humans, that women have babies, that animals are domesticated for human use, that sexual attraction is part of human relationships, and so forth. We seek to define what the order is because it gives direction in life. It is not natural for plants to eat people and knowing that helps us feel some measure of control and even security as we relate to plants. The natural order helps provide an ethic for what is right and wrong. It provides some order in the midst of chaos. But every once in a while, the order seems to break down, and we experience chaos in our lives.

In struggling with that turbulence in our lives, we discover that though God does have an order to the universe, our view of it is often too narrow and restrictive. Most of the judges in Israel, for example, were men. But in the chaos of Canaan's oppression, God raised up Deborah to save Israel. "For the Lord will sell Sisera into the hands of a woman." The natural order of things, as perceived by a male-dominated world, was broken open. What other "natural orders" are too narrow and will be exposed as we trust God in our chaotic times? Perhaps one of the reasons we have such a difficult time responding to the changes in the church that are happening around us, is that we have become more wed to our perception of what is right than in our trust that God will lead us.

Psalm 123

As the eyes of servants look to the hand of their master, as the eyes of a maid to the hand of her mistress, so our eyes look to the Lord our God, until he has mercy upon us. — Psalm 123:2

This psalm is the prayer of a pilgrim arriving in Jerusalem after a long journey. Because the psalms teach us how to pray, they can become our prayer as we approach God in worship. Out of a weary and stressful world, we enter an experience in which we are to focus our complete attention on God (v. 1). While many powers and pressures in life buffet us, we recognize that only one power really determines our well-being. In a challenging image of God experienced as both male and female, the psalmist uses the analogy of a servant to a master or a maid to a mistress (v. 2), to depict this recognition that God is truly in charge of our future. As many clergy know, it is very easy to measure our lives by the response of those around us and to be deeply wounded by the contempt that we frequently experience from others. The psalmist guides us to pray, "Have mercy upon us, O Lord, have mercy upon us, for we have had more than enough of contempt." It is appropriate to lay such pain before God.

As we approach God in prayer, we do so as souls who sometimes feel as if we are drowning in the pain of the insensitive who seek their limited security by exercising power to put others down. So the psalmist invites us to pray, "Our soul has had more than its fill of the scorn of those who are at ease, of the contempt of the proud." For a moment, in prayer, we step aside from the endless power games that so numb our psyche and blunt our ministry to others. We give up the need to exercise power and gain control and instead look to God for mercy. The world will await our return, but for a moment, we focus our attention on the one who can heal our numbness by her mercy and restore us to right living that focuses on the needs of our neighbor.

1 Thessalonians 5:1-11

> *... let us be sober, and put on the breastplate of faith and love, and for a helmet the hope of salvation.*
> — 1 Thessalonians 5:8

Paul challenged those who like to engage in speculation about the end time. He insisted that there was no way to calculate the timing of such an event. While Jesus would come "like a thief in the night," his coming would not catch believers by surprise because "you are all children of light and children of the day...." While Paul clearly challenged the silly speculations that are made by the "Left Behind" series, he also encouraged Christians to live as if that day would come at any time. He contrasted those who are drunk with those who are sober. The implication is that a sober person is alert and responsible in how they live. Paul was fully aware that the life of faith was a struggle against an enemy and required an alert and active response. We protect ourselves with faith and love. Faith requires us to trust in the God who calls us, and love guides our actions toward others. While the battle may seem endless, we are sustained by the hope of salvation. We do not have an inside knowledge of when God will act decisively to reconcile the world to Godself. We do trust, however, that all acts of faith and love contribute to God's consummation of the plan of salvation that God intended from the beginning.

Matthew 25:14-30

> *... You have been trustworthy in a few things, I will put you in charge of many things, enter into the joy of your master.*
> — Matthew 25:21

There is a mystery of inequality to life that we cannot explain. The parable acknowledges that there is inequality among the population. It also suggests that once God has blessed us, we are given a great deal of freedom in deciding how we are going to use what we have. At the same time, the parable reminds us that all we have is not our own but on loan to us, and how we choose to use this loan will reflect on our Master. It is another way of reflecting on our being created in the image of God. This parable holds out the daunting reality that how any of us use the resources and abilities that come into our lives does reflect on God. The parable also suggests that our choices of use may well reflect our response to the image of God that we hold. If we see God as an angry, vindictive God, then we may well act out of fear as the man with one talent did. The result is that we focus our attention on the scarcity of resources rather than the generosity of the giver. We begin to see God and life as harsh and unforgiving. We expect judgment rather than grace. The result is that we live life defensively. However, if we see God as a generous and merciful God, we are much freer to act in an expansive manner that produces much fruit. While the first two slaves were given differing amounts, they each responded to their given possibility to expand the pleasure of their master. By responding to grace, they experienced even more grace.

Christ The King
Proper 29

Ezekiel 34:11-16, 20-24

> *I will seek the lost, and I will bring back the strayed, and I will bind up the injured, and I will strengthen the weak, but the fat and the strong I will destroy. I will feed them with justice.* — Ezekiel 34:16

One can see this passage as the foundation for several of Jesus' parables, as well as the church's understanding of who Jesus was. When you hear, "I myself will search for my sheep, and will seek them out," the parable of the lost sheep comes to mind (Luke 15:3-7). When you read, "I myself will judge between the fat sheep and the lean sheep," one sees the basis for Matthew's parable of the separation of the sheep from the goats (Matthew 25:31-46). John's image of Jesus as the good shepherd surely is based on this passage, as well. Ezekiel was speaking to a people who had lost all hope. The nation had been destroyed, and the people had been carried into exile. The human possibility of the people regaining their status as a nation seemed almost as impossible as the ancient Abram and Sarai having a child. All depended on the miraculous intervention of God.

Yet, as always is true, some had profited from this tragic situation. Even as they prayed for God's intervention, there was the realistic understanding that God's restoration would not be good news for everyone. "I will seek the lost ... but the fat and the strong I will destroy." God's presence among us is both a sign of hope and of uneasiness. As we celebrate Christ the King Sunday and God's presence among us in Christ, we are faced with the challenge of God's concern for the weak and the injured. In Ezekiel's words, when God comes among us, "I will judge between sheep and sheep." Strong churches and successful Christians must wonder at God's words, "I will feed them with justice." Perhaps we need to pay more attention to helping our weaker churches if we want to be prepared to meet our Lord.

Psalm 100

> *Make a joyful noise to the Lord, all the earth.*
> — Psalm 100:1

This psalm is a command to praise God that is issued to the whole world (v. 1). The essential quality of life is the praise of God seen in our serving God's purpose with gladness. We are to "come into his presence with singing." Life is to be a song that joins the earthly chorus in praising God. It is in praising God that we recognize that God is Lord of our life, that we belong to God, and that we depend on God for our well-being like sheep depend on the one who places them in good pasture. "It is he that made us, and we are his; we are his people, and the sheep of his pasture." While the image of verse 4 is of a people coming to worship in the temple, in the context of the preceding verses, the temple becomes symbolic of the whole earth. What happens in the temple, or the church, is to be a provisional image of what will eventually be true for the whole earth. We are to enter life with thanksgiving and praise and allow our life to be a thanksgiving that blesses God's name (v. 4). The true purpose of our life is to praise God because the author of life is good (v. 5a). This goodness is experienced in a steadfastness of love and a faithfulness that has endured from one generation to the next (v. 5b). When one reflects on the language of heaven, as depicted in the book of Revelation, we are offered the image that the language of heaven is truly a song. Singing God's praises here on earth prepares us for the communion of the saints.

Ephesians 1:15-23

> *And he has put all things under his feet and has made him the head over all things for the church, which is his body, the fullness of him who fills all in all.*
> — Ephesians 1:22-23

If Christ is king and you take what happened to his body as a reflection of the world's response to the incarnation, does this suggest what we might anticipate in the church as Christ's body? He came not to dominate but to serve, and the church is called to serve others rather than exercise power over them. Jesus rejected attempts to make him king, and the church is called to reject the same temptation of assuming the reigns of power. Jesus fed the hungry, healed the sick, included the excluded, was tender to children, and rejected pompous piety. Does this provide parameters for the ministry of the church? Jesus' body was scourged by soldiers and left hanging on the cross. Any observer would have concluded that Jesus' body was weak and helpless before the world.

In an age that disparages the church, what does it mean that the church is Christ's body, "the fullness of him who fills all in all"? Some have tried to respond to this challenge by separating the institutional, or visible, church from the true church. If the church is the "body of Christ," is it possible that the church, with all its visible flaws, is Christ crucified and that its failings are the wounds of Christ bleeding in the world? Are those who claim Christ as Lord but abandon the church similar to the disciples who ran away at Jesus' arrest? Is the manic busyness, the power plays, petty jealousies, and the dullness and lethargy of so many churches part of Christ's woundedness? To know the "hope to which we are called," the "richness of his glorious inheritance," and the "immeasurable greatness of God's power," do we have to understand the resurrection as God's empowerment of Christ's body? How do we rediscover the power of Christ as king in a body that appears weak? Is it possible that to fully acknowledge Christ as king over all "rule and authority," we have to follow Christ's exhibition of authority as servant?

Matthew 25:31-46

... Lord, when was it that we saw you hungry and gave you food or thirsty and gave you something to drink?
— Matthew 25:37

This parable has evoked the compassion of Christians throughout the world and captured the imagination of even those outside the faith. There are several challenging features of this parable that should be noted. First, there is the suggestion that we are not talking about just the believers but all people. This is more than an individual standing before God. It is clear that it is the nations, not just individuals, that are gathered. We are talking about a worldwide perspective. Second, those who are welcomed into the kingdom have focused on deeds of mercy and not on correct religious beliefs. Those who were blessed for their deeds were not even aware that they were serving God. As we are confronted by the religious pluralism of our world, it is significant that the parable suggests how nations treat their less fortunate may determine their fate before God.

There is even the suggestion that we may be talking about national survival since the consequence of having failed to do deeds of mercy resulted in the nation's destruction. In this vision of the last judgment, loving your neighbor is the way you demonstrate love of God. "Truly I tell you, just as you did do it to the least of these who are members of my family, you did it to me." For many, this has caused them to see Christ in the stranger. This image is fulfilled in the resurrection story on the road to Emmaus when the stranger they invited to stay with them turned out to be Christ. Finally, it should be noted that the king of the parable refers to all creation as members of his family. While religion, race, and nationality may divide us, in God's eyes we are all of one family. (See also Acts 17:26.) A good family is both sensitive to and generous in sharing their resources with the ones who are most needy.

www.ingramcontent.com/pod-product-compliance
Lightning Source LLC
Chambersburg PA
CBHW060339170426
43202CB00014B/2820